HUMAN

KINDNESS

AND

THE SMELL

OF

WARM

CROISSANTS

HUMAN

KINDNESS

AND

THE SMELL

OF

WARM

CROISSANTS

AN INTRODUCTION TO ETHICS

Ruwen Ogien

Translated by Martin Thom

Columbia University Press
New York

Columbia University Press
Publishers Since 1893
New York   Chichester, West Sussex
cup.columbia.edu

Library of Congress Cataloging-in-Publication Data
Ogien, Ruwen.
  [Influence de l'odeur des croissants chauds sur la bonté humaine. English]
  Human kindness and the smell of warm croissants : an introduction to ethics /
Ruwen Ogien ; translated by Martin Thom.
      pages cm
  Includes bibliographical references and index.
  ISBN 978-0-231-16922-6 (cloth : alk paper) —
  ISBN 978-0-231-16923-3 (pbk. : alk. paper) —
  ISBN 978-0-231-53924-1 (e-book)
  1. Ethics.   I. Title.

BJ1063.03413   2015
170—dc23   2014037136

Columbia University Press books are printed on permanent and
durable acid-free paper.
This book is printed on paper with recycled content.
Printed in the United States of America

c 10 9 8 7 6 5 4 3 2 1
p 10 9 8 7 6 5 4 3 2 1

Cover design by Jennifer Heuer
Cover photograph by Hiroshi Higuchi, © Getty Images

CONTENTS

Preface: An Antimanual of Ethics   *vii*

Acknowledgments   *xi*

Introduction: What Is the Use of Thought Experiments?   *xiii*

PART I.
PROBLEMS, DILEMMAS, AND PARADOXES:
NINETEEN MORAL PUZZLES

1. Emergencies   7

2. The Child Who Is Drowning in a Pond   11

3. A Transplant Gone Mad   15

4. Confronting a Furious Crowd   17

5. The Killer Trolley   24

6. Incest in All Innocence   42

7. The Amoralist   56

8. The Experience Machine   65

9. Is a Short and Mediocre Life Preferable to No Life at All?   71

10. I Would Have Preferred Never to Have Been Born   73

11. Must We Eliminate Animals in Order to Liberate Them?   76

12. The Utility Monster   89

13. A Violinist Has Been Plugged Into Your Back   91

14. Frankenstein, Minister of Health   94

15. Who Am I Without My Organs?   100

16. And If Sexuality Were Free?   104

17. It Is Harder to Do Good Intentionally Than It Is to Do Evil   107

18. We Are Free, Even If Everything Is Written in Advance   109

19. Monsters and Saints   113

PART II.
THE INGREDIENTS OF THE MORAL "CUISINE"

20. Intuitions and Rules   131

21. A Little Method!   134

22. What Remains of Our Moral Intuitions?   138

23. Where Has the Moral Instinct Gone?   142

24. A Philosopher Aware of the Limits of His Moral Intuitions
    Is Worth Two Others, Indeed More   151

25. Understand the Elementary Rules of Moral Reasoning   154

26. Dare to Criticize the Elementary Rules of Moral Argument   163

    Conclusion   173

    Glossary   *181*
    Notes   *191*
    Index   *219*

PREFACE

AN ANTIMANUAL OF ETHICS

This book is a general introduction to ethics.[1]

But it has neither the pretension to instruct anyone how to live, nor the mission to teach the history of moral ideas from their origins to our own time, in chronological order.

Its ambition is far more modest: to put at the disposal of those who might be interested a sort of *intellectual toolbox* enabling them to brave the moral debate without allowing themselves to be intimidated by the big words ("Dignity," "Virtue," "Duty," and the like) and the grand declarations of principle ("You must never treat anyone simply as a means" and so on).

If these titles had not become registered trademarks, I might have called it *Antimanual of Ethics* or *Little Course of Intellectual Self-Defense Against Moralism.*

Since we have to do with a book of philosophy and not a detective novel, I presume no one will be frustrated if I "kill the suspense" by presenting my principal ideas straightaway.

They can be summarized in the form of two propositions:

1. It is not true that our moral beliefs would have absolutely no value if it were impossible to have them rest upon a single, indisputable principle (God, Nature, Pleasure, Feelings, Reason, and so on): in ethics, we can do without "foundations."

2. Conceding a certain form of pluralism of doctrines and methods is the most reasonable option in ethics.

I am obviously not the only one to uphold these kinds of antifoundationalist and pluralist ideas.[2]

But I would venture to say that the originality of my defense of them lies in the fact of its resting almost entirely upon the critical examination of two basic ingredients of the moral "cuisine": *intuitions* and the *rules of reasoning*.

What is a moral intuition?

What is a rule of moral reasoning?

MORAL CUISINE

Certain moral arguments are extremely simple. They take the form of raw judgments as to what is good or bad, just or unjust, which no one bothers even to justify, since they appear self-evident. For example: When we see a child who is drowning, we try to save him. It would be monstrous to do nothing to help him get out of the water.[3] In order to describe these direct, spontaneous, and purportedly self-evident judgments, philosophers have become accustomed to saying that they are *moral intuitions*.

Other moral arguments are more complicated. They bind intuitions together by means of *relations of thought*, elementary rules of moral reasoning.

Thus, in order to denounce the clear conscience of the rich, who do nothing or almost nothing to put an end to famine and the terrible poverty that there is in the world, Peter Singer, a philosopher whose fame rests upon his uncompromising fight against factory farming, advances the following argument: By giving nothing or almost nothing to the organizations that seek to combat famine in the world, you are letting children in many countries die. You are behaving in just as monstrous a fashion as if you were letting them drown before your very eyes in a pond and without lifting a finger to save them.[4] It would be really very astonishing if the argument sufficed to convince the wealthy to share their wealth. But it is very interesting so far as its construction is concerned. Peter Singer puts on the same moral plane the fact of letting a child who is drowning before your very eyes die and that of letting a child in a distant country die. He asserts that the two forms of behavior are equally monstrous. It is a comparison that is certainly open to dispute. But what interests me is the fact of its appealing implicitly to one of the elementary rules of moral reasoning: *like cases must be treated alike.*

In reality, complex moral arguments always have roughly the same form. They rest, on the one hand, upon simple intuitions relating to what is good or bad, just or unjust, and, on the other hand, upon rules of moral reasoning that tell us how they can be applied.

Intuitions and rules of reasoning are the two basic ingredients of the moral "cuisine." How could we deepen our understanding of moral thought without undertaking a systematic analysis of them, and without trying to answer the philosophical questions they pose?

What are they?

QUESTIONS REGARDING THE RULES AND THE INTUITIONS

Three elementary rules of moral reasoning are well known: "ought implies can" ("no one is held to the impossible"); "one cannot derive an ought from an is" ("one must not confuse judgments of fact and judgments of value"); and, finally, "like cases must be treated alike" ("it is unjust to use two different measures for two different weights").

We can ask ourselves if there are others, if they are sufficiently clear and precise, if they are consistent with one another, and if they are a sort of unassailable "dogma" or propositions open to being contested.

Many questions are also raised with regard to moral intuitions. How are we to know them? Are they the same everywhere and with everyone, or do they differ from one society to the next and from one individual to the next? Are they *innate, learned,* or a bit of both at the same time? Are they purely emotional reactions or spontaneous judgments that do not necessarily have an affective content?

What part do moral intuitions play in the justification of grand moral theories?

In order to try to answer these questions, I make extensive use of what we call "experimental moral philosophy."

WHAT IS EXPERIMENTAL MORAL PHILOSOPHY?

Experimental moral philosophy is a discipline still in gestation, and one that mixes the scientific study of the origins of moral norms in human and animal societies with reflection upon the value of these norms, without our yet knowing exactly in what direction it will ultimately tend, or what the nature of its contribution to philosophy (if there is one) will be.[5]

For its most enthusiastic promoters, it is a revolutionary style of investigation that is turned toward the natural sciences with a view to finding the means to clarify or resolve the traditional questions of philosophy.[6]

Other promoters, who are somewhat less enthusiastic, or somewhat less deft, prefer to say that there is absolutely nothing new about this style of investigation. According to them, experimental moral philosophy simply renews the ties between the natural sciences and philosophy, which formerly were very close, and which should never have been sundered, since it is thanks to them that human knowledge has progressed.[7]

This is a dispute in the history of ideas into which I do not propose to enter. What interests me is the fact that experimental moral philosophy proposes five classes of empirical data susceptible to making a contribution to moral reflection:

1. Investigations into the moral intuitions of each and every one of us.
2. Investigations into the moral reasonings of each and every one of us.
3. Laboratory experiments regarding human generosity or human cruelty.
4. Psychological researches into the moral development of children.
5. Anthropological accounts of the diversity of moral systems.

It would be absurd, in my opinion, *to decide in advance* that such works would in no way serve to clarify questions of moral philosophy, under the pretext that they have to do with facts and not values or norms, and that there is a yawning abyss between the two kinds of investigation.

For certain philosophers, the opposition between scientific research and moral reflection is no longer defensible. It is a dogma that is dead.[8] Without going as far as that, we can inquire as to its exact meaning and see to it that it remains open to critical scrutiny.

ACKNOWLEDGMENTS

I owe particular thanks to the following people:

Patrick Savidan, who believed in this project, backed it from start to finish, and, through his skill, generosity and friendship, helped me to give it its final form.

Maryline Gillois, for her unfailingly correct ideas, and for her unswerving and affectionate support, as well as Albert Ogien, Jacky Katuszewski, Valérie Gateau, Nathalie Maillard, Christine Tappolet, Patricia Allio, Florian Cova, Vanessa Nurock, Bernard Baertschi, Danièle Siroux, Solange Chavel, Jean-Cassien Billier, Corine Pelluchon, and Peggy Sastre. They were my first readers. All of their observations were illuminating, and I owe them a huge debt.

Charles Girard, Patrice Turmel, Stéphane Lemaire, Charles Larmore, Luc Faucher, Nicolas Tavaglione, Monique Canto-Sperber, Cora Diamond, Sandra Laugier, Pierre Livet, Nicolas Baumard, Marc Fleurbaey, Marta Spranzi, Marie Gaille, Edwige Rude-Antoine, Roberto Merrill, Speranta Dumitru, Isabelle Pariente-Butterlin, Simone Bateman, Gustaf Arrhenuis, Caroline Guibet-Lafaye, Bernard Joubert, Martin Gibert, Francis Wolff, Eva Keiff, Florence Burgat, Bertrand Guillarme, Jean-Luc Guichet, Frédéric Worms, Catherine Larrère, and Jean-Yves Goffi. Through their objections, observations, and reformulations of my questionings, they helped me a great deal, either with the whole or else with specific parts of this book.

Sonia Kronlund, Sarah Chiche, Patricia Richer-Clermont, Myriam Ogien, Sophie Dufau, and Dagmar Dudinsky, who brought their ideas, encouragement, and enthusiasm.

I also think often of Kristina Hauhtonen, of all that she has given me, when she herself is engaged in so difficult a fight.

INTRODUCTION

WHAT IS THE USE OF THOUGHT EXPERIMENTS?

Imagine a lifeboat caught in a storm, adrift in the open sea. On board are four men and a dog.

All five will die if no man is willing to be sacrificed, or if the dog is not thrown overboard.

Is it morally permissible to throw the dog into the sea simply because it is a dog, without further argument?[1]

What do you think?

Let us now suppose that these men are Nazis on the run, perpetrators of barbaric massacres, and that the dog is a heroic rescuer whose actions enabled dozens of persons to escape a terrible death after an earthquake.

Would this change anything in your approach to assessing their respective rights to remain in the lifeboat?

The problems involved in sacrificing animals for the good of members of our own species, whatever they may be, do not only arise in moral fictions. In 1984, in the United States, a surgeon proposed to the parents of a baby born with a congenital heart defect and who was faced with the prospect of a very early death that their child be offered the transplant of a baboon's heart.

The operation went ahead. The baby survived, but for no more than a few weeks.

This episode, known as the "Baby Fae" affair, gave rise to a very heated debate.

What certain antivivisection societies condemned out of hand was not the fact that the child had been treated as a sort of guinea pig or the fact that the species barrier between human and baboon had been breached.

What scandalized such societies was rather the fact that it had been deemed natural to sacrifice a living and intelligent animal in a bid to save a baby whose chances of survival were slender in the extreme![2]

It seems to me that the majority of philosophers will judge that the "Baby Fae" affair repays close scrutiny, even if they are not specialists in animal ethics.

My sense is that they will be more divided over thought experiments.

Some will tell you that they have nothing against the use of fictions in ethical reflection, so long as they involve rich and open-ended literary works, which lead the reader to become aware of the difficulty of formulating a moral question correctly, rather than schematic examples that tell him in advance what direction his research should take.[3]

They will perhaps not go so far as to maintain that, in order to understand the moral questions raised by our relationship to animals, we would do better to read Lassie Come Home than a somewhat absurd story about a lifeboat with dogs and Nazis, but they will not fall very short.

Others will reject such thought experiments on the pretext that they are so abstract, so far removed from reality, that from them we can deduce absolutely nothing of any interest or value regarding our own lives.[4]

Are these two arguments well founded?

TOO POOR?

Thought experiments are little fictions, specially devised in order to arouse moral perplexity.

Since we have to do with narratives that are simple, schematic, short, and wholly without literary merit, every imaginable manipulation of the narrative elements serving to advance moral reflection is possible.

For example, in the above story I saw fit, without feeling guilty at having wrecked a work of art, to introduce a small change into the original lifeboat scenario, by saying something about the past of the four men and the dog. It was supposed to serve as a way of measuring the respective importance in our moral judgment of belonging to a species and of individual qualities.

There would be little sense in proceeding in the same fashion with great literary works like *Anna Karenina* or *Madame Bovary*.

No doubt they too are "thought experiments," since they present invented characters, in morally complicated hypothetical situations. Yet their contribution to moral reflection seems to arise from the hypothetical situation such as the author has described it, in its particularity, with all its details and its complexities.[5]

We would therefore lose everything they are supposed to teach us if we simplified them, as in summaries in Wikipedia or in Pass-Notes, or if we strayed too far from the narrative by posing bizarre questions such as "what if Madame Bovary were a man or a transsexual?" and "what if Anna Karenina were a housewife?"

Simplified fictions can obviously not play the same edifying role as great literary works. Yet they allow us to identify more clearly the factors that influence our moral judgments, such as belonging to a species or possessing particular individual qualities. In my opinion this is a contribution that is by no means negligible.

TOO FAR REMOVED FROM REALITY?

The second reproach we can level at moral thought experiments is that they are too abstract, too far removed from the problems people face in real life, to give us anything else but the futile, and purely intellectual, pleasure of amusing ourselves with ideas.[6]

The same is said of certain thought experiments in physics.

In a thought experiment in physics, if, in our imagination, we place in fictitious hypothetical conditions a fictitious object that is too different from real objects and too far removed from real conditions, what do we get? Science fiction at best, and at worst fictitious results that will serve no purpose at all, not even to amuse us.[7]

But thought experiments in ethics have nothing to do with thought experiments in physics! Their *ultimate* aim is not to help us to attain a better knowledge of reality, but to know *if there are reasons to keep it as it is or to change it.*[8]

Thus, precise description of the animal condition is of great importance in stimulating reflection. But it is insufficient *when we ask in what direction things should develop.*

If, for example, we seriously think that animals are not things, what are the implications? Should we not completely foreswear owning them, selling them, buying them, and eating them?

Would that not lead to the complete disappearance of all animals that were not wild? Is that really what we want?

I do not see how, in endeavoring to shed a little more light upon these complicated moral and political questions, we could do without thought experiments.

I should add that, far from being novel, this method has a venerable pedigree.

The most famous moral thought experiment is perhaps the one proposed by Plato, over twenty-four hundred years ago.

PSYCHOLOGY AND PHILOSOPHY

Do you know the story of Gyges's ring? It is evoked by Plato, and all those who have done a little moral philosophy will probably have heard tell of it. For those who may perhaps have forgotten, I will give the gist of it, though mindful that Plato specialists may well raise an eyebrow over points of detail.

According to an ancient legend, a shepherd, the ancestor of a certain Gyges, found a gold ring that enabled him to render himself invisible when he turned its setting toward the palm of his hand, and to become visible again when he turned it outward. The ring thus bestowed the power to be visible or invisible at will—and to commit the worst of crimes without being seen or detected!

In book 2 of *The Republic*, one of the characters, Glaucon, speaks and asks us to imagine what two individuals, one assumed to be just and the other unjust, would do if each of them possessed a ring of Gyges.[9]

Would it still be possible to distinguish between them? Would they not behave in exactly the same way?

Would the just man remain honest? Would he refrain from stealing from shop windows when he could do it with impunity? And what would one really think of him, if he remained honest, if he did not profit from the power the ring gave him? Would one not take him, at bottom, for some sort of idiot, despite all the praises one would indeed be obliged to heap upon him?

Such are the questions that feature in the narrative.

At first glance, the story of Gyges's ring is a psychological thought experiment, in the sense that it solicits our judgment as to what people will do if placed in a certain hypothetical situation.

We can give it a quasi-scientific form.

Suppose that we offer two persons, one honest and the other dishonest, a ring that enables them to render themselves invisible and to commit all sorts of crimes without being either seen or recognized.

HYPOTHESIS

The honest person will behave in exactly the same way as the dishonest person. There will no longer be any moral difference between the two of them.

JUSTIFICATION OF THE HYPOTHESIS

The only thing that keeps us from being dishonest is the fear of being caught and punished. If the honest person no longer runs the risk of being caught and punished, he will behave in exactly the same fashion as the dishonest person.

Interpreted thus, the thought experiment proposed by Plato does indeed resemble a psychological thought experiment.

It would not be specific to moral philosophy. It might interest a criminologist, or an economist who was conducting research into the motivations behind fraud on public transport or theft in a large department store. Who would pay for their seat on a bus or for their purchases in a large store if they were invisible?

But when we view this thought experiment as a whole, we come to realize that there is nothing psychological about it. It is a *conceptual* inquiry into what it means to be just or to be honest, or, more generally, into the idea of justice.[10] What the experiment in fact aims to show is that a really just person is not one who behaves in a just fashion simply because he is afraid of being caught and punished.

In reality, the aim of the experiment is not to *predict* a behavior in certain hypothetical conditions, as a psychologist might do, but to clarify the idea of justice.

A thought experiment in ethics can serve to show that a psychological problem is in reality a *conceptual problem*. It is, so to speak, one of its philosophical functions. Once we have understood this, a whole range of factual questions that we could pose in regard to it become a little ridiculous. For example: "This story about rings makes no sense. If you steal objects from a large department store while being invisible, that does not mean that the objects stolen will be invisible too. Do you imagine that no one would be surprised at Hermès scarves and Rolex watches floating toward the exit? You are treating people like idiots. You will be caught straightaway!"

Another example: "We do not know enough about the characters involved to be able to answer the question that has been put. You ask if an honest person will become dishonest were he able to become invisible at will. My answer to you is that it depends upon the people involved. Some honest persons would indeed become dishonest if they could steal or defraud without any risk of being caught. Others, however, would remain honest because they have had a good education or because they would nonetheless be afraid of being caught. Without supplementary information on these persons, their past, their interests, their preferences, and their occupations, all prediction would be futile, even haphazard."[11]

A third objection might seem more pertinent: "The hypothesis according to which the only thing keeping us from being dishonest is the fear of being caught and punished is an unproven assertion. Without supplementary arguments, the hypothesis is unwarranted."

I nonetheless have the impression that this third objection is as misplaced as the previous one, inasmuch as the rightly disputed hypothesis is itself empirical.

What Plato's thought experiment is in the end supposed to give us is the definition of a moral concept (in this instance, being just).

Thought experiments can, however, be constructed for a very wide range of other purposes.

In present-day moral philosophy, the method of the thought experiment serves above all to identify our moral intuitions with a view to testing the validity of the great moral doctrines.

The standard procedure is as follows:

1. Construct bizarre cases in order to reveal our moral intuitions.
2. Assert that the doctrines which are not to our liking are false, since they contradict these same intuitions.

It is this procedure that interests me.

THREE WAYS OF CONCEIVING OF MORALITY

Deontologism and consequentialism are the two main theories in contention within present-day moral philosophy.[12]

Deontologism (from the Greek *deon*, "duty") is to a large extent inspired by Kant. According to this theory, there exist *absolute constraints upon our actions*, things *that we should never do*: "do not lie" and "do not treat a human person simply as a means" are examples of this kind of constraint.[13]

For a consequentialist, what counts morally is not blindly respecting such constraints but rather acting so that there is, *in total, the most good or the least possible evil in the universe*. Indeed, if in order to attain this goal it is necessary to free ourselves from these constraints, we must do so, or at any rate attempt to do so.[14]

The most famous consequentialists are the utilitarians. For the latter, the good is pleasure, and what we must do is produce the most pleasure and the least pain for the greatest number. We can, however, be consequentialist without being utilitarian. It is sufficient that we not reduce the good to pleasure.

For some time now, these two great theories have been confronted with the spectacular return of a more ancient conception, namely, a *virtue ethics* inspired by Aristotle.[15] It is sometimes called "aretist" (from the Greek *arete*, "excellence"). A virtue ethics of this kind asserts that the only thing that matters morally is *personal perfection*, being someone who is good, a person of good character, generous, affectionate, courageous, and so on. The rest—that is to say, showing respect for great principles or working for the greatest good of the greatest number—is secondary. For virtue ethics, morality does not only involve relationships with others, since it is also a concern for one's own self. It must preach temperance as regards the pleasures, the monitoring of desires and of emotions, and so on.

What is the best moral theory? Is it possible to amend them? Do several different versions of these theories exist?[16] Which is the most reasonable? Must we prefer the one that is most in harmony with the greatest number of moral intuitions?

Can a moral intuition serve to disqualify one or another of these moral theories, much as certain physical facts serve to wreck a scientific hypothesis?

In order to refute the idea that all swans are white, it suffices, by and large, to show that there exists a black swan (which has not been colored by a practical joker).

In order to refute Kantian ethics, which absolutely excludes any right to lie, even out of "humanity,"[17] is it sufficient to recall the intuition granting you permission to lie to cruel murderers who come looking for an innocent hidden in your house?

In order to refute utilitarian ethics, is it sufficient to recall the intuition that forbids you to have an innocent hanged, even if it is to save a large number of human lives?

In order to return virtue ethics to the pigeonhole of outmoded moral ideas, is it sufficient to recall the intuition which requires of us that we not put on the same plane the concern for self and the concern for others, murder and suicide, and, more generally, the harm done to others and the harm we cause ourselves?

MUST WE DEMOCRATIZE
THOUGHT EXPERIMENTS?

The philosophers have often found no better way of discrediting a moral theory than to say of it: "It's absurd. It contradicts our ordinary intuitions!"[18]

Even supposing we admit that this is a pertinent objection, we still need to know what these "ordinary" intuitions actually are. Numerous philosophers are content simply to say "we" think, "one" thinks, "most people" think, "no one" thinks, without asking themselves whether this is not simply what they and a few colleagues in their philosophy department think.

It is worth saying that this is not always for want of rigor. Some, indeed, reckon that they are not obliged to give a concrete or sociological meaning to the notion of an "ordinary" intuition.

They may reckon that the notion, in their use of it, does not refer to the spontaneous judgments of the *majority of people*, but to the "well-formed" judgments of persons who are "enlightened," "well-informed," "aware of moral questions," capable of "neutralizing their own interests" and their "prejudices," and so on.[19]

There exists, moreover, a venerable elitist tradition in moral philosophy, in the characterization of persons who were deemed competent to voice an ethical opinion, or whose "intuitions" were held to count in any moral debate.[20] But why give more weight to the judgments of this "moral elite" than to those of each and every one of us?

Another way of presenting "ordinary" intuitions, entailing no reference whatsoever to the ideas of each and every one of us, consists in claiming that they are propositions it would be irrational not to accept.[21]

Is it true, though, that all persons who are rational, well informed, and aware of moral questions would accept these propositions? Must we not in fact conduct concrete and systematic research in order to know whether this is so?[22]

It is with these questions in mind that a number of philosophers open to the empirical disciplines have begun to take an interest in the works of sociologists and psychologists that bear upon the spontaneous moral judgments of all manner of different people across the world, philosophers and nonphilosophers, as well as people of different ages, genders, educational attainments, religions, languages, cultures, and social categories.

They have undertaken to put to the greatest number the strange questions that professional philosophers used to ask themselves (and other philosophers):[23]

"Is it permissible to kill one person in order to remove his organs and thereby save the lives of five other persons awaiting a transplant?"

"Is it permissible to divert a trolley that threatens to kill five persons onto a siding upon which only one person will be crushed?"

"Can incest be practiced in all innocence?"

"Is it immoral to clean a toilet with the national flag?"

This is how experimental moral philosophy was born.[24]

EXPERIMENTS ON BEHAVIORS

Experimental moral philosophy is not only concerned with thought experiments. It is also interested in experiments on behaviors, where it encounters other obstacles.

Thought experiments, those of philosophers and those that are subjected to the sagacity of everyone, do not pose any moral problem.

There is no harm in wondering what one should *think* of a person who refuses to take in his car the victim of a road accident who is bleeding profusely, *so as not to ruin his brand-new leather seats.*[25]

We can put the question to a host of people with a fairly good chance that they will answer us calmly, if they have the time to spare.

Experiments on so-called moral or immoral behaviors are not so innocent from the moral point of view.

Arranging a mise-en-scène in order to assess how drivers *really* behave when going past the heavily bleeding victim of an accident is not without risk.

What would the reaction be of someone held up to ridicule for preferring to save his brand-new leather seats rather than a human life? We cannot be certain that this experiment would amuse.

The idea of performing experiments on behaviors in order to confirm hypotheses on "human nature" is in fact ancient.

Kant was keen on this exercise, although he perhaps did not have much of a talent for it. One of his hypotheses was that a woman will sulk for longer if we tell her that she is old (that's objective) than if we treat her as ugly (that's subjective).[26]

One could consider the experimental study of so-called moral or immoral behaviors to be a research program that is designed to test hypotheses of the same kind, but where the interest in these hypotheses is more evident, while the methods used are a little more serious and a little more respectful.

In what respect might this scientific program concern moral philosophy? According to certain researchers, the best service that these experiments on behaviors could render moral philosophy would be to help it to eliminate the more unrealistic theories, those that take absolutely no account of "human nature."[27]

Yet they can also help to rid us of all manner of clichés regarding "human nature." Certain well-known experiments show that it takes very little to get you to behave like a monster: an experimenter in a white coat who gives you orders in a firm but polite voice, a role as prison warder and the uniform that goes with it, and, hey presto, you are ready and willing to torture your fellow human being!

However, other experiments, somewhat lesser known, tend in quite another direction. They show that precious little is likewise needed for us to behave like saints: the smell of warm croissants that puts us in a good mood, a little free time stretching ahead of us, and so on.[28]

Before advancing grandiose claims as to a purported "natural inclination" of man to do evil (or good), we should perhaps take an interest in the results of these modest experiments.

It is at any rate one of the questions that experimental moral philosophy also raises.

The majority of the nineteen cases that I present in the first part of this book belong to the "corpus" of experimental moral philosophy.

I have tried to present the others in such a way that they could, in the future, be the subject of this kind of research. They lend themselves to being studied by means of the methods of experimental moral philosophy, even if hitherto they have not been handled thus.

Among the philosophers who are interested in these case studies, some have a profoundly reverential attitude toward the methods and results of everything that claims to be "scientific" (statistical inquiries, speculations on the natural history of our species, cerebral imaging, and so on).

Others are completely uninterested in normative questions, that is to say, in what is just or unjust, desirable or undesirable. They are content simply to record these biological, psychological, or social facts without wondering how they might contribute to the elaboration of morally acceptable norms.

Yet I believe that this research can be put to other uses, without relinquishing a critical sense as regards their outcomes, and without renouncing normative concerns.

HUMAN
KINDNESS
AND
THE SMELL
OF
WARM
CROISSANTS

PART I
PROBLEMS, DILEMMAS, AND PARADOXES

Nineteen Moral Puzzles

THE PROGRAM

Thought Experiments

I begin by presenting five thought experiments that have attracted a great deal of comment: Emergencies; The Child Who Is Drowning in a Pond; A Transplant Gone Mad; Confronting a Furious Crowd; The Killer Trolley.

They have been devised in order to try to discover to what extent our moral intuitions, that is, our spontaneous judgments as to what is good or bad, just or unjust, tally with deontological or, conversely, with consequentialist conceptions of ethics.

Are we deontological and therefore obsessed by the notion of manifesting unconditional respect for certain moral rules such as "do not lie" and "never treat a human person simply as a means"?

Or are we consequentialist, and therefore concerned to act in such a way that there is the most good and the least evil possible in this world, even if it entails not always respecting certain rules?

These thought experiments also demonstrate the importance, in our moral judgments, of elementary rules of moral reasoning such as "like cases must be treated alike."

Next I have recalled the case of Incest in All Innocence, which enables us to pose a question that seems to me to be central to morality. Why do we have a tendency to see morality everywhere, that is to say, to invent all manner of "victimless moral crimes," such as incest between consenting adults? In order to clarify this question, and to try to furnish the rudiments of an answer to it, I employ two experimental sources: psychological research into the moral development of children, and comparative anthropological researches into moral systems.

The Amoralist is a thought experiment devised in order to get us to reflect upon the two arguments moral philosophers use in order to obstruct the character who undermines their claims by saying "what if everyone did the same thing?" or "how would you like it if the same thing were done to you?"

The Experience Machine, Is a Short and Mediocre Life Preferable to No Life at All?, and I Would Have Preferred Never to Have Been Born all relate to the most traditional moral questions: "How are we to live?" "What is a life worth living?" Although I should say right from the outset that they do not provide an answer.

There then follows a discussion about animal rights, which takes into account the results of the previous case studies regarding lives worth living. Its point of departure is a series of fairly famous experiments known as the "Life Raft," the purpose of which is to make us reflect on our tendency to consistently favor the members of our own species.

The Utility Monster concludes this discussion by pushing the utilitarian argument further, to the point of absurdity.

A Violinist Has Been Plugged Into Your Back particularly interests me because it demonstrates the importance of thought experiments in moral debate. More specifically, it modifies the terms of the philosophical discussion surrounding abortion. Philosophers who contest the right to abort rely upon the idea that fetuses are persons, whose right to life is beyond dispute. This imaginary case, which derives more from science fiction than from a news item, allows us to envisage the possibility that, even if fetuses were persons, the voluntary interruption of pregnancy would still be legitimate. We could view it as an act of self-defense against aggression threatening existence itself or the quality of life. The whole question would then be that of knowing the conditions under which self-defense would be legitimate.

I have assembled under the title Frankenstein, Minister of Health a series of hypotheses concerning the future of human nature, were certain scientific projects to be implemented (reproductive human cloning, the genetic enhancement of human physical and mental capabilities, the freezing of ova, and so on)

The aim here is to assess the merits of the argument that says that we must not "tamper with nature" or "take ourselves for God."

The reactions to these thought experiments also enable us to assess our propensity to employ the slippery slope argument in this domain.

Who Am I Without My Organs? addresses the question of personal identity from the ethical perspective. What are the implications for our ways of conceiving of human "responsibility" and "dignity," the relations we establish between our persons, our bodies, and the organs or particles of which they are composed?

In order not to break completely with my earlier philosophical preoccupations, I present one thought experiment on sexuality. It aims to challenge our tendency to hierarchize the reasons we might invoke for having a sexual relationship, whereby love is placed at the top of the scale.

Finally, I propose two thoughts titled respectively It Is Harder to Do Good Intentionally Than It Is to Do Evil and We Are Free, Even If Everything Is Written in Advance, which are designed to tease out our intentions concerning the reality of our liberty and the moral importance of the idea of intention. I use them to draw certain conclusions regarding the difference between metaphysical and ethical thought experiments.

Experiments on Behaviors

In moral philosophy, experiments on behaviors have but one purpose, namely, to evaluate *virtue ethics*, an ancient notion revived with loud fanfare in contemporary moral debate. According to an ethics of this kind, there are exemplary moral "personalities," which remain such irrespective of the context. Yet experiments on behaviors seem to show that such personalities do not exist. There is thus no such "hard kernel" of the personality, something stable, unified, and unvarying from one situation to the next.

The idea that there could be "monsters" or "saints" anywhere else but in fairy tales or legends is therefore illusory.

Trivial or insignificant factors could alter our conduct in a "moral" sense (as with behavior whereby assistance is given, which is altruistic, helpful, generous, and so on) or else in an "immoral" one (as with destructive behaviors, which are violent, cruel, or humiliating).

The experiment I have chosen to represent destructive behaviors is famous. Devised by Stanley Milgram, this experiment is supposed to reveal the mechanisms underlying *submission to authority*. Though one of the earliest thought experiments, it remains authoritative (which is the very least you would expect).

Another experiment, conducted in the same spirit, is due to Philip Zimbardo. Here volunteers play the part of prison warders, the aim being to see how far, and how rapidly, they come to behave as badly as those whose roles they have assumed.[1] The experiment is not a cause for optimism. It did not take certain volunteers very long to become sadistic little executioners. All "reality TV" seems to take its inspiration from this same experiment.

I have set Zimbardo's experiment to one side, not because it is unduly depressing, but because the one devised by Milgram seems to me to suffice.

For helping behaviors, I present a number of small experiments. The least known, but not the least interesting, studies *the influence of the smell of warm croissants on human happiness*.

Because it seems to me unjust that this experiment has attracted so little comment, I took it as the title of the original, French edition of the present book.

To what extent do these experiments affect virtue ethics? This is the question that everyone—among those concerned with such matters—asks themselves.

One final observation, of an aesthetic rather than a conceptual order. My case studies vary markedly in length, a fact that may offend those who cherish balance and harmony. Some are very long, others very short, and still others somewhere in between. It is easier to justify length than brevity.

Thus, the case of The Killer Trolley has generated a staggering quantity of sometimes utterly baroque variants. It has sparked a huge number of studies and debates (with millions of hits on the World Wide Web), sometimes so sophisticated that only a few initiates are still able to follow them. We have got to the point that we can say ironically, although with a modicum of truth nonetheless, that a new scientific discipline—*trolleyology*—has been born.[2] The number of pages I devote to scrutinizing this case reflects the success of this "discipline."

Alongside these lengthy expositions, I give some very short case studies accompanied by equally short questions. This does not necessarily mean that the debate surrounding the case in question is any less rich.

I have simply sought to use such cases in order to introduce or to conclude succinctly a series of cases. For example, The Utility Monster serves to round off a sequence of reflections on utilitarianism, while Emergencies serves to introduce a set of questions on the opposition between killing and letting die.

1
EMERGENCIES

Is it acceptable to kill an imprudent pedestrian in order to avoid letting five severely injured people, whom you are rushing to the hospital, die?

SCENARIO 1: FAILURE TO RENDER ASSISTANCE TO A PERSON IN DANGER

You are dashing to hospital with, in your car, five people who have been seriously injured in an explosion. Every second counts! If you waste too much time, they will die.

All of a sudden, you see by the roadside the victim of a terrible accident, who is bleeding profusely.

You could save this person too, if you were to load her into your vehicle. If you fail to do this, the victim of this accident will certainly die. But if you do stop, you will waste time, and the five persons being rushed to hospital will die.

Should you stop even so?

SCENARIO 2: KILLING THE PEDESTRIAN

You are dashing to hospital with, in your car, five persons who have been severely injured in an explosion. Every second counts! If you waste too much time, they will die. But all of a sudden, you see in the middle of the road a pedestrian crossing in an imprudent fashion. If you brake you will skid and waste time, and the five persons being rushed to hospital will die. If you do not brake, you will kill the pedestrian. Should you brake even so?[1]

The hypothesis of the philosophers who invented or commented upon this experiment is that the majority of people will reckon that these two cases are not morally equivalent.

They will be more indulgent toward the driver who leaves a wounded person by the roadside to die than toward the one who kills a pedestrian, *even though the consequences are exactly the same.*

Is this difference in moral approach justified?

The philosophical debate surrounding the distinction between killing and letting die provides us with a few pointers for our attempt to answer this question.[2]

KILLING AND LETTING DIE

For some consequentialists, there is not a profound moral difference between killing and letting die. The outcome is the same in either case, since the victim dies.

Aretists (the friends of virtue ethics) and deontologists (the friends of Kant, among others) are not in agreement. For the aretist, you have to be a horrible individual to kill with your own hands (or with your own steering wheel), whereas anyone, or nearly anyone, can let a person die by way of calculation or through negligence without their being particularly morally repugnant.[3] Hence the harsh reaction toward someone who kills and the relative indulgence shown to someone who lets a person die.

But this explanation turns the *moral* distinction between killing and letting die into a *psychological* difference, which may pose a problem for those who take the two to be radically opposed.

It is on the basis of the criterion of intention that the deontologist distinguishes between killing and letting die. According to the deontologist, we cannot settle for evaluating an action in terms of its consequences without taking intentions into account. If we could do so, we would no longer be able to distinguish between killing someone by cutting him or her in half with a chainsaw, with the intention of punishing him or her (because he or she has not paid their debts, for example), and fleeing the scene of this horrible crime without attempting to bring succor to the victim, with the intention of saving one's own life.

Intention possessing a central moral value for the deontologist, he will naturally ascribe such an importance to the distinction between killing and letting die, and reject the consequentialist's skepticism regarding the question.

Yet there are cases in which we can readily see the difference between killing and letting die, but with greater difficulty discern the difference in intention.[4]

1. You are impatient to inherit from your uncle. You find him on his own and at home, lying in his bath, the victim of a heart attack. A doctor could still save him. You do not call a doctor. It is clear that, without killing your uncle, you are letting him die. It is also clear that you wish to get rid of him so that you can inherit.

2. You are impatient to inherit from your uncle. You crush him with your car. It is clear that you are not content to let him die. You are *killing* him. It is also clear that you wish to get rid of him so that you can inherit.

If the deontologist remains on the plane of intention, how can he distinguish between the first case, which is an example of letting someone die, and the second, which is an example of killing, since the intention informing the action is the same, namely, getting rid of the uncle in order to inherit?

More generally, that is to say, independently of consequentialist, aretist, or deontological explanations, we may wonder whether it is possible to save the moral distinction between killing and letting die in cases in which the effort required in order to not let someone die is negligible.

What moral difference would there be between killing a child and letting the child die, if we could save the child simply by clicking once on our computer?[5]

Even the deontologists and aretists would have to admit that, in such cases, the moral distinction between killing and letting die is nonexistent.

In order to persevere with the same line of argument, or, in other words, in order to show that the conflict between consequentialists, deontologists, and aretists over the distinction between killing and letting

die could be transcended, we might venture the hypothesis that this conflict does not depend upon the principles involved but *upon the point of
view adopted when describing the action.*

In reality, when philosophers address the distinction between killing
and letting die, they often adopt the agent's perspective: ambulance drivers in a hurry, unscrupulous heirs, or doctors whose patients are suffering from terminal illnesses. From this point of view, the difference
between killing and letting die does often appear glaringly obvious.

Yet if we put ourselves in the victim's or the patient's shoes, things look
quite different: the pertinence of the distinction between killing and letting die becomes less obvious.

Thus, for the terminally ill patient who wishes to go on living, it matters little whether the doctors intervene actively in order to cause him to
die or whether they let him die by terminating the care that was keeping him alive. The patient *wants neither the one nor the other option.* He
judges both of them to be equally bad. From his point of view as a patient
who does not want to die, the moral difference is nonexistent.

The same argument should apply to the case of a terminally ill person
who *no longer wants to live.* It matters little whether the doctors intervene actively in order to cause him to die or whether they let him die by
curtailing the treatment that was keeping him alive. The patient *wants
either option.* He judges both of them to be equally good. From his point
of view as a patient who no longer wishes to live, the moral difference
is nonexistent.[6]

If the above hypothesis is correct, we might then wonder: if there
is no *moral* difference for the patients, why should there be one for
the doctors?

2

THE CHILD WHO IS
DROWNING IN A POND

What would you do to save a child's life?

SCENARIO

By chance you are passing a pond and you notice a very small child who is in difficulties. He is drowning. Neither parents, nor nanny, nor any other bystander is in the vicinity to come to his aid. You could very easily save his life. All you have to do is to run immediately toward him without taking the time to strip off and drag him as swiftly as possible to the bank. You do not even need to know how to swim, for the pond really is not too deep and in fact resembles a large puddle. If you enter it, you merely risk ruining the beautiful shoes you have just treated yourself to and arriving late for work. Would it not be monstrous to let the child die in order to preserve your new shoes and to avoid being under some pressure at work?

If you answer yes to the above question, you should also answer yes to the question as to whether it is monstrous to allow children from the poorest countries to die of hunger when you would simply have to devote a tiny part of your income to saving them. We are in fact concerned here with *like cases having to be treated alike*.[1]

This thought experiment very plainly refers to the two basic notions in moral thought, namely, intuitions and rules.

The intuition may be phrased as follows: "letting a person die before our very eyes when we could very easily save them is monstrous."

The rule of reasoning is *"like cases must be treated alike."*

It may be applied as follows: if it is monstrous to let a drowning child die before your very eyes in a pond when you could easily save him by grabbing him by the hand, it is likewise monstrous to let a starving child die in a faraway country when you could easily save him by sending a small check to Oxfam.

This thought experiment may lead us to draw on two other elementary rules of moral reasoning: (1) "One cannot derive an ought from an is." It may be applied as follows: from the fact that the rich have a tendency not to devote of their own free will a significant part of their income to helping the poorest, it does not follow that this is good, or that it is what we must do. (2) "Ought implies being able to" (or, in more everyday terms, "no one is held to the impossible"). It may be applied as follows: Is it not completely unrealistic to demand of people that they sacrifice a significant part of the time and resources that are at their disposal and at that of those close to them in order to devote them to distant people whom they do not know? Is it not a *psychological impossibility*?

When all is said and done, this thought experiment may lead us to reflect upon three elementary rules of moral reasoning. Yet it is the rule "like cases must be treated alike" that bears the brunt of the argument.

We should be on our guard, however.

It is possible to dispute the value of the moral intuition ("letting a person die before our very eyes when we could very easily save them is monstrous") and the pertinence of the rule ("like cases must be treated alike").

THE INTUITION

It is far from being obvious that the failure to render assistance to a person in danger is a *monstrous* crime, that is, as serious as or more serious than, for example, a murder preceded by barbarous acts (although in this particular instance it would be a somewhat difficult case to defend).

One could add that no one has a *duty* to act like a saint or like the Good Samaritan. If the cost is too high, rendering assistance to a person in danger may be deemed discretionary. If, moreover, deciding what is "too high a cost" is left to each individual, the duty to assist a person in danger risks being reduced to almost nothing.

THE RULE

It is not obvious that the two situations described are sufficiently alike for it to be just to treat them alike.

One could, for example, point out that it is absurd to equate an act that you alone are able to do (save the child) with another that numerous people could also carry out (send a check to a charity combating famine).

Can the question of knowing if situations are sufficiently alike to be treated in the same fashion be given an absolutely definite answer in each case? Is it not more reasonable to hold that we will never be able to do better than find pragmatic solutions, recipes which allow us to judge that situations are sufficiently alike for it to be just to treat them in the same fashion?

MORAL QUESTIONS

Is not helping someone as serious morally as doing him harm?

Can the failure to render assistance to a person at risk of death, which amounts to not causing a good, be put on the same moral plane as murder, which amounts to causing an evil?

Are not saving a child who is drowning before our very eyes and letting thousands of children very distant from you die really similar cases?

Is our responsibility the same in both cases?

THE PROBLEM OF NEGATIVE RESPONSIBILITY

For a utilitarian, the fact that we have not personally committed any act aimed at causing hunger in the world in no way absolves us from our responsibility for this state of affairs, insofar as, at any rate, we could act to change it. Admittedly we are concerned here with a *negative* responsibility, but a responsibility nonetheless.[2]

For the critics of utilitarianism, this idea of negative responsibility empties the notion of responsibility of any content, because it applies the notion to something other than what we have voluntarily or intentionally caused. They admit only *positive* responsibility, that is to say, responsibility for something of which we are voluntarily the cause.

To which the utilitarian replies by insisting upon the absurd implications of deontological doctrines that only admit positive responsibility. Thus, Kant asserts that it is categorically forbidden to lie. According to him, we have to do here with a moral duty that, as such, admits of no exceptions. It even applies to the dramatic circumstance in which, when you are sheltering in your house an innocent pursued by cruel assassins, these latter present themselves at your door and ask you if their victim is within.[3]

It is hard to grasp Kant's position unless we take into account the fact that, for him, we are only responsible for what we do intentionally. The immoral acts that others perform while taking advantage of our moral commitments cannot morally be chalked up to us personally. In the circumstance in question, we are absolutely not responsible for what the criminals will do. Besides, we can never be sure of what they will do after our intervention, whereas we can be sure of having defiled our souls if we lie.

Finally, it is because Kant excludes negative responsibility that he can allow himself to assert that we must always tell the truth, no matter what the consequences may be, and even to criminals lacking all scruples. Is the absurd—or, at any rate, counterintuitive—nature of Kant's argument definitive proof of the validity of the idea of negative responsibility? The utilitarians, for their part, certainly think so. Yet is this argument as counterintuitive as all that? This is a point that does perhaps merit further scrutiny.

3

A TRANSPLANT
GONE MAD

Is it acceptable to kill a person who is in good health in order to transplant his organs into five patients with a life-or-death need of them?

SCENARIO 1

A highly gifted surgeon, specializing in the transplanting of organs, is caring for five patients who risk imminent death if they do not undergo a transplant. The first needs a heart, the second a kidney, the third a liver, the fourth a stomach, and the fifth a spleen. They all have the same blood type, a very rare one. By chance, our surgeon happens upon the medical file of a young man in excellent health, who likewise has this blood type. It would not be difficult for the surgeon to inflict a gentle death upon him, and then to remove his organs and through them to save the lives of the five patients.

What should he do: cause the death of the young man or let the five others die?[1]

SCENARIO 2

The highly gifted surgeon is tired. He prescribes in error product X to five patients, the horrifyingly negative effects of which differ, however, from one patient to another. In two of them, it affects the kidneys, in another, the heart. In the fourth, it is the liver, in the fifth, the lungs.

On account of the surgeon's fatal negligence, all five patients urgently need an organ transplant.

If the surgeon, who is directly responsible for their state, fails to find any organs to transplant, he will have *killed* five patients.

However, if he sacrifices the young man, he will only have killed one person.

Is that a sufficient reason to give the surgeon moral permission to sacrifice the young man?

Is it not *less immoral* to kill one person rather than five, taking everything else into account?

The hypothesis of the philosophers who invented these thought experiments is that most people will judge the surgeon to be committing a morally monstrous act, were he to sacrifice the young man along the lines of scenario 1. He should let his five patients die.

It would be just as monstrous, according to the philosophers, to sacrifice the young man along the lines of scenario 2.

It seems obvious to them that, if the surgeon fails to find any other solutions, he should let the five patients die. Given the surgeon's personal responsibility for their plight, this would mean that he would have killed them. In other words, he should resign himself to having killed five persons when he could have killed only one.

But if killing is a far more serious thing than letting die, how can we come to the conclusion that it is better, morally, to kill five persons rather than just one?

Is that not absurd?

4

CONFRONTING A FURIOUS CROWD

‾‾

Is it permissible to have one innocent executed in order to avert a massacre?

‾‾

SCENARIO 1: A FURIOUS CROWD

A judge confronts a crowd of demonstrators, enraged by the barbaric murder of a member of their community. They are demanding that the author of this barbaric crime be found. If this fails, they threaten to avenge themselves by attacking the quarter in which another community, whom they suspect of shielding the murderer, now lives. The judge does not know who the author of the crime is. In order to avert the sack of the entire quarter and the massacre of a great number of its inhabitants, he decides to accuse an innocent person and to have him executed.[1]

SCENARIO 2: A RESPONSIBLE PILOT

A pilot whose plane is about to crash steers toward the least populated zone of the city, knowing that he will inevitably cause the death of some of its inhabitants, in order to avoid killing a far greater number of them.[2]

For many philosophers, scenario 1 is thought to lend credence to our so-called deontological intuitions.

Indeed, the idea that there are things that we cannot do, no matter what the beneficial consequences for ourselves or for society as a whole may be, is the pivot of the deontological conception.[3]

The principle that states that we must never use a person simply as a means in order to obtain an outcome, even if it were desirable, is an expression of this conception. So too is the thought that there exist fundamental rights that we cannot in any circumstances violate.

If we have intuitions of this sort, we will reject with some distaste the utilitarian arguments that allow us to justify the sacrifice of an innocent for the good of society.[4] We will rule out, a priori, without brooking any argument, the moral possibility of executing an innocent person in order to avoid bloodshed.

The second scenario contradicts these conclusions. It does indeed seem that, in this sort of circumstance, the idea that it is legitimate to sacrifice a small number of people in order to avoid killing many others does not run counter to our intuitions. We will reckon, in all likelihood, that what the pilot does is rational, and even that it is his moral duty. We will judge him to have behaved in a "responsible" fashion.

If we think that what he does is fine from all these points of view, this means that our intuitions are not systematically deontological or antiutilitarian. They may give utilitarian thought the credit for possessing a degree of moral value.

The antiutilitarians could, however, retort that our deontological intuitions are not completely annulled by the belief that the pilot does well to go and crash into the least populated zone of the city. They will say that we probably have the feeling that our fundamental, inviolable, inalienable, and intangible rights are not threatened in this case, whereas they are when an innocent is sent to the gallows.

Executing an innocent person is violating his fundamental rights to a fair trial and to not being tortured or killed without an acceptable public justification. None of these rights is violated, however, when a pilot chooses to crash into the least populated zone of the city.

This is why the deontologist might reckon that he can, without contradicting himself, judge it to be repugnant to have an innocent executed in order to preserve the lives of numerous persons, and morally permissible for someone to crash their plane in a fairly uninhabited zone of a large city in order to kill fewer people.

Having an individual executed in order to avoid bloodshed is a decision that should, in principle, shake our deontological principles, supposing we have any, to their very foundations. It contradicts the notion
that there are things we must never do, and that violating the fundamental rights of persons is one of them. But the judge could reply that it is
precisely because he has a lofty idea of these fundamental rights that he
decides to have the innocent executed. He calculates that violating the
rights of a person is justified if it is with a view to avoiding violations
of the still greater rights of other persons. Now, if a residential quarter
of the city is sacked and its inhabitants massacred, the *quantity of fundamental rights violated will be huge*, or greater, at any rate, than if one
innocent were executed. The judge reckons that his action is just because
he has acted in such a way that the sum total of fundamental rights violated is the smallest possible. Can he be reproached for this?

In actual fact, I am putting into the mouth of the judge, who is perhaps
not a great expert in moral philosophy (and has no need to be such), the
so-called consequentialist arguments upon which utilitarian ideas rest.[5]

According to these arguments, what we must do is maximize the
good or minimize the evil in general, whatever our conception of good
and evil may be. In asserting that the good is pleasure, well-being, or
the satisfaction of people's preferences, and that evil is suffering, misery,
or whatever goes against people's preferences, the utilitarians are simply
rendering this principle specific. But a consequentialist can quite readily define the good in terms of respect for rights, and evil in terms of
violation of rights. A good attitude so far as he is concerned would entail
maximizing respect for rights and minimizing violation of rights.[6]

This is exactly the kind of idea that causes the adversaries of consequentialism to howl with derision! For them, the mere fact of *thinking of
making calculations of this kind* suffices to morally discredit those conceptions that allow them.[7] This is the proof that their minds are "corrupted,"
as Elizabeth Anscombe has put it.[8] In order to illustrate this unsympa-
thetic judgment, she proposes the following thought experiment:

Imagine that ten persons, the victims of a shipwreck, are stranded on a
rock on the open sea, without water or food. Some distance away another
shipwrecked person has managed to cling to another rock. He does not
have any water or food either. All of them will die very quickly if no one
comes to their aid. A navigator in the vicinity will have enough time to save

either the group of ten or the individual on his rock. Let us suppose that he decides to help the isolated person rather than the ten others, although not for a morally ignoble reason (for example, the isolated individual is white, the ten others are black, and the navigator is white and a racist).

Will he have done something wrong if he chooses to save one ship-wrecked person rather than ten?[9]

Elizabeth Anscombe thinks that he will have done nothing wrong. She justifies her position by saying that the ten people abandoned and left for dead would have no cause to complain.

Was something that was their due denied to them? No. Had they a greater entitlement to be helped than the isolated person? No. What wrong in the end has been done to them? None whatever.

What reproach could they then level at the navigator?

None, if his motive was at no point an "ignoble contempt."[10]

Elizabeth Anscombe does not use her thought experiment to test theories, whether consequentialist, deontologist, or of some other kind. She denies the value of moral theories in general, that is to say, the idea that we could *know in advance* what the most morally pertinent factors in a given situation are (rights, consequences, and so on). But she by no means rules out the possibility that the consequences might be pertinent in a *particular situation*.[11]

What, on the other hand, she appears to exclude in the thought experi-ment of the Shipwrecked is the notion that questions of quantity have any moral value whatsoever. She seems to think that, provided that one does not have a "corrupt" mind, they are questions that *one should not pose*.[12]

I am not sure that I understand what she means by a "corrupt" mind, or that I am able to give a clear account of it. I will therefore use a thought experiment to make my point.

Suppose someone asks you: "who should beat a wife who has been unfaithful, her brother, her father, or her husband?"

You will reply that it is an absurd, badly framed question, and that you do not wish to answer it, for it is already tainted by a way of thinking that you reject. It assumes that unfaithful wives must be beaten, a scandalous notion in itself.

The same goes for the navigator. If someone asks you, "Whom should he help, the ten who are shipwrecked, or the one who is all alone on the rock?" you must reply, "That's a badly framed question. It assumes that the navigator ought to take into consideration the fact that there are *more* shipwrecked persons on one rock than on the other.[13] Yet I reckon that nothing justifies this assumption from the moral point of view."

If this is indeed Anscombe's argument, it is clear enough, but I have to say that I do not find it convincing. It in fact implies that if the navigator has decided to save one person, rather than ten, he will have done nothing wrong. Indeed, there will be nothing to discuss. Anyone posing such a question probably has a "corrupt" mind, by dint of their envisaging a moral situation in terms of quantities.

Yet I do not see why "is it better to save ten persons rather than one?" is a question that we should refuse to pose.

Does Anscombe's conception imply that a pilot whose plane is going to crash into a big city asks himself a question *he should not pose* if he wonders how best to steer toward the least densely populated zone?[14]

Does it imply that if the pilot chooses to crash into the most densely populated zone, he will not have done anything wrong, for its inhabitants will have no cause to complain (well, when all is said and done, it will no longer be very much of an issue for them, so perhaps we should say rather that their families will have no cause to complain!), since they will not have been refused something that was due to them?

Who could agree with this? We can of course deny the moral value of quantities, but *this way of refusing a debate* does not seem to me to be philosophically justified. We know perfectly well, moreover, that the reasons for rejecting thought experiments are not always very good ones.

In a psychology test, the following question was posed: "what is the color of bears living on an ice floe where everything is white, bearing in mind the fact that bears are always the same color as their natural habitat?"

Some rejected the question, saying that they could not possibly know, never having been on an ice floe. If the inquirer insisted, specifying that the answer was contained in the question and that they simply had to reread it, they would refuse to do so.[15]

There is also the well-known story of the schoolboy. When a maths teacher said to him, "Let X be the number of sheep," the schoolboy objected, "But . . . what if X isn't the number of sheep?"[16]

In short, we need to know whether Elizabeth Anscombe's a priori rejection of consequentialism in general, and of one of its expressions, namely, taking quantities into moral consideration, is not equally unjustified, even if it cannot be, of course, equally absurd.

An empirical inquiry into the ideas we really form of consequentialist calculations should perhaps help us to not take this high-sounding vocabulary too seriously.[17]

We are concerned here with a comparative study of students from, on the one hand, the United States and, on the other, the Republic of China, to whom the story of the judge and the furious crowd was told.

The respondents had to indicate whether they found the judge to have made an "immoral" decision in having the innocent executed, on a scale of 1 (total disagreement) to 7 (complete agreement).

The American students tended to award the judge a grade of 5.5, signifying "agreement with the assertion that the judge's decision is immoral," but not "complete agreement." They did not award him 6.5 or 7: we do not find the total agreement that the anticonsequentialists should expect.

Furthermore, the students from the Republic of China, responding to the assertion that the judge's decision was immoral, awarded, on average, a grade of 4.9. They were even less likely than the American students to be in complete agreement with the notion that the decision was immoral.

Can it be that all these students, representing as they do vast populations, have minds "corrupted" by consequentialism?

According to the authors of the investigation, the minor differences between American and Chinese students are statistically significant. In their view, they indicate a more pronounced tendency on the part of students from the Republic of China to not disapprove of the judge's decision to have the innocent person executed.

But we should not conclude from this that there exists a profound "cultural" difference between the American and the Chinese students. The divergences in the grades awarded are not huge.

At any rate, it would be absurd to conclude, on the basis of these answers, that the students from the Republic of China are less rationalist or universalist than the American students, although that is precisely what the most relativist philosophers, those keen to persuade us that people "think differently in the East," might do.

In mounting a stronger defense of the judge's decision, the Chinese students simply show themselves to be more consequentialist than deontological. But being consequentialist is just as rational or universalist a stance as being deontological!

In making "calculations" of quantity with respect to the rights of persons, is the judge proving right those who think that consequentialism and utilitarianism are profoundly immoral doctrines?

Yet how could the aim of minimizing evil or of maximizing good be immoral?

5

THE KILLER TROLLEY

Is using a person simply as a means always unacceptable?

THE DRIVER'S DILEMMA

The driver of a trolley realizes that his brakes have gone when he is hurtling down a valley hemmed in by steep banks.

On the track, ahead of him, but some way off, there are five trolley workers carrying out repairs.

If the runaway trolley continues in its course, the five trolley workers will inevitably be crushed, since there is not enough room alongside the track for them to take cover.

However, as luck would have it, the main line divides shortly before reaching the five people, leading onto a narrow secondary track. The driver can avoid killing them if he diverts the trolley.

But, unluckily, another trolley worker is repairing the secondary track. The situation is much the same as on the main line, since there is not enough room alongside the track for the trolley worker to take cover, and the driver's maneuver will inevitably result in his being crushed.

The driver is therefore faced with the following dilemma: he could choose not to intervene and let the five trolley workers be crushed on the main line, or he could intervene and divert the trolley, thereby causing the death of the trolley worker on the secondary line.

Is it morally permissible for the driver to divert the trolley?[1]

This thought experiment was devised by Philippa Foot in 1967.[2]

Her idea was to contrast the driver's dilemma with the numerous other cases in which philosophers wonder whether it is morally permissible to sacrifice one person in order to save several others.

One of the most celebrated cases she evokes is that of a spelunker so fat that he gets stuck when attempting to get out of a cave and will have to be blown up with dynamite in order to save the lives of the other spelunkers trapped within.[3] Would it be morally permissible to do this?

But Philippa Foot preferred to compare the trolley driver's dilemma with the actions of a surgeon who kills a person in good health, dismembers them in order to remove the organs, and transplants them into five patients in order to save their lives.

According to her, *we all have the intuition* that it is not permissible for the surgeon to do what he does, but *we all also have the intuition* that it is permissible for the trolley driver to divert his engine toward one trolley worker in order to save five others. Yet in both cases it is a question of sacrificing one person in order to save five. Wherein does the difference lie? Are these intuitions not contradictory? How is one to justify them?

In a series of articles extending over more than thirty years, Judith Jarvis Thomson has proposed several variations on the original theme, in an attempt to refine the argument.[4] What follows are the two most important variations.

THE DILEMMA OF THE WITNESS WHO COULD THROW THE POINTS LEVER

You are strolling beside the tracks when you witness the scene described above. You quickly grasp that a trolley driver who is hurtling down a valley hemmed in by steep banks has lost consciousness. You see the five trolley workers trapped on the track and doomed to be crushed. What should you do? As luck would have it, there is a points lever right next to you. If you throw it, the trolley will be sent down a secondary track.

But, as bad luck would have it, another trolley worker is working on the secondary track. If you throw the lever, the trolley worker will inevitably be killed.

You are therefore faced with the following dilemma: either you fail to intervene and you let the five trolley workers be crushed on the main track, or else you intervene by throwing the points lever and cause the death of the trolley worker on the secondary track.

Is it morally permissible for you to throw the lever?

THE DILEMMA OF THE WITNESS
WHO COULD PUSH THE FAT MAN

You are on a footbridge when you see on the track beneath you a trolley hurtling along and, on the other side of the bridge, five trolley workers working on the rails. You grasp immediately that the trolley will not be able to stop. But you know enough physics to understand that if a large object were to be thrown at that moment onto the track, the trolley would inevitably stop. Now, a fat man, who seems to have the necessary volume and weight, is in fact on the footbridge right next to you. He is leaning over the parapet. He is waiting for the trolley to pass, suspecting nothing. Just a flick of the finger would send the fat man toppling over onto the track.

Is it morally permissible for you to do this?

Judith Jarvis Thomson informs us that "most people" when told these two stories reckon that it is morally permissible to throw the points lever, but not to push the fat man onto the track in order to stop the runaway trolley. She herself shares these intuitions. But how is one to justify them? How is one to account for this *moral asymmetry*? After all, when we push the fat man, we are doing nothing else but causing the death of one person in order to save the lives of five others, that is to say, exactly the same thing as when we deliberately divert the runaway trolley onto the secondary line where there is just the one person.

Is it not somehow inconsistent to judge that there is a significant moral difference between the two examples?

Thomson does not think so. On the contrary, she reckons that our intuitions are consistent because they enable us to grasp *the problem of rights* that has been raised.

According to her, two features in fact characterize the dilemma of the witness at the points lever:

1. The agent saves the five persons by transferring to one isolated person the danger that threatens them.
2. The agent does not resort to any means liable to constitute in itself a violation of the rights of the isolated person.

Taking up again a comparison I have already used, I would say that, for Thomson, the situation resembles to some degree that of a pilot who would opt to crash his plane into the least densely populated zone of a big city.

It is a way of minimizing the number of deaths liable to be caused by a threat that anyway already exists, and that will bring about deaths whatever the agent does. We are simply "diverting the fatality" without infringing the fundamental rights of anyone whatsoever.

According to Thomson, in the dilemma of the fat man, we are also simply "diverting the fatality." We save five persons by transferring to one isolated person the danger that threatens them. *But we do it by violating the fundamental rights of the fat man.* It is because we are aware of this difference that we judge the two cases so differently.

Judith Jarvis Thomson constantly refers to "ordinary intuitions." She contests sophisticated philosophical conceptions by invoking "what people think," that is to say, what she thinks people think. But what do people really think? How do they justify their judgments?

FROM THOUGHT EXPERIMENT TO "SCIENTIFIC" STUDY

The most ambitious inquiry into these questions was conducted by a team of psychologists directed by Marc Hauser in the context of a massive investigation on the Internet between 2003 and 2004.[5]

The results were published in 2007, in other words, half a century after Philippa Foot's thought experiment (one proof, among many, that a little story can have major consequences in the sphere of moral reflection).

Analysis of the answers to the whole set of experiments by and large confirms Judith Jarvis Thomson's intuitions: for most people it is morally permissible to throw the points lever but not to push the fat man onto the track in order to stop the runaway trolley. However, these answers do not validate Thomson's interpretation so far as rights are concerned.

THE INQUIRY

Hauser's inquiry involved around twenty-six hundred people, of both sexes and from several age sets, religions, levels of educational attainment, and ethnic or cultural groups, as well as in several different countries, namely, Australia, Brazil, Canada, India, the United States, and the United Kingdom.

Some respondents had been exposed to moral philosophy (a little over five hundred of them), while others had not. Several scenarios were outlined on separate sheets of paper and selected at random.[6] They differed in various respects from the original thought experiments devised by Philippa Foot and Judith Jarvis Thomson.

In the driver's dilemma, it is a passenger who has to seize the controls if need be, for the driver fainted when he realized that his brakes had failed. The witness's dilemma has been replaced by a pair of much more complicated dilemmas, which I will present separately below in order not to confuse the reader too much.

These scenarios are designed to enable us to determine whether reference to the *doctrine of double effect* can make it possible to understand the moral thinking of each and every one of us.

What is the "doctrine of double effect"?

When the psychologists conducting the inquiry use this term what they have in mind is a very simplified version of a complex notion that philosophers have elaborated over centuries of debate.

This moral doctrine, the original formulation of which is ascribed to Thomas Aquinas, designates two effects, one good, the other bad, of an action that, considered in itself, is good, or at any rate neither good nor bad.

One might think of the bombarding of a bunker in which the high command of a cruel army waging an unjust war is hiding, but in which civilians are also sheltering. One of these effects—the elimination of unjust aggressors—is good. This is what the action is designed to achieve, what its authors want. The other effect—the killing of innocent civilians—is bad. The authors of the action anticipate it, deeming it to be an inevitable "collateral effect." But it is not this latter effect that is *aimed at*, or *intended by its authors*. It is not even conceived as a *means* of arriving at the result aimed at.

According to the doctrine of double effect, this kind of action having two effects is morally permissible under these conditions (the bad effect is not aimed at, it is neither an end nor a means). But the harm caused (in terms of innocent victims, for example) must not be *disproportionate*.[7]

The psychologists conducting the inquiry seem sometimes to be reducing this complex and controversial doctrine to Kant's formula: "Act in such a way that you always treat humanity, whether in your own person or in the person of any other, never simply as a means, but always at the same time as an end."[8]

But they are not required to be the exegetes of medieval theories, and once we see with sufficient clarity what they have in mind when they speak of the "doctrine of double effect," everything is fine. It is the notion that we must distinguish between those cases in which we treat a human person *simply as a means* (the fat man) and those in which we do not do so (the driver who diverts the trolley, the witness at the points lever).

What is important and enables us nonetheless to place the empirical inquiry on the same plane as the thought experiment is the fact that the three significant differences between the variants have been respected:

1. action aimed at *diverting a threat* (to the five trolley workers) or action creating a *new threat* (to the fat man);
2. action causing the death of one of the persons as a *means* of stopping the runaway trolley (pushing the fat man) or as a *collateral effect* of the fact of having diverted it (by throwing the points lever);
3. action causing a death in an *impersonal* fashion (by diverting the trolley or by throwing the lever) or in a *personal* one (by giving the fat man a shove).

We must also insist upon the fact that, in the original thought experiments, no mention was made of personal ties between the participants, of how visible the trolley was, or of the possibility of stopping it by some other means. The inquiry treats all these things as given.

What were the results?

A PAIR OF THOUGHT EXPERIMENTS: DIVERTING
THE TROLLEY AND PUSHING THE FAT MAN

Of all the people taking part in the experiment, 89 percent judge it to be morally permissible to divert the trolley onto the secondary track on which there is a trolley worker, thus deliberately causing his death. There is no significant variation in terms of age, religion, gender, culture, educational attainment, or knowledge of moral philosophy.

Only 11 percent of the persons taking part in the experiment judge it to be morally permissible to push the fat man onto the track, thus deliberately causing his death.[9] There is no significant variation in terms of age, religion, gender, culture, educational attainment, or knowledge of moral philosophy.

These results are in complete harmony with Judith Jarvis Thomson's predictions. Indeed, all of the respondents deem it morally permissible to divert the trolley, but only a tiny minority judge it to be morally permissible to push the fat man.

What strikes all those interested in these results is the unlikely convergence of the answers despite differences in age, religion, gender, culture, educational attainment, and exposure to moral philosophy.

The more optimistic proclaim that, thanks to the help given by psychologists, the philosophers have at last discovered a universal moral datum. The problem is that such data seem rather to show that what is universal in our moral reactions is their inconsistency!

THE PROBLEM

For 89 percent of respondents, it is morally permissible to divert the trolley and thus deliberately cause the death of one person in order to avoid letting five die. Upon reading this result, we could conclude that the respondents are overwhelmingly consequentialist, since it seems to them morally permissible to carry out an act that minimizes evil, independently of any consideration relating to the nature of the act itself. But only 11 percent judge it to be morally permissible to push the fat man in order to achieve the same outcome. What has become of the consequentialist intuition that seemed to inform the first judgment? If we think that it is morally permissible to deliberately cause the death of one person in order to avoid letting five other people die, why would it not be morally permissible to throw the fat man onto the track? Is it not a form of inconsistency to judge that there is a significant moral difference between the two?

Such is the problem we have to address here.

THE RESPONDENTS ARE ASKED
TO JUSTIFY THEIR JUDGMENTS

When the respondents are asked to justify their judgments, they divide into three groups.

1. *Those who offer satisfactory justifications.*

They readily grasp what the significant differences between the cases are: physical contact or the lack of it; using another as a means or not doing so; averting an existing threat or introducing a new one.

They seek to justify their answers by taking such differences into account. They will say, for example, that it is permissible to divert the train but not to push the fat man onto the track, because it is acceptable to divert a threat but not to create a new threat.

2. *Those who offer unsatisfactory justifications.*

Some simply say that they are unable to justify their judgments. They find themselves declaring without any further justification that, in the one case, you cannot do other than let someone die, that it was inevitable, whereas in the second case you can abstain from killing. Others offer a consequentialist justification in the one case (it is better to save five persons than one, diverting the train is a lesser evil, and so on) and a deontological justification in the other (it is morally prohibited to kill, we have no right to take ourselves to be God and to decide who is to live or to die, not causing a wrong is more important than going to someone's aid, and so on). But they are not able to see the contradiction and do not attempt to explain why we should be consequentialist in the one case and not in the other.

3. *Those who offer justifications that are not pertinent* (but that are at the same time more amusing). They have not grasped the significant differences and offer any old thing by way of justification: "A man's body cannot stop a train," "It's an absurd story: the trolley workers would have heard the train coming and would have fled," and so on.

According to Hauser, 70 percent of the respondents are incapable of justifying their spontaneous judgments.

The 30 percent who offer satisfactory justifications have no particular characteristics so far as religion, age, or gender are concerned.

The only significant factor, that is to say, the only factor that would have enabled us to predict the satisfactory justifications, is *exposure to moral philosophy*. Of the philosophers 41 percent (as against only 27 percent of the nonphilosophers) are capable of giving satisfactory justifications of their spontaneous judgments. But these figures also show that the simple fact of having studied moral philosophy is no guarantee that we will be able to justify our judgments in a consistent fashion, since 59 percent of the philosophers were incapable of doing as much (but perhaps they had not attended every course!).

Hauser, who devised the experiment, was not surprised by this outcome. One of his original hypotheses was that there exists a *dissociation* between moral intuitions—the rapid, and often not conscious, reactions that we all have—and their justifications, which we are often incapable of giving.

On the other hand, for Hauser moral intuitions, despite their rapidity and intensity, are not purely emotional reactions. We may without a doubt be concerned here with spontaneous judgments devoid of any affective content, with the kinds of principle applied with the utmost rapidity and unconsciously, and with complete conviction. This hypothesis is pivotal to Hauser's construct. Indeed, it is this that he seeks to prove at all costs, since he is thereby able to envisage the possibility of our all being Kantians without being fully aware of it.

By means of his experiments, Hauser seeks to confirm that intuitions cannot be reduced to irrational emotional reactions lacking in moral relevance. This accounts for his bias in favor of a deontological interpretation of the results, one that is, however, not self-evident.[10]

There are in fact several ways of interpreting the spectacular difference between the results relating to the permission to divert the runaway trolley and those concerning the prohibition on pushing the fat man, even though the consequences of the two actions are identical.

THE CONSEQUENTIALIST INTERPRETATION

We formed a consequentialist judgment when we were faced with the dilemma of the witness who wonders whether he should throw the points lever. We judged that it was morally permissible to kill one person rather than five, when the alternative presents itself thus. If we were consistent, we ought not to change our conceptual framework when addressing the dilemma of the fat man. We should remain consequentialist and judge that it is morally permissible to push him even if, *personally, we would rather not do it*. But that is manifestly not what happens. We react in the second case as if we had suddenly become fanatical deontologists who absolutely rule out certain actions even when they are for a higher good. Why is this?

One of the hypotheses that would account for this inconsistency has it that we are naturally "programmed" (through the evolution of our species) to be shocked by violent physical contact, and psychologically incapable of remaining coolly rational when faced with such a sight or thought.[11] The idea of pushing the fat man unleashes emotional reactions so intense that they block the processes of rational thought. This is why we would tend to distinguish between diverting the train and pushing the fat man, when the two cases are in fact morally equivalent.[12]

THE ROLE OF THE EMOTIONS

In order to sustain the above conclusions, which rank deontological reactions with irrational madnesses (with which perhaps not all deontologists will be best pleased), some researchers have invoked techniques borrowed from the neurosciences.[13]

When the possibility of pushing the fat man is evoked, it is the emotional areas of the brain that are presumed to be aroused. When the possibility of throwing the lever is evoked, it is the rational areas of the brain that are supposed to react.[14]

I obviously cannot pronounce upon the validity or otherwise of the data, having no particular competence in what is by common consent a highly problematic field of science, namely, that concerned with cerebral localization.[15]

The philosophical objection that I might nonetheless raise here is that, in a very general sense, from the fact of an action being motivated or accompanied by emotional reactions, it does not follow that it is itself irrational.[16]

THE DEONTOLOGICAL INTERPRETATION

It was in order to establish the inadequacy of this consequentialist and irrationalist explanation that Marc Hauser submitted to the respondents the following two cases, which are variants of the case of the witness throwing the points lever proposed by Thomson.[17]

We are concerned here with situations in which the fat man is *used* to block the runaway trolley, *but without his having been pushed by the witness.*

This time we must imagine that the secondary track onto which the witness can divert the trolley by throwing the points lever describes a loop and then returns to the main track.

THE CASE OF THE FAT MAN ON THE LOOP

A fat man is on the loop. In hitting the fat man and causing his death, the trolley will be greatly slowed down, and this will give the five trolley workers time to flee and to save their lives.

Is it morally permissible to throw the lever?

THE CASE OF THE MASSIVE OBJECT
AND THE TROLLEY WORKER

There is a massive object on the loop behind the trolley worker. In hitting the object, the trolley will be greatly slowed down, thus giving the five trolley workers time to flee and to save their lives. But the trolley worker who is in front of the massive object will inevitably be killed.

Is it morally permissible to throw the lever?

In the pair of scenarios "with a loop," the action taken is impersonal, without there being any violent physical contact with the victim.

However, in the first scenario, the witness who throws the points lever treats the fat man *simply as a means* to block the runaway trolley, which leads us to assimilate this case to the one in which the fat man is directly pushed.

In the second scenario, the trolley worker's death is inevitable, but *as a collateral effect of the fact that the trolley is heading for the massive object.* The trolley worker is not treated simply as a means.

In this second scenario 72 percent of the respondents judge it to be morally permissible to throw the lever (the trolley worker is not treated simply as a means).

But in the first scenario only 56 percent judge it to be morally permissible to throw the lever (the fat man is treated simply as a means).

According to Hauser, the difference is statistically significant. It allows us to conclude that in the four scenarios, with and without a loop, the respondents judge that we can cause the death of one person in order to save five, *if we do not treat him simply as a means*. Furthermore, when the trolley is stopped on a loop, there is no violent personal contact, which enables us to eliminate the irrationalist interpretations.

For Hauser, taken as a whole, these results display a kind of consistency. In his view, everything happens as if the respondents were intuitively applying the doctrine of double effect, as it is understood by the authors of the experiment.

It is deontological, in the sense that, in the authors' opinion, it absolutely excludes treating intentionally a human person simply as a means.

In the two scenarios "without a loop," the doctrine might be phrased: it is permissible to divert the train but not to push the fat man. By diverting the train, we are certainly causing the death of the trolley worker, *but we are not treating the trolley worker simply as a means to save five lives.* On the other hand, that is precisely what would happen if we were to push the fat man.

But this pair of scenarios can admit an irrationalist interpretation, since there had been violent physical contact. In the two scenarios "with a loop," the "violent personal physical contact" factor is eliminated. Yet the respondents continue to judge it to be far more inadmissible to treat the fat man simply as a means than to cause the death of one person as a collateral effect.

For Hauser, these results bear out his hypothesis: it is not the idea of violent personal physical contact that explains why we overwhelmingly reject the idea of pushing the fat man, but *the thought that we are treating him simply as a means.*[18]

The results thus lend credence to the idea that the sample in question tends to employ the doctrine of double effect (as interpreted by Hauser).[19]

In other words, the best interpretation of the *full set* of the results would not be consequentialist and irrationalist but deontological and rationalist. It shows that what counts for most people is their not treating a person simply as a means.

This interpretation is still contested by the irrationalists, on the basis of the following hypothesis. And if it were possible to cause the fat man to fall onto the track, with the aim of blocking the runaway trolley, without any violent physical contact, simply *by opening up a trapdoor beneath his feet*?[20] Would we be so shocked? Probably not.

However, we would thereby have treated the fat man simply as a means, and in exactly the same fashion as if we had pushed him! Before asserting that what shocks, when we push the fat man, is not the violent physical personal contact, but the fact that we are treating him simply as a means, we should perhaps devise some tests based upon thought experiments as simple as that of the trapdoor that opens up beneath the fat man's feet.[21]

A DRAW BETWEEN DEONTOLOGISTS AND CONSEQUENTIALISTS

Marc Hauser is confident of having shown that people rapidly and unconsciously apply the doctrine of double effect (in his sense of the term).

If people find it permissible to throw the points lever but not to push the fat man, it is because a person is turned into a simple means in the second case but not in the first. Their moral intuitions are consistent, rational, and . . . deontological! But the consequentialists continue to defend the notion that the refusal to push the fat man is inconsistent, irrational, and due to the involvement of emotional factors. They reckon that the deontologists have not conclusively demonstrated that a feeling of revulsion at the idea of brutal, personal physical contact was not an important explanatory factor, but was perhaps in fact the decisive factor accounting for the different judgments regarding the fact of, on the one hand, throwing the points lever and, on the other, pushing the fat man.[22]

The debate surrounding the best interpretation of the spontaneous judgments of people exposed to the different scenarios of The Killer Trolley therefore ends up, at any rate for the time being, in "a draw."

THE POVERTY OF MORAL INTUITIONS

Numerous other research projects have been devised with a view to evaluating the above results. The latter should in fact lead us to doubt the solidity of our moral intuitions. For all we have to do is to add certain data to our presentation of the dilemmas, or simply to modify the way in which they are presented, and our moral intuitions alter.[23]

Various hypotheses lending credence to this supposition are plausible. Some of them have received empirical backing.

Our intuitions relating to the moral right to throw the points lever or to push the fat man might vary:

1. *According to the presumed moral qualities of the people involved.* We should be less doubtful about the idea of pushing the fat man if we were told that it was he who had put the lives of the five trolley workers at risk by sabotaging the trolley, or if we learned that he was a sadistic torturer who went on footbridges to watch accidents.[24]

2. *According to whether the people at risk are relatives or are unknown to us.* We would tend to be more moved by the fate of the trolley worker who was to be sacrificed if he were a friend or a member of the family.

3. *According to the age of the people at risk of being sacrificed.* We would tend to be more moved by the fate of the person who was to be sacrificed if they were young or very young.

4. *According to whether the people at risk of being sacrificed resemble us or not.* We would be less inclined to sacrifice people who resemble us. Women would thus be less inclined to sacrifice their sisters, and men their brothers![25]

5. *According to the degree of responsibility of the people at risk.* We would be less inclined to sacrifice people who were in no way to blame for being at the precise spot they happened to be at or whose duty it was to be where they were.[26]

6. *According to the energy needed to obtain the result.* We would be sensitive to the fact that more effort is required to push a fat man from a footbridge (especially if he resists) than to operate a points lever.[27]

7. *According to whether the result is obtained by violent physical contact or not.* We would be more shocked if the fat man were to be toppled by

brute force than if his fall were to be brought about by opening a trap-door beneath his feet.

8. *According to whether the threat is diverted or created.* We would tend to find less grave the action of diverting an existing threat without creating a new one (by throwing the lever) than that of creating a new threat (which is aimed at the fat man), even if it were with a view to diverting an existing threat.

9. *According to the position occupied by the characters in the narrative.* It would be a graver matter to threaten a person who was in a safe place (the fat man on the footbridge) than a person who was in a tight spot (the trolley workers).

10. *According to the order in which the stories are told.* When we have been exposed first of all to a scenario of sacrifice as hard to bear as a transplant gone mad (one person is killed so that their organs can be removed and the lives of five other sick people saved), we will be less inclined subsequently to deem it permissible to throw the points lever, thereby causing the death of one person in order to save five.[28]

11. *According to the choices on offer.* If the decision is taken to present only the case of the witness who pushes the fat man and at the same time to insist that there is no other way of saving the five trolley workers, the rejection of it will be less overwhelming.[29]

12. *According to the position that the respondent is supposed to assume.* We all tend to be more moved by the fate of the trolley worker to be sacrificed when we ourselves are presumed to be responsible for throwing the points lever (in answer to the question "what would you do?") than when we are presumed to be in the position of a moral judge who does not intervene (in answer to the question "what do you think about it? is it morally permissible?").[30]

If all of these hypotheses were to be confirmed, the upshot would be that the intuition whereby it is permissible to sacrifice one person in order to save five is operative only in cases in which:

1. We have to do with unknown persons, with whom we have no familial ties and no bond of proximity or friendship, and who have no gender or age, no rights, and no responsibilities;

2. Our point of view is that of a moral judge who does not intervene.

One cannot say that this would be a result decisively in favor of the idea that our moral intuitions are on balance consequentialist. It might simply allow us to think that our consequentialist intuitions, if we have any, are, most of the time, neutralized, because the cases in which they could be pertinent are very rare.

From another perspective, if all the above hypotheses were confirmed, the intuition "it is not permissible to treat a person simply as a means" would be completely neutralized or anaesthetized:

1. when treating a person simply as a means is the only choice possible;
2. when treating a person simply as a means does not require any violent physical contact;
3. when the person whom we treat simply as a means is morally repugnant;
4. when the person whom we treat simply as a means is at the origin of the threat;
5. when the person whom we treat simply as a means is responsible for the risks he has taken.

Results of this kind could establish that our minds do not have a tendency to orient themselves, in every case, consciously or unconsciously, around the principle: it is not permissible to treat a person simply as a means.

One cannot say that it would be a conclusive result in favor of the notion that our moral intuitions are on balance deontological. It might merely allow us to think that our deontological intuitions, if we have any, are often blocked because, in numerous cases, they do not take priority.

THE FRAGILITY OF MORAL INTUITIONS

One author has wondered whether, by increasing the quantity of people who could be saved by pushing the fat man (a hundred persons saved, let us say, instead of five), the intuition that forbids us to do it could be blocked. This does not seem to always be the case.[31]

But that does not rule out the possibility of there being certain "threshold effects" that weaken this type of intuition. The difficulty is in knowing where these thresholds are situated, and for what kind of people.[32]

Is it morally permissible to push the fat man in order to save a hundred, a thousand, two thousand, a million innocent adults?

And what if it were to save children, let alone *our own* children?

Once cases become too complicated, once the numbers exceed a certain threshold, once the qualities of people obtrude, our intuitions lose their solidity.

To summarize:

For a great many researchers, the problem posed by the experiment of The Killer Trolley is that of the consistency of the answers.

Why is there such an asymmetry between our ways of judging the act of throwing a lever to divert a runaway trolley toward one person, thereby bringing about his death, and those of causing the death of one person by pushing him off a footbridge in order to block a runaway trolley?

According to the so-called consequentialist interpretation, The Killer Trolley experiment shows that we are inconsistent, being under the sway of our irrational emotional reactions.

According to the so-called deontological interpretation, The Killer Trolley experiment shows that we are consistent. We apply rapidly, naturally, and effortlessly a principle that is well known in moral philosophy, whereby we are prohibited from treating a person simply as a means.

How are we to come to a decision?

The most difficult questions arise when we change the way in which we present dilemmas, adding particular details to the cases under discussion. We then realize that our intuitions change too. These intuitions appear to possess neither the robustness nor the degree of independence from their theoretical contexts that we generally expect to find in an intuition. The philosophical questions raised are then the following:

If we really do not have robust intuitions that could come to the rescue of deontological theories, how could we justify such theories?

If we really do not have robust intuitions that could come to the rescue of consequentialist theories, how could we justify such theories?

According to certain philosophers, appealing to moral intuitions is as vain and hopeless in ethics as it is in mathematics.[33] Is the comparison pertinent?

It seems to me that the contribution of experimental moral philosophy to armchair moral philosophy is a little clearer at present.

The empirical results show that the philosophers who defend theories, be they deontological or consequentialist, cannot rely upon ordinary intuitions to justify their point of view.

But that does not mean that they are wrong or that no other means of justifying a moral theory exists save that of appealing to ordinary intuitions.

Besides, other interpretations of these intuitions, of a kind that neither Hauser nor his critics have envisaged, are possible.

I have in mind here the interpretation in terms of rights that Judith Jarvis Thomson defended and that has never really been tested.[34]

We can also try to advance interpretations that would be founded neither on the doctrine of double effect, nor on the emotions, nor indeed on rights.

6

INCEST IN ALL INNOCENCE

Are certain actions inappropriate or immoral, even if they have not caused anyone any concrete harm? Are these victimless moral crimes?

SCENARIO

Julie and Mark are brother and sister, both of them adults. They spend their holidays together in the South of France. One evening, happening to be in a chalet by the sea, they say to each other that it would be interesting and amusing to try to make love. Julie has been on the pill for some time, so that the risk of her becoming pregnant is negligible. Yet to make doubly sure, Mark uses a condom. They derive pleasure from making love but decide not to repeat the experiment. They recall with fondness a night that gave them a sense of being closer to each other, but keep their secret to themselves.

What do you think about this? Was it morally permissible for them to make love?[1]

These questions have been put to population samples differing in "culture," social origin, age, gender, religion, and so on.[2] The spontaneous judgments were on the whole convergent. The majority of respondents voiced their immediate disapproval. Yet their more considered justifications were ill formed.

In order to explain why what Julie and Mark did was not "appropriate," they evoke the possibility of Julie becoming pregnant and giving birth to a handicapped child. The experimenter then reminds them that the couple had taken every precaution to avoid such an outcome.

The respondents then resort to another justification: the relationship could inflict a psychological trauma. The experimenter reminds them that no such thing occurred.

They change tack once more: the relationship might offend society. The experimenter again specifies that it will remain secret.

In the end, the respondents are obliged to admit that they have run out of reasons, which does not prevent them from continuing to voice their disapproval: "I know it's wrong, but I cannot say why."

As in The Killer Trolley experiment, there is a sort of dissociation between the spontaneity and vigor of the judgments and the inadequacy of the rational justifications.[3]

But in the case of incest, the judgments of spontaneous disapproval are so robust, so resistant to argument, and also so universal that it is not altogether absurd to suppose that they are just, natural, and innate.

This, however, is a hypothesis that stands in need of verification. From the fact of a response being universal, it does not follow that it is innate. It could be inculcated by force into all human societies for the very same reasons (such as the need to extend the circle of social exchanges outside the family, narrowly defined, by taking sexual partners and spouses elsewhere and so on).[4]

In order to add a slight note of skepticism, I would also venture to point out that some researchers reckon that the question is badly phrased, for in their view it is not true that incest and cannibalism (to give another example of a supposedly universal prohibition) are everywhere and always disapproved of. They assert that many societies tolerate or even advocate incest (to varying degrees of proximity) or cannibalism (by, for example, authorizing or requiring the consumption of those one has slain in battle, but not of others).[5]

Is it true that universal moral prohibitions exist?

Is it true that our intuitive responses are independent of our considered judgments?

Is it true that our intuitive responses are natural and innate?

These are interesting questions of fact to which different answers are possible.

Nevertheless, this type of research does not have particular moral implications, aside from the general and banal conclusion that if our intuitions are innate and not susceptible to being modified, any moral conception that did not take them into account would be unrealistic.[6]

But what interests me in this thought experiment are its particular implications for moral philosophy. From this point of view, the questions raised by Incest in All Innocence are the following:

Is it true that, for the majority of people, certain actions are inappropriate or immoral, even if they have not caused any concrete harm to anyone?

Can one legitimately consider victimless crimes to be immoral?

THE PROBLEM OF "VICTIMLESS MORAL CRIMES"

In order to describe actions judged to be inappropriate or immoral, even though they have not *caused any nonconsensual harm to any concrete persons*, one can speak of "victimless moral crimes" or "victimless moral wrongs."[7]

This category includes personal relationships between consenting adults (incest, homosexuality, prostitution), violations of abstract entities (blasphemy against gods or ancestors), and action directed at the self (suicide, the control of hair or of sexual secretions).[8]

A number of studies of moral psychology have addressed this question of "victimless crimes." In fact, two major conceptions are opposed in this regard:

1. We tend to judge only crimes *with* victims to be immoral.
2. We tend to judge some victim*less* crimes to be immoral.

The first conception may be termed "minimalist," because it presupposes our underlying morality to be impoverished through the fact of its excluding victimless crimes.

By the same token, the second conception may be termed "maximalist," because it presupposes our underlying morality to be rich inasmuch as it admits many victimless crimes.[9]

MINIMALISM

Various different experimental studies lend credence to the thesis of the poverty of our underlying morality. The most important are those by Elliot Turiel and Larry Nucci.[10]

One such study consisted of interviews with young or very young subjects (from the age of five to adolescence) who had had a strict religious education in milieux relatively untouched by the liberal values surrounding them (Amish-Mennonites, Calvinist Protestants, conservative and orthodox Jews).[11] This study was concerned with the spontaneous judgments and justifications given by respondents as regards the following subjects:

Moral rules: is it permissible to steal, to strike, to speak ill of someone, to destroy their property, and so on?

Nonmoral rules linked to religious authorities and rituals: is it permissible not to respect the Sabbath, the obligation to cover or uncover oneself, or dietary prohibitions, as well as not to practice circumcision?

Where religious rules, such as those concerning circumcision or kosher food, are concerned, answers tended on the whole to converge.

1. Religious rules are inapplicable to the members of other religions. They only apply to those who share the same faith. Those who are not Jews are not obliged to be circumcised or to eat kosher food!
2. If there were no reference to these obligations in the Bible, or if no religious authority prescribed them, there would be no need to abide by them.

Where moral rules are concerned, the answers likewise all tend to converge.

1. Moral rules are applicable to the members of other religions. They apply to everyone.
2. Even if there is no reference to these obligations in the Bible, one should nonetheless abide by them.

These general tendencies are presumed to establish that the young distinguish between what pertains to morality and what forms part of the religious domain.

In the moral domain, the rules are presumed to be universal and in no way need to be guaranteed by a human authority, a sacred text, or a supernatural being. According to the respondents, it would be wrong to steal or to strike someone, even if there were no mention of a ban upon such acts in any passage from the Bible.

Turiel finds an answer given by an eleven-year-old conservative Jew to be particularly representative.

He is asked the following question:

"Would it be permissible to steal if it were written in the Torah that it is *obligatory* to do so?"

The boy replies:

"Even if God says it, we know he can't mean it, because we know it is a very bad thing to steal . . . maybe it's a test, but we just know he can't mean it."[12]

When asked to explain why God would not mean it, the boy replies: "Because we think of God as very good—an absolutely perfect person."

Where this boy is concerned, it is the good in a moral sense that is the measure of what *God can think*. For him, religion is not the measure of what is good in a moral sense.

Young people raised within the Calvinist religious tradition are supposed to honor the divine commandments. Yet they too think that, if God commanded one to steal, the act of theft would not thereby be rendered good, and that in any case God could not ordain such a thing.

Like the young Jewish boy, the young Protestant, who is fifteen years old, says that God could not ordain such a thing "for he is perfect and if he said that we should steal he would not be perfect."

To summarize, these answers show that, for the respondents, religious commandments are only obligatory for the members of that faith, whereas moral obligations are binding for everyone.

These answers lend weight to the hypothesis concerning the independence of the moral and the religious domains. They also show that when there is interference between these two domains, it is not always religion that dictates what is good. It is the moral ideas that serve to evaluate the religious rules and not vice versa. Finally, these answers show that, for these children, the rules that are supposed to apply to everyone and not only to their own community are minimalist. They only concern actions that, like stealing, are presumed to harm others.

In short, according to this theory, when we are young we do not see morality everywhere but only in a specific domain: that of our relationships with others and, more precisely, of wrong done to others.

The hypothesis that a long social apprenticeship is needed in order to become a "moralizer" in every domain, including one's relationship with oneself, becomes plausible.

These studies have been reproduced in various countries, Western and non-Western alike, in order to evaluate the scope of these results. They have been conducted among subjects professing different religious beliefs.

They have culminated in the elaboration of the most interesting and most controversial theory of moral development to be encountered today.[13]

No matter what the social or cultural milieu, we would very early on make a distinction between three different domains:

1. The *domain of morality*, from which we universally exclude those actions that involve harming others.
2. The *domain of conventions*, from which we exclude certain actions whereby the harm done to others is not obvious, as with eating pork or dressing in pink at a funeral. These rules are only valid for the community in question and are justified or guaranteed by a sacred text or a word uttered by authority.
3. The *personal domain*, which is only supposed to concern oneself and which has to do with individual preferences (it could, for example, involve a liking for some sport or another or for some kind of bodily decoration).

Such a differentiation into three domains may become further refined during moral development, from childhood until the entry into adulthood, but it exists from the earliest years.

MAXIMALISM

The scientific community was obviously never going to be indifferent to so complete and so bold a theory. In order to test its validity, similar

experimental scenarios have been devised.[14] The theory's leading chal-
lenger has been Jonathan Haidt, an American psychologist.

His central hypothesis, diametrically opposed to that of Elliot Turiel,
is that a natural or universal tendency to restrict the domain of morality
to actions that harm others does not exist.

In order to verify this hypothesis, Haidt presented population samples of differing ages, cultures, and socioeconomic levels with a range
of "vignettes" recounting stories of behaviors that are deemed to be
thoroughly shocking but that cause no direct harm to anyone.

The scientific wager was as follows. If these actions causing no direct
harm to others are judged to be "immoral," the theory according to
which only actions harming others can be judged to be immoral would
obviously be refuted.

More generally, if, for certain populations, there are *victimless moral
crimes*, the theory according to which our baseline morality is built upon
the idea that there is no victimless moral crime would be refuted.

The samples consisted of individual young adults, rich and poor,
from Philadelphia (the United States), Recife (Brazil), and Porto Alegre
(Brazil), 360 in all. Eight little stories were printed on the vignettes:

Swing: A little girl wants to play on a swing. But a little boy is already
on it. She gives him a violent shove. He falls and hurts himself very badly.

Uniforms: A boy goes to school in his everyday clothes even though he
knows that the rule is that one must come in uniform.

Hands: A man always eats with his recently washed hands, both at
home and in public.

Flag: The mistress of the house finds an old Brazilian (or American)
flag in a cupboard. As she is not particularly keen to keep it, she tears it
up into rags, which she uses to clean the bathroom.

Promise: A dying woman asks her son to see her and gets him to
promise that after her death he will visit her grave every week. The
son so loves his mother that he makes her this promise. But after his
mother's death, he fails to keep his promise, having too many other
things to do.

Dog: The family dog is killed by a car just outside the house. The members of the family have heard that dog meat is delicious. They decide to
prepare the dog for the pot, and dine well off it.

Kisses: A brother and a sister love kissing each other on the mouth. They find a spot where no one can see them so that they can kiss passionately on the mouth.

Chicken: A man goes each week to the supermarket to buy a dead, plucked chicken. Before putting it in the oven, he masturbates in it.[15]

What is important so far as Haidt's hypothesis is concerned is the fact that only the first vignette (*Swing*) presents a story of a crime *with* a victim: the physical harm done to an innocent child. All the others recount *victimless crimes*.

If people exposed to the vignettes having to do with *victimless crimes* find these actions to be immoral, we will be able to conclude that it is mistaken to think that only crimes *with* victims are judged to be immoral.

Haidt calls "permissive" those who limit the domain of legitimate moral judgment to crimes *with* a victim, and "moralizing" those who extend this domain to include certain crimes *without* a victim.

The conclusion of Jonathan Haidt's first studies, published in 1993, is that, strictly speaking, there does not exist any "natural" or "universal" propensity to be moralistic. There is merely a set of more or less significant correlations between economic and social status as well as other factors of the same nature such as "Westernization" and "urbanization" and the scope given to moral judgment.

People whose economic and social status is high and who are "Westernized" are, by and large, less moralistic than those whose economic and social status is lower and who are less "Westernized." The former admit fewer victimless moral crimes than the latter.

When we enter into the statistical details, we find that the poor are more alike from one country to the next than the rich are.

Those people whose economic and social status is the lowest are on the whole moralistic, be they in Recife, Porto Alegre, or Philadelphia. But those people with the highest economic and social status are divided. They are more moralistic, or less permissive, in Recife and in Porto Alegre than in Philadelphia. Apparently it is not only economic and social status that counts: the factor of "Westernization" seems to have a certain pertinence also. But there are so many other factors left unexamined by this kind of study that it is not necessary to rush to endorse this "culturalist" conclusion.

THE NATURALIZATION OF THE "MINIMALISM" VERSUS "MAXIMALISM" DEBATE

Subsequently Jonathan Haidt set off in a different direction, far removed from his initial sociological relativism. He has maintained that studies in moral psychology were often skewed by certain "progressive" and "Westernizing" prejudices.[16] They start from the assumption that the whole of morality can be boiled down to the concern to not cause harm to others, and they admit, without any valid reason, that everyone traces very clear boundaries between morality, religion, and social conventions.

But in every human society, there are obligations and prohibitions that go beyond this minimal concern to not cause concrete harm to other individuals but that, for the members of these societies, do come *under the same type of judgment.*

The majority of prohibitions, whether sexual (the prohibition on incest between consenting adults included) or dietary (not eating pork, shellfish, and the like), are considered by those who respect them as "universal" bans and obligations, that is to say, as rules valid for everyone and not only for the members of a specific community. The same applies to obligations toward our own selves (shaving our heads, letting our beards grow, not drinking alcohol or taking drugs, and so on) and the dead (not burying them, burying them on the bare ground, and so on). *"Moral" obligations or prohibitions are therefore involved.*

However, these obligations and prohibitions concern actions or relations that do not cause any concrete wrong to anyone in particular (even in the case of incest between consenting adults) and seem not to raise questions of justice or of reciprocity.

It may be the case that in the Western world the moral domain has in fact become very narrow. But it may also be the case that it is the cultural prejudices of the researchers that cause them to see things thus.

Be this as it may, if we take the trouble to go and look elsewhere, we realize that a moral system based upon wrongs, rights, and justice is not the only one conceivable. Thus Schweder distinguishes three great moral systems: *an ethics of autonomy, an ethics of community, an ethics of divinity.*[17]

ETHICS OF AUTONOMY

In an ethics of autonomy, the person is viewed as a structure of individual preferences. Their autonomy and their capacity to choose and to control their life are considered to be moral values to be protected.

The moral code here insists upon the notions of wrongs, rights, and justice. These notions are elaborated in a refined fashion in the legal and moral systems of secularized Western societies. This code corresponds exactly to the moral domain as Turiel conceives it.

ETHICS OF COMMUNITY

In an ethics of community, the person is viewed as the bearer of a role in a collective, interdependent venture that transcends him.

The moral code here insists upon duties, respect, and due obedience to the authorities. Actions are supposed to be in accordance with the requirements of the roles attached to gender, caste, age, and so on.

ETHICS OF DIVINITY

In an ethics of divinity, the person is viewed as a spiritual entity who must, above all, remain pure, avoid being defiled, and aspire to sanctity. All sorts of acts that are supposed to defile or degrade the spiritual nature of the person are punished even if they cause no harm to others. This moral code, centered upon bodily practices, seems bizarre to the members of Western societies. Yet it has given birth in India to an unbelievably complex system of rules of purity and defilement, and in the Old Testament to a complex series of sexual and dietary prohibitions.

Haidt's cunning lies in having deposited these three systems in each of us at birth, so to speak. The inhibiting or development of one or another of them would depend upon the social environment.

In his more recent publications, Haidt has taken naturalization a step further. He supposes our minds to be naturally equipped with five modules, that is, autonomous psychological apparatuses with a specific purpose, which act in a quasi-automatic manner, like reflexes, and whose activity is triggered by precisely determined social stimuli:

1. Actions that cause suffering or pleasure,
2. Just or unjust actions,
3. Expressions of betrayal or of loyalty toward the community,
4. Signs of deference,
5. Signs of personal purity and impurity (respect for hygienic, dietary, and sexual rules).

These modules have typical emotional expressions:

1. *Compassion* toward those who suffer,
2. *Anger* toward those who cheat and gratitude toward those who help,
3. *Pride* in the membership group and *indignation* toward "traitors,"
4. *Respect* for prominent personalities,
5. *Disgust* for those who transgress against the rules of decency or of dietary or sexual purity.

These emotions help to nurture particular virtues: generosity, honesty, loyalty, obedience, and temperance (chastity, piety, purity). In each society, they are triggered by specific stimuli: baby seals and soccer teams arouse feelings of compassion or of pride in certain societies and not in others.

In every society they answer to functional imperatives and present advantages from the point of view of the survival of groups or of individuals: protection of the youngest and most vulnerable, the benefits of cooperation and respect for hierarchies, the protection of health, and so on.

All in all, these reactions that are "innate," "natural," "automatic," "intuitive," and "emotional" in character underlie more complex cognitive constructions, which for their part are the concern of a process of socialized apprenticeship, which might explain the divergences in the public conceptions of the scope of the domain of ethics.

Even more recently Haidt added two other modules to those he had already described, which means that he has got to seven, although I should add that he has been assisted by a colleague.[18] With a little imagination they will find others, for there is not really any reason to stop.[19]

To summarize: For Haidt, our basic morality is very rich. We develop very early a tendency to judge as immoral all kinds of actions without clearly identifiable victims: homosexual relationships between consenting adults, blasphemy, suicide, profanation of tombs, the consumption of impure food, ways of dressing ourselves or treating our bodies that are deemed to be impure, and so on. Haidt went so far as to maintain that the sheer incomprehension with which liberals greet this natural morality is at the origin of profound scientific and political errors. But the principal question remains that of knowing whether Haidt has really succeeded in proving that entire populations tend to judge certain victimless crimes as "immoral" and not simply as contrary to religious or social rules.

THE CASE OF FEMALE GENITAL MUTILATION

There is no shortage of people who reject female genital mutilation. What is this rejection based upon? Haidt reckons that the following judgment, recorded in the course of an investigation, is particularly significant: "It is an obvious example of child abuse. Not protecting these young women from these barbaric practices, which deprive them forever of the right to the physical wholeness God has given us, is a form of inverted racism."[20]

According to Haidt, this judgment, though apparently simple, brings into play several different reactions that involve independent or "modular" psychological mechanisms or micro-operations of the mind: one mechanism sensitive to the physical sufferings of others, and other mechanisms, each independent, sensitive to injustice, to the fact that a divine commandment protecting physical integrity has been violated, or that personal purity has been defiled.

What would give moral disapproval of excision so profoundly intransigent a character would be not only the fact of its causing a concrete physical wrong to a particular individual, but that of its infringing a divine commandment and values of physical integrity and of personal purity. This reaction would be irreducible to the indignation aroused by a concrete wrong inflicted upon a flesh-and-blood individual.

But the minimalists could object that it is the revulsion at the wrong done to another that in reality bears all the weight of the moral judgment. The reactions of indignation at the infringement of the physical integrity and personal purity that God protects by an inviolable law would, admittedly, be important but they would have a religious, and not a *moral*, character.

Finally, the choice between the two interpretations depends not upon the facts but upon the theory used at the outset. If we reckon that the moral and the religious domains are entirely independent of each other, the minimalist interpretation will seem to be preferable. We will say that what is ostensibly a moral reaction is simply revulsion at the wrong done to another. The remainder pertains to what is not moral.

If we judge, on the other hand, that the moral and the religious domains are not entirely independent from each other, the maximalist interpretation will then become plausible. We will be justified in saying that the feeling that a divine commandment has been breached, or that personal purity has been profaned, does itself come under the heading of a moral reaction.

Can we distinguish between moral conceptions in terms of their propensity to invent victimless moral crimes (such as homosexual relationships between consenting adults)?

How far could a moral system go in inventing victimless moral crimes? Could it go so far as to judge certain ways of dressing or doing our hair to be immoral?

How far could a moral system go in excluding victimless moral crimes? Could it go so far as to leave people free to do as they wish with their bodies, including the selling of it as separate body parts?

In the light of recent research in moral psychology, we might be led to suppose that human beings are not only more moral than they have usually been taken to be, but *much more moral*, that is to say, far too much inclined to judge others, to act as moral policemen, to nose around in other people's affairs, and to take themselves to be saints.

This is what John Stuart Mill was implying when he wrote: "it is not difficult to show, by abundant instances, that to extend the bounds of what may be called moral police, until it encroaches on the most unquestionably legitimate liberty of the individual, is one of the most universal of all human propensities."[21] Yet it is a controversial claim. In reality, researchers entertain two opposed hypotheses.

For some, our basic morality is poor, indeed, minimal, and a considerable social labor is needed to turn us into moralizers unable to tolerate styles of life different from our own and always tempted to poke our noses into other peoples' affairs.

For others, our basic morality is rich, and a considerable social labor is needed to turn us into liberals able to tolerate styles of life different from our own and respectful of the intimate lives of others.

Which is the more convincing hypothesis?

We do not yet know.

7

THE AMORALIST

"What if everyone did the same thing?"—"How would you like it if the same thing were done to you?"

WHAT ARE THESE ARGUMENTS WORTH?

Just as you are leaving a restaurant, a storm breaks. You cannot afford to wait for it to pass and you haven't got an umbrella. By a lucky chance (lucky for you), other, more prudent customers have come out with their umbrellas, and left them in a stand.[1]

You glance swiftly to the left and to the right. No one is watching you.

You grab an umbrella and you leave nonchalantly, neither seen nor recognized, as if you were wearing the ring of Gyges, which if it is turned renders the wearer invisible, allowing him, according to the myth, to commit any number of crimes with complete impunity.[2]

You are more or less conscious of wronging in some measure a person whom you do not know, and who has not done you any harm. Yet you do not really take this fact into account.

Plainly this is not a sufficient reason to prevent you from taking the umbrella.

You are one of those amoralists who have been bothering philosophers (and nonphilosophers) ever since they began to reflect upon morality.[3]

They stubbornly seek the knockout argument that might release the amoralist from his indifference and, in this particular case, prompt him not to steal an umbrella from an unknown person on the night of a storm.

They wish to give a decisive answer to the question that has always preoccupied them: "Why be moral?"

WHY BE MORAL?

Among the reasons for doing or not doing certain things, there are some that are a matter of personal prudence. If you drink what is really too much beer, you risk damaging your health. If you wish to stay healthy, there is a good reason for you to drink a little less beer.

There is also the desire to be approved of, and the fear of being disapproved of, by others, the desire to obtain rewards and to avoid punishments. If you really drink too much beer, you risk being subjected to moral lectures all day long (among other inconveniences). If you prefer to avoid such lectures, there is a good reason for you to drink a little less beer.

One can envisage a great number of other reasons for doing or not doing certain things—religious reasons, such as the unconditional love of God or the fear of the punishments God might inflict (particularly terrible after death), and so on.

Certain philosophers reckon that alongside these prudential reasons, social or religious, for acting or refraining from acting, there are "purely" moral reasons. No definition of these reasons wins unanimous support, but there is a tendency to characterize them as follows:[4]

1. They are more to do with others than with ourselves: this is what distinguishes them from reasons of personal prudence.

2. We are not supposed to abide by them out of the hope of being rewarded or the fear of being punished: this is what distinguishes them from social reasons.

3. They are not fixed in an arbitrary fashion by a supernatural authority: this is what distinguishes them from religious reasons.

4. There is a tendency to think that everyone should follow them, which is not always the case where social or religious reasons are concerned.[5] Indeed, these latter are often seen as valid reasons solely for the

members of such-and-such a society or for the believers of such-and-such a religion. Jews and Muslims do not eat beef that has not been bled. Yet they in general acknowledge that if you are not Jewish or Muslim, you are not obliged to do as they do. On the other hand, they reckon that everyone should refrain from stealing, even those who do not practice their religion.[6]

5. They have to do with matters that strike us as important (such as life, death, happiness, the meaning of life, the common good, and so on) rather than trivial (the color of the socks you will wear in order to go fishing). Certain philosophers at least reckon that one of the criteria by which to identify moral rules is the intensity of the reaction that the transgressing of them provokes. They add that if the transgressing of moral rules provokes more intense emotional reactions than a failure to respect a no parking sign, it is because of their importance in our lives.[7]

Those researchers who concern themselves with ethics often give the impression of thinking that these criteria are enough to enable us to distinguish moral reasons from others. Yet this is a controversial idea. Given that it is not very easy to characterize "purely" moral reasons other than in this pointillist fashion, we can be tempted to deny their specificity and to reduce them to a congeries of reasons of personal prudence and of social or religious conformism.

Besides, there are several candidates for the title of moral reason.

The main ones are *deontological* and *consequentialist* reasons. The former are reasons for never doing certain things, such as lying, killing, or torturing, no matter what the benefits may be for ourselves or for society. The latter are reasons for promoting the good of the greatest possible number or, more precisely, for aiming at maximizing the good or minimizing the evil.

We may come to think that, from this consequentialist point of view, it is morally permissible to cause the death of one individual in order to save ten thousand of them or to torture one child in order to save a hundred thousand of them.[8] At the same time, it may also be the case that we are absolutely not inclined, personally, to kill someone even if it is in order to save ten thousand lives, or to torture a child even in order to save a hundred thousand of them. It is not out of cowardice or incomprehension of what a moral requirement is. It is because our deontological moral reasons then clash with our consequentialist moral reasons.

Be they deontological or consequentialist, these "purely" moral reasons pose a particular problem.

It is fairly easy to understand why reasons of prudence or the fear of God or of society might hold us back from performing certain acts (stealing, humiliating someone, causing pointless suffering) or inspire us to carry out others (helping someone, working for the common good). It is more difficult to know why we should be sensitive to moral motives. What are we to say to someone who is ignorant of such motives and is satisfied simply to follow rules of personal prudence and the laws of the city, while transgressing them from time to time when it suits him and when, like our borrower of umbrellas, he is sure of not being caught?[9]

There exist two arguments that crop up time and time again among philosophers, as well as among nonphilosophers.

"What if everyone did the same thing?"

"How would you like it if the same thing were done to you?"

What exactly do they mean? Are they conclusive?

I do not believe so.

WHAT IF EVERYONE DID THE SAME THING?

It is necessary to distinguish between the "what if everyone did the same thing?" argument and the Kantian criterion of "universalization without contradiction" with which it is often confused.

The Kantian idea is that certain rules of personal action would become absurd or contradictory if they were presented as great moral principles valid for all and in all circumstances.[10]

Take the little idea that may go through your mind (but not too often of course): "I only keep my promises when it suits me."

Turn it into a universal principle: "He who makes a promise is only obliged to keep it if it suits him."

The problem is not that if each person followed this principle, the practical consequences would be disastrous. It is that this principle is absurd and irrational, for it is contradictory in itself. It authorizes us to make promises that we have no intention of keeping, that is to say, promises devoid of the properties that make them promises.

The Kantian test of universalization proposes a criterion by which to evaluate our principles. It measures their *conceptual consistency.*[11]

For its part, the "what if everyone did the same thing?" argument asks us to *imagine practical consequences.* One can put it that it is a sort of thought experiment, an "imaginary generalization."[12]

At first glance, it is above all a machine for producing platitudes, that is, true propositions whose intrinsic interest is not evident: "If everyone went at the same time to the local swimming pool, there would no longer be any room to swim."

Or, to give another equally fatuous example: "If everyone went out into the street at the same time, we would no longer be able to move."

But the imaginary generalization "what if everyone did the same thing?" can also have an interesting explanatory role.

We must distinguish, at any rate, two sorts of case. The generalization concerns either morally neutral actions or else actions judged to be morally flawed.

MORALLY NEUTRAL ACTIONS

Posing the question "what if everyone did the same thing?" is supposed to help us to grasp that actions that are neither bad nor irrational in themselves can become so if several persons perform them, for example, in certain situations of mutual dependence and at the same time.[13]

Consider the action of withdrawing all of your assets (supposing you have any) from the bank, an action that in itself has nothing bad or irrational about it. If everyone did this at the same moment, the outcome risks being disastrous.

Consider likewise a fire that devastates an overcrowded nightclub, when there is only one way out. There is nothing evil or irrational about wishing to save your own life by rushing toward the exit. If everyone does it at the same moment without caring about others, the outcome risks being catastrophic.

MORALLY FLAWED ACTIONS

In the cases that preoccupy us, however, the question "what if everyone did the same thing?" does not have to do with morally neutral actions like withdrawing our savings from a bank.

It concerns actions that are each, at first glance, morally flawed, such as taking an umbrella from an unknown person on the night of a storm, line-jumping, or being a scrounger who turns up at a get-together empty-handed and helps himself to whatever others have put upon the table.

What use is this question?

None whatsoever, according to the deontologist. For him, the question "what if everyone did the same thing?" may perhaps have a social interest: we can wonder whether the tolerance of such acts would be stronger or weaker if they were more frequent. But it has no moral interest. We clearly recognize its fatuousness when it concerns crimes whose gravity is admitted. In order to condemn a barbarous murder, no one needs to appeal to the "what if everyone did the same thing?" argument.

Obviously, line-jumping and scrounging are not crimes of the same seriousness. But they are not actions that are just either. For a deontologist, it is a sufficient reason to disapprove of them. It is pointless to add: "what if everyone did the same thing?" It is *one argument too many.*

Nevertheless, if the aim is to find an argument that could convert the amoralist, it is absurd to think that a deontological moral reason like "you must not do it because it is wrong, period!" could do the business, since indeed he is not sensitive to this kind of reason. We have to put to him an argument of another kind. And it is this that the question "what if everyone did the same thing?" is supposed to supply. How?

At first glance, it is not by harping on the personal interests of the amoralist. "What if everyone did the same thing?" does not mean "if you line-jump, if you scrounge, if you steal another's umbrella on the night of a storm, it is *you* who will be hurt." It would anyway be absurd to highlight this argument, for it is manifestly false.

However, the argument "what if everyone did the same thing?" has something to do with the consequences. It does indeed seem, in fact, that appealing to this argument is meant to make the line-jumper, the scrounger, and the one who "borrows" an umbrella on the night of a storm understand that they are simply living as "parasites" upon the moral system.[14]

If no one any longer respected lines, if no one any longer brought any food or drinks to parties, and if no one any longer left umbrellas in stands, they would no longer be able to line-jump, take advantage, or purloin an unknown person's umbrella on the night of a storm. Those who do such things rely upon the fact that most people respect moral rules, and the former thus profit from the advantages offered by not respecting them.

It is not obvious, however, that the amoralist would be unduly impressed by an accusation of parasitism. It is a moralistic qualification to which he would have every reason to remain indifferent.

Is the argument "how would you like it if the same thing were done to you?" more effective in causing the amoralist to doubt?

"HOW WOULD YOU LIKE IT IF THE SAME THING WERE DONE TO YOU?"

We must distinguish the argument "how would you like it if the same thing were done to you?" from the *law of talion*, the principle of revenge that entitles us to render evil for evil: "An eye for an eye, a tooth for a tooth!"[15]

"How would you like it if the same thing were done to you?" is a rhetorical question. The answer expected is "I wouldn't like it," when you have caused harm to someone, such as breaking their tooth. But this answer says nothing at all about the punishment that you ought to undergo (or even if you ought to undergo one). It certainly does not entitle the one whose tooth you have broken to break one of yours too.

"How would you like it if the same thing were done to you?" would seem to be more akin to the famous *golden rule* than to the law of talion. This rule says: "do not do unto others what you would not have them do unto you," or "do unto others what you would have them do unto you." It is not a principle of revenge but one of benevolence.[16]

However, like the law of talion, the golden rule is a principle of reciprocity with a certain content.[17] It specifies what we have to do: do unto others what we would have them do unto us, and do not do unto others what we would not have them do unto us.

If we follow the rule blindly, moreover, we arrive at absurd conclusions. A masochist would be allowed to torture others (do unto others what you would have them do unto you). A doctor who would prefer not to have his appendix removed ought not to remove one from a patient (do not do unto others what you would not have them do unto you).[18] For its part, the argument "how would you like it if the same thing were done to you?" does not have any precise content. It is simply a general test of impartiality.

How might it be applied to the case of the umbrella?

Suppose we start from the principle that you would not like it if your umbrella were taken on the night of a storm (for otherwise the argument does not work).

If you are impartial, you cannot think: if it is *my* umbrella that is taken, then it is morally important, but if it is the umbrella of anyone but *me*, it has *no moral importance.*

Of course, if it is your umbrella that is taken rather than that of another, this will probably make a *psychological* difference to you. But if you view things from an impartial point of view, it will not have, for you, any *moral* difference.

From this impartial point of view, at any rate, you will have a reason not to take an unknown person's umbrella on the night of a storm. It is exactly the same reason as the one that ought to stop others taking yours.[19]

The problem (there always is a new one looming in moral reflection) is that this reason will not necessarily dictate your actions.

You could have one reason to do or to not do such-and-such a thing, and another, stronger reason not to behave in accordance with this reason.

You could have one reason to do or to not do such-and-such a thing and lack a *personal motive* to behave in accordance with this reason.[20]

LEAVE THE AMORALIST IN PEACE!

If the problem of the amoralist is not that he lacks moral reasons for doing such-and-such a thing, but rather that he lacks personal motives for acting in accordance with them, it is futile to preach at him.

What's the use of repeating what he already knows?[21]

All that we could do to release him from his moral inertia would be to reinforce his personal motives for behaving in accordance with these moral reasons, that is to say, acting not on the reasons for his action, but on its *causes*, be they psychological, sociological, or biological.

In order to change the amoralist, we would have to subject him to a program of moral conditioning, perhaps not as radical as that imagined by Anthony Burgess in *A Clockwork Orange*, but one whose moral value would also be far from obvious.[22]

Rather than undertaking this kind of project, would it not be better to leave the amoralist in peace?

Is it not preferable to try to live with him as he is (while being a little wary even so, from time to time)?

8

THE EXPERIENCE MACHINE

Would you swap your real life, marked as it is by frustrations and disappointments, by partial successes and unfulfilled dreams, for a life of experiences that were desirable but entirely artificial, being occasioned by chemical or mechanical means?

Suppose there existed a machine that could enable you to live every form of experience that you wished to have.

Brilliant neuropsychologists would be capable of stimulating your brain in such a way that you would be able to believe and feel that you are engaged in writing a great novel, making a good friend, reading an interesting book, or doing whatever else your heart desired. But, in actual fact, you would be permanently in the machine, with electrodes plugged into your skull. It is you who decides the program of experiences that you wish to have for, say, two years. Subsequently you would have a few hours out of the machine to choose the program for the following two years. Of course, once in the machine, you would not know that you were there; you would think that everything was really happening.

Would you plug yourself in?

Do not worry about minor details, such as knowing who would run the machines if everyone were plugged in![1]

This thought experiment has been used to demonstrate that so-called hedonistic conceptions were false.[2]

In actual fact, for the hedonists what counts is the having of agreeable experiences or, more broadly, experiences that correspond to our preferences. The fact of these experiences being real or illusory, deep or superficial, chemical or natural, their being fixed upon a person with a stable character or not ought not to have any sort of moral importance. Artificial paradises are just as valuable morally as natural ones, and a loss of self has nothing immoral about it.

But if the hedonists were right, everyone would be tempted to plug into the experience machine!

Now, according to Robert Nozick, the inventor of this thought experiment, we (humans) will not be tempted to plug ourselves into the experience machine. He advances three reasons of an intuitive kind in favor of this hypothesis:

1. We want to do things and not only have the experience of doing them.
2. We want to be a certain kind of person and not an indeterminate object into which electrodes are plugged.
3. Contact with reality and authenticity have a crucial importance in our lives.

Suppose the main hypothesis is correct, that is, the majority of people will not be prepared to plug themselves into the experience machine. Suppose even that, in a large-scale investigation, it appears that 100 percent of respondents refuse to plug themselves into the experience machine. One question would remain unresolved. For Nozick, the only possible interpretation of this general refusal would be that pleasant experience is not the only thing that counts in our lives. Is this really the only possible interpretation?

No! One could suppose, for example, that this refusal has its origin in an irrational psychological revulsion toward everything that is not "natural," or in an anxiety at the idea of having electrodes plugged into the brain, and so on. But the best "alternative" explanation has cropped up only very recently. A good deal of cunning was needed on the part of a philosopher to propose it.[3]

THE TENDENCY TOWARD INERTIA

If we refuse to plug ourselves into the experience machine, it is not because experience counts less than reality or authenticity. It is because we would change too much the state in which we are currently if we were to agree to plug ourselves in.

In actual fact, we have a certain *tendency toward inertia*. We do not want to undergo too violent a change of state, and this is what justifies the prediction that we will reject the experience machine.

Nevertheless, according to the same model, if we were plugged into the experience machine, we would not be willing to leave it. That too would be too violent a change, and one that would contradict our tendency toward inertia.

The philosopher's cunning lay in having thought of this pair of hypotheses, and above all of the second, which, if it were confirmed, would prove that *we are not at all opposed in principle to living in an experience machine*.

Now if it is true that we are not at all opposed, in principle, to living in an experience machine, Nozick is wrong, as are all those philosophers who have been persuaded over almost half a century that he dealt hedonism a knockout blow.

This hypothesis is founded upon an explanatory model inspired by certain works by economists, which they call the *bias in favor of the status quo*. In order to verify it, we simply have to change the way in which the thought experiment is presented. The question would no longer be: "Are you prepared to leave your real life and to plug yourself into the experience machine?" It would be: "Would you prefer to stay in the experience machine or to return to your real life?" This is what was done with a set of students with no particular expertise in philosophy. The thought experiment of the experience machine was reformulated as three scenarios according to the principle: You are in the experience machine. You are given the option of returning to real life. Do you accept?

SCENARIO 1

One morning, you hear someone knocking at your front door. You open it. An official makes the following announcement:

"We are very sorry to inform you that you have been the victim of a grave error. You have been plugged into an experience machine by some brilliant neuropsychologists able to stimulate your brain. You believed that you made friends, that you were engaged in writing a great novel, reading some interesting books, or doing whatever else your heart desired.

"But in reality it was all merely cerebral stimulation. You were permanently in the machine, with electrodes on the skull.

"We have realized that the request to be plugged in had been put to us by someone else.

"We therefore propose to you, with our sincere regrets once again for everything that has occurred, the following two possibilities: either stay in the machine or else return to your real life."

Choose.

Tell us why.

SCENARIO 2

The same story as in scenario 1. But at the end it is specified:

"In real life, you are in the high-security wing of a prison.

"Do you prefer to stay in the experience machine or to return to real life?"

Choose.

Explain why.

SCENARIO 3

The same story as in scenario 1. But at the end it is specified:

"In real life, you are a stupendously rich artist living in a palace.

"Do you prefer to stay in the experience machine or to return to your real life?"

Choose.

Explain why.

To summarize, the three scenarios are as follows:

1. *Neutral*: Do you prefer to stay in the experience machine or to return to your real life?

2. *Negative*: Do you prefer to stay in the experience machine or to return to your real life, in which you are in the high-security wing of a prison?
3. *Positive*: Do you prefer to stay in the experience machine or to return to your real life, in which you are a stupendously rich artist living in a palace?

In the negative scenario, if you choose real life you return to the high-security wing of a prison.

Of respondents, 87 percent declare their preference for staying in the experience machine.

This result can hardly be said to be very startling. The fact remains that it could be enough in itself to prove Nozick wrong. Reality is not *always* preferred!

In the neutral scenario, 46 percent only prefer to remain in the machine.

In addition, 54 percent prefer the return to real life without asking themselves any questions as to its quality, which seems to send the pendulum in the other direction.

But the positive scenario should give the ultimate advantage to the idea that reality is not necessarily preferred.

In this scenario, if you choose real life, you return to a palace as a multi-millionaire. Nonetheless, 50 percent do prefer to remain plugged into the machine. This result is disconcerting. Knowing that you will be able to live like a nabob, why remain in the experience machine?

This is where the hypothesis of a preference for the status quo, whatever it may be, intervenes.

You have a somewhat irrational preference for the state in which you already are, which means that you will choose to remain in the experience machine, even when the prospects offered by a return to real life are splendid.

From this investigation we can draw certain conclusions as to the validity of hedonism simply by noting that Nozick's experiment is not sufficient to refute it.

But it seems that we can also derive from it a more general and more important conclusion, regarding the validity of our moral intuitions.

If we ask, "Are you prepared to plug yourselves into the experience machine?" people are supposed to answer, "No."

We must conclude that human intuitions do not agree with hedonism.

If we ask, "Are you prepared to leave the experience machine?" the answers are more various. But by and large, the tendency is toward inertia. We prefer to remain in the machine.

We must conclude that human intuitions agree with hedonism.

We are therefore saddled with two contradictory conclusions: *our intuitions are and are not hedonistic.*

It is possible to rescue consistency by bringing in the hypothesis of the status quo. In both cases, violent changes of state are rejected owing to conservatism.

But if the hypothesis of a preference for the status quo holds, that means that our moral intuitions are systematically affected by a psychological flaw: conservatism or inertia.

Does that deprive them of all value as a means to moral knowledge? That would have to be proved.

In any case, if we reckon that this tendency toward inertia is irrational, we are the heirs to a problem in moral epistemology.

How could irrational intuitions serve to confirm or invalidate a moral theory, be it hedonistic or of another kind?

9

IS A SHORT AND MEDIOCRE LIFE PREFERABLE TO NO LIFE AT ALL?

Under what conditions can a child say to his mother that she has made a mistake in letting him be born?

RISKY PREGNANCIES

Two women are both looking forward to having a child.[1] The first is already three months pregnant when the doctor tells her one piece of good news and one piece of bad. The bad news is that the fetus she is carrying has a defect, which, even if it is not so grave as to render the child's life wretched or not worth living, will greatly diminish its quality of life. The good news is that this defect can be easily treated. All the mother has to do is to take a pill without side effects and the child will avoid his handicap.

The second woman sees her doctor before becoming pregnant, and when she is just about to stop all contraception. In this case too the doctor tells her one piece of good news and one piece of bad. The bad news is that because of the state of her health, if she conceives this child in the next three months, he will have a significant handicap that will have the same impact on the child's quality of life as in the previous case. This handicap cannot be treated. But the good news is that the woman's pathology is temporary. If she waits three months before getting pregnant, her child will avoid the handicap.

Let us suppose that the first woman forgets to take her pill and that the second does not wait to get pregnant, which means that the two children are born with precisely the same serious handicap.

Are the moral implications identical? This is by no means obvious.

The first child can say to his mother: "By not taking the pill, you have wronged me. My life would be better if you had taken the pill."

But the second child cannot say: "By not waiting three months before becoming pregnant, you have wronged me. My life would be better if you had waited."

If he cannot say it, it is quite simply because, had his mother waited, he would not have been born at all!

Is a life with a grave handicap, but not so miserable as to not be worth living, preferable to no life at all?[2]

10

I WOULD HAVE
PREFERRED NEVER TO
HAVE BEEN BORN

---

*Would it have been better never to have been born even if the life you
live is worth living?*

A friend tells you:

"My life is happy, full of pleasures and even of moments of ecstatic joy.
It consistently brings me profound affective and professional satisfaction. I have the sense of being entirely fulfilled. And, don't you see, this
feeling of happiness is not fleeting: it is present all the time, and in my life
it has always been so."

You observe that it is not April Fool's Day, that your friend is not joking, and that he has not been drinking, and nothing suggests that he is
any more mad than the average person. It is quite simply an exceptional
case of authentic happiness!

You congratulate your friend, you declare that you are happy for him,
which should increase his happiness yet more. He thanks you, then adds:

"My life is worth living. But I would have preferred never to have been
born."

For the philosopher Bernard Williams, your friend is talking nonsense! He contradicts himself in one and the same sentence.

For Williams, indeed, asserting that "I would have preferred never to
have been born" implies "my life is not worth living."[1] There is not even

any need to specify this if the person you are addressing has a modicum of common sense.

When you say to that person, "I would have preferred never to have been born," they must spontaneously understand, "my life is not worth living."

Consequently "my life is worth living but I would have preferred never to have been born" is a contradictory proposition.

Is Williams right? Is it really incoherent to say, "My life is worth living, but I would have preferred never to have been born."[2]

The first problem posed by this kind of statement is the fact that the question of knowing what "a life worth living" is does not have an answer that obtains unanimous agreement.

Some demand that objective criteria be employed to define this kind of life. Others leave it up to each person to decide. I will consider both cases.

The second, still more complicated problem is that it is hard to understand what "a preference for never having been born" means.

It cannot *literally* be a question of a preference for the state in which we are in when we are not born. We do not know what state we are in when we are not born. How could we "prefer" it, choose it, say that it is better than the state in which we find ourselves?

It is therefore more reasonable to think that the judgment "my life is worth living but I would have preferred never to have been born" relates to the life that we have.

But in this case, how can we fail to agree with Bernard Williams? How can we not think that, if we would have preferred never to have been born, it is because something is amiss in the life we are living, even if we are incapable of knowing what. "My life is worth living, but I would have preferred never to have been born" would mean: "I believe that my life is worth living, but in reality, objectively, it is not, for otherwise I would not say, 'I would have preferred never to have been born.'"

WOULD IT HAVE BEEN BETTER NEVER TO HAVE BEEN BORN RATHER THAN TO LIVE AN IMMORAL LIFE?

It seems nonetheless that it is possible to give a meaning to "my life is worth living but I would have preferred never to have been born" that does not rest upon the idea *that we deceive ourselves regarding the quality of our life.*

Suppose we consider the following propositions:

1. My life is worth living, but so much effort was needed to make it such that I would have preferred never to have been born.[3]
2. My life is worth living, but so many terrible trials had to be endured for it to be such that I would have preferred never to have been born.[4]
3. My life is worth living, but there will be an end to it, I am going to die, and this prospect so distresses me that I would have preferred never to have been born.[5]
4. My life is worth living, but I had to commit so many immoral acts for it to be such that I would have preferred never to have been born.[6]
5. My life is worth living from a personal or subjective point of view, but it has no meaning from an impersonal or objective point of view, and this feeling of absurdity is so deep that I would have preferred never to have been born.[7]

All these answers are ambiguous. They may indeed signify: "my life is worth living, but I would have preferred never to have been born." But they may also mean: "*all things considered,* my life is not worth living, which is why I would have preferred never to have been born." Is it possible to find an unambiguous meaning in the proposition "my life is worth living, but I would have preferred never to have been born"?

11

MUST WE ELIMINATE ANIMALS IN ORDER TO LIBERATE THEM?

If animals are not things, we should probably renounce the selling, buying, and eating of them. Would that not lead to the complete disappearance of all animals that are not wild? Is this really what we wish for?

THE LIFE RAFT AND THE CHIMPANZEES

A life raft caught in a storm on the open sea is full to the brim.

It is occupied by some humans—adults who are comatose or who are senile—and by an equivalent number of young chimpanzees, who are lively and in perfect health.[1]

All will die if the raft is not rid of its excess weight.

Would it be right to throw overboard one or several chimpanzees, even if they are more reasonable or sociable than the comatose and senile old people, simply because they are not human, without any further argument?

We talk of "limit" or "marginal" cases in describing this kind of particularly shocking scenario.[2]

These "limit cases," which we must obviously accord the status of thought experiment, without any political implication, serve in fact to illustrate the following reasoning:

1. There exist properties and capacities that serve as criteria for belonging to the moral community, that is, the class of beings that we cannot treat simply as things that are merely good to eat, to exploit, and to throw away once they have outlived their usefulness. Among these criteria, the most frequently advanced are self-consciousness and the capacity to plan and to anticipate, to deliberate and to choose, to feel sensations such as pleasure and pain and emotions such as fear, joy, and anger, and so on.

2. Now certain nonhuman animals possess these properties and capacities more than certain human animals do. Thus, according to Jeremy Bentham, "a full-grown horse or dog is beyond comparison a more rational, as well as a more conversible animal, than an infant, of a day, or a week, or even a month, old."[3]

3. The argument from marginal cases consists in asking ourselves whether there exists a moral justification for the fact of according, in case of conflict, our preference to the human who possesses these properties and these capacities to a lesser degree than the nonhuman.

4. Those who are called "speciesists" assert that, even in these cases, the preference should go to the humans, while those who are called "anti-speciesists" dispute the moral legitimacy of this choice.

In actual fact, the speciesists opt for a sort of *positive discrimination* toward humans.

Positive discrimination consists in according a systematic preference to certain people (as regards university entrance, in public life, and so on) not because their individual (intellectual or physical) qualities are superior, but because they belong to a certain category (the poor, ethnic minorities, and so on)

By the same token, the speciesists accord a preference to the members of the human species, from the moral point of view, among others, even when their individual capacities are inferior to those of animals.

The whole question, of course, is that of knowing what justifies this "positive discrimination" toward the members of the human species.

The antispeciesist argument of the "limit cases" is *continuist*. It disallows any moral abyss between human and nonhuman animals. Each individual is judged according to certain qualities (such as the capacity to suffer or to understand) that may be common to the members of the two species.

For certain philosophers, the continuist argument is a mystification pure and simple. It rests upon criteria of distinction between humans and animals that are readily used to establish continuity between the two, such as the faculty of experiencing pleasure and pain or of living in company. But, they say, in order to reinstate the abyss between human and animal you merely have to alter the criteria. Some justify this abyss on the basis of the Kantian opposition between beings of nature and beings of liberty. Others highlight the criteria of the "normal character-istics of the species," bodily form or social belonging.

None of the above criteria is conclusive.

"NATURE" AND "LIBERTY"

Luc Ferry: "In the name of what rational or even merely reasonable criterion could we claim in every scenario to be obliged to respect humans more than animals? Why sacrifice a chimpanzee in good health for a human being reduced to a vegetable? If we adopted a cri-terion according to which there is continuity between men and beasts, Singer would perhaps be right to regard as 'speciesist' the preference accorded to a human vegetable. If, on the other hand, we embrace the criterion of liberty, it is not unreasonable to admit that we should respect humanity, even in those who only manifest residual signs of it."[4]

What Luc Ferry calls "liberty" is the possibility of positing actions that are disinterested, irreducible to selfish interests or to the pursuit of pleasure or the avoidance of pain, things that nonhuman animals are incapable of.

But his sarcastic illustration of this point completely misses its mark. He writes that we "have already seen men sacrifice themselves for whales," whereas the converse is rarer.[5] Now, examples of altruistic, disinterested acts are really not lacking in the animal world, sometimes even between members of different species,[6] including acts for the benefit of humans. Does Luc Ferry think that dogs sacrificing themselves for their masters is a thing that only happens in cartoon strips?

INDIVIDUAL AND SPECIES

Alberto Bondolfi proposes that we replace the criterion of actual individual capacities with that of potential individual capacities and of the capacities of the species to which an individual belongs.

His arguments go as follows: "The first [difficulty] is linked to what are called 'marginal cases.' Let us recall that man is 'in general' endowed with reason and free will but that these faculties are not to be found in all the members of the species. There are newborn babies, embryos, the mentally handicapped, or those who are asleep or in a coma, and no one wants to exclude them from the human species. For what reason, then, do we respect their right to life? We must review the overhasty speciesist arguments and advance a more compelling criterion."[7]

According to Bondolfi, this criterion should be the principle of the potentiality of the members of a species: "It does not rest so much on the qualities and capacities to experience pain on an ad hoc basis in man or in the animal but on the habitually admitted capacities and qualities."[8]

It is hard to see how this criterion could not be applied to human embryos and to the incurably and terminally ill, thereby wresting all legitimacy from voluntary interruptions of pregnancy and from medically assisted dying. But it is a conclusion that is too much at odds with numerous reasonable convictions to be readily accepted.

SOCIAL BELONGING AND BODILY FORM

Jean-Luc Guichet seeks to show that antispeciesism rests upon the forgetting of several criteria, such as social belonging and bodily form.[9]

Social belonging: "Marginal human cases are really not so marginal as all that: they do not come out of nowhere, they are linked to other humans by parental and familial attachments, they have a surname, and so on. Dealing with such-and-such a man, even one who is mentally handicapped, is therefore a matter of dealing not simply with him, but also with his kin, and more broadly with the particular communities (ethnic, regional, socioprofessional, national, and so on) with which he has some relations of belonging and which may stand in for him and hold me to account."

Bodily form: "The overall form of the human body is not irrelevant to us, but serves us as a veritable ethical signal. We do not in fact have the time to ascertain that the humans we encounter daily are indeed human, and we are therefore forever habituated to considering them to be such, simply on the basis of their bodies, being thus conditioned to a veritable reflex of ethical recognition. The human body as such, without speech, naked, without expression, even entirely divested and minimal, that is, even purely "animal," retains in our eyes something that transcends animality: an ethical value that it has attained for us since our own acceding to consciousness."

But, as Jean-Luc Guichet himself points out: "What is to be done with regard to a human being so monstrous that we could not intuitively recognize him as such on the basis of his body?"

Besides, we may wonder just how the fact of invoking ties of belonging to human groups could morally justify speciesism. Mafiosi likewise invoke belonging to a group in order to justify preferential treatment. But they find it very difficult to convince others of the moral value of this criterion.

In other words, the criterion of bodily form is neither necessary nor sufficient, since there exist disfigured and mutilated monsters whom we still judge to be "human." As for the criterion of social belonging, its moral value is doubtful.

In actual fact, it is hard to find good arguments that could justify the existence of a moral abyss between humans and animals. But the attempts to completely align the status of nonhuman animals with that of humans seem likewise doomed to failure. They culminate in paradoxical conclusions, at best.

If we were to treat nonhuman animals as we should treat humans, by absolutely excluding all forms of exploitation and instrumentalization and by completely abrogating their status as property, we would end up not with the liberation of nonwild animals but with their disappearance pure and simple, through extinction, liquidation, or sterilization.[10] Under these conditions, we cannot help but ask ourselves the following question, no matter how we view the fate to which animals are subjected: can we find the means to avoid the paradox that consists in causing the disappearance of all the individuals belonging to certain classes of nonhuman animals in the name of their liberation?

The fact that the question can be put for animals marks a huge difference between the animal liberation movement and the movements for the liberation of women, slaves, gays, and other minorities. To militate for the liberation of women from masculine domination may ultimately bring about the disappearance of certain traits that characterize women in societies with a high degree of sexual segregation, such as submissiveness or prudishness. But if militating for the liberation of women should bring about the disappearance of women *as individuals*, the project would certainly be judged quite differently.

WHAT CRITERIA?

There is no criterion that could serve to justify the moral abyss between humans and animals without arousing controversy.

Does there exist a criterion that would enable us to establish moral continuity between humans and animals in an incontestable fashion?

Bentham has proposed such a criterion, namely, sentience, at the end of a famous argument that I have already evoked and that deserves to be cited in full: "The day *may* come, when the rest of the animal creation may acquire those rights which never could have been withholden from them but by the hand of tyranny. The French have already discovered that the blackness of the skin is no reason a human being should be abandoned without redress to the caprice of a tormentor. It may come one day to be recognised that the number of the legs, the villosity of the skin, or the termination of the *os sacrum* are reasons equally insufficient for abandoning a sensitive being to the same fate. What else is it that should trace the insuperable line? Is it the faculty of reason, or perhaps, the faculty of discourse? But a full-grown horse or dog is beyond comparison a more rational, as well as a more conversible animal, than an infant, of a day, or a week, or even a month, old. But suppose the case were otherwise, what would it avail? The question is not, Can they *reason*? nor, Can they *talk*? but, Can they *suffer*?"[11]

Is this criterion incontrovertible?

IS THE CRITERION OF SUFFERING SUFFICIENT?

For Bentham, the only moral question that we should ask ourselves with regard to animals is not "Can they *reason*? nor, Can they *talk*? but, Can they *suffer*?"[12]

Is this really the only question that we should ask ourselves?

We may reckon that the criterion of suffering is necessary. But it seems to me that the idea that it is sufficient can be ruled out, for the following three reasons:

1. It does not allow us to draw a clear distinction between harm (meaning "moral wrong," a setback to another's interests or rights) and injury (meaning physical, psychological, or economic pain).
2. It rules out all moral debate on the massive but painless slaughter of animals (supposing of course that industrial slaughter without suffering is conceivable, which is doubtful).
3. It does not really take into account the possibility that a short and mediocre life may be preferable to no life at all.

INJURIES AND HARM

The simple fact of causing physical suffering or of helping through our actions to cause the scales of pleasure and pain to tip to the side of pain does not in itself yet serve to establish that an injustice has been committed. Why? Simply because not every infringement of another's integrity, not every suffering that has been inflicted upon him, is constitutive of a *harm*.

The routine physical injuries occasioned in violent sports such as Thai boxing or rugby football, or even in a surgical intervention to which one has agreed and which has proceeded according to the normal medical protocol, are not considered to be wrongs or harms.

A wrong or a harm is a kind of injury about which we must be able to say that it is unjust in one or another important respect.[13] By marrying someone, for example, you deprive all the other suitors of this possibility, and you certainly do them an injury thereby. But can we for all that speak of "harm"? It is hard to see what there is that is unjust in the fact of uniting your life with that of another, of privileging him in this fashion.

Besides, for there to be "injury," the state in which the person who is supposed to have suffered it must *be worse* than that in which they were before. A one-legged person who demanded, after an accident, to be compensated for the leg that he did not have prior to the accident could not expect to be taken seriously.

In certain cases, the prior state is difficult to establish. Let us suppose that a child were born with a handicap against the wishes of its parents, who had been deceived by a reactionary doctor clandestinely combating a woman's right to interrupt a pregnancy voluntarily. In order to assess the injury that the child has suffered, must we compare his state with the state that *would have been his if he had not been born* (as his parents had wished)? But what kind of state is the state of "one who has not been born"?

The question obviously arises for animals consumed as food and serving as pets. The choice for them could well be between a short and painful life and no life at all. Which is preferable? In short, the passage from pain to harm raises complicated problems.

A final example: We admit that, in certain cases at any rate, consent cancels out a wrong: injuries suffered in combat sports are the most striking examples (if I can put it like that). But if animals are incapable of consenting in a sufficiently clear and explicit fashion, they cannot cancel out any wrong that is done to them. Must we conclude from this that the class of actions that can inflict wrongs upon animals is potentially much larger than the class of actions that can inflict wrongs upon humans?

This is the approach we take toward children. We can inflict many more wrongs on children than upon adults, for the simple reason that they can in no way consent to the injuries they suffer.

This is certainly a paradoxical conclusion for animals, for we tend rather to think that we cannot inflict as many wrongs upon them as upon humans, from the fact of the question of consent not arising at all so far as they are concerned.

We tend rather, it seems to me, to align the status of animals with that of fetuses than with that of newborn infants. Even those most opposed to abortion consider it to be a more serious thing intentionally to wound or to mutilate a fetus than to cause it to disappear altogether.[14]

And everyone seems to reckon that, even if it is better, in every case, not to do harm to a newborn child, it is less grave, on the scale of crimes, to wound it intentionally than to kill it.

One could say that, for animals as for fetuses, we consider it to be less grave to kill them than to cause them to suffer or to mutilate them while alive. The right to kill animals for certain ends presumed to be

useful is, for the time being, broadly accepted. But the right to mutilate gratuitously, and to cause animals to suffer pointlessly, is less and
less conceded.

A SHORT AND MEDIOCRE LIFE OR NO LIFE AT ALL

Suppose we admit that the existence of moral limit or marginal cases
is sufficient to establish a certain moral continuity between human and
nonhuman animals. We could draw two contradictory normative conclusions from this:

1. We must treat humans like animals.
2. We must treat animals like humans.

If spelled out, the first conclusion would mean that it is not illegitimate to treat humans as we treat animals today, that is, as beings whose
exploitation knows no limits, whom we can kill, cause to suffer, ridicule,
reduce to the state of an object for a scientific experiment if we have the
means to do so and if it suits us. Conceding this principle would anyway
only be putting right in accordance with the facts, and not conceding it
would be purely hypocritical.

The second conclusion states that we must treat animals as we recognize that humans must be treated today, that is, positively by taking their
interests into account and negatively by excluding all forms of exploitation or instrumentalization, and by abrogating their status as property.
Humans should not be treated as slaves or as objects of consumption or
experimentation. Animals should not be so treated either.

The first conclusion is unacceptable from the moral point of view: no
moral conception, even one entirely at odds with the one to which we are
accustomed, recommends this sort of conduct.

The second conclusion, though apparently more sympathetic, likewise poses problems.

If we treat nonhuman animals exactly as we should treat humans, positively by taking their interests into account and negatively by excluding
all forms of exploitation or instrumentalization, and by abrogating their
status as property, we will end up not with the liberation of domestic

animals, be it their purpose to be consumed or to amuse, but with their disappearance pure and simple through extinction or liquidation.

EXTINCTION

According to the utilitarian philosopher Richard Hare, if we stop consuming animals, the meat market will collapse. There will be fewer and fewer animals bred for the purposes of consumption.[15] They could still be reared and exploited, because they produce milk and eggs, but in fewer numbers. Among those who will reproduce themselves, certain will become wild or domestic animals: they will lose the characteristics by which we know them.

Thus, cows, chickens, and pigs will gradually disappear, which will reduce the quantity of personal happiness of all those who appreciate them aesthetically and gastronomically, and also the sum of animal well-being.

For Hare, the moral argument "based on the wrongness of *killing* animals collapses completely in the face of the objection that by accepting it we should in practice *reduce* the number of animals, and thus the total amount of animal welfare."[16]

For the argument to be acceptable, the sole criterion of animal well-being would have to be pleasure or the absence of pain, and we would have to be prepared to endorse what Parfit calls the "repugnant conclusion."[17]

THE CRITERION OF PLEASURE AND PAIN

It is only if the slaughter of animals is completely painless that their consumption post mortem will not diminish too much the sum total of their well-being. This is how Bentham argued. Invoking reasons of general utility, he did not see any obstacle to the painless slaughter of animals: "we are the better for it, and they are never the worse. They have none of those long-protracted anticipations of future misery which we have."[18]

It is the same reasoning that today allows utilitarians committed to the animal cause such as Peter Singer to justify scientific experimentation on animals. It should be permitted, they say, if its advantages in terms of general well-being are incontestably greater than the suffering it causes, and if it is impossible to substitute another, equally effective procedure for it.

What the utilitarian excludes, on the other hand, is every act resulting in wounding or *gratuitously* distressing an animal, which seems to be the case in cock fights, the corrida, recreational hunting and fishing, zoos, circuses with animals, and the testing of makeup. The pleasures or advantages we derive from them would then be out of all proportion to the bundle of sufferings thereby engendered.[19]

On the basis of these utilitarian premises, Richard Hare offers us a thought experiment that might agree with the idea that the breeding of animals for consumption is not necessarily an evil: "And if we put ourselves in the place of farmed trout?" Hare reckons that it cannot be so unpleasant for a trout to live in the waters of English fish farms, even if it is hardly a thrilling existence. He adds that, as a trout, he would not find it unfair to then be killed in order to be eaten, provided that he had been stunned beforehand: "I am fairly certain that, if given the choice, I would prefer the life, all told, of such a fish to that of almost any fish in the wild, and to non-existence."[20] In this thought experiment, Hare seems to endorse the "repugnant conclusion." What does it consist of?

THE REPUGNANT CONCLUSION

According to Parfit, an enormous quantity of short and miserable lives could have the same value in the calculation of the sum total of happiness as a small quantity of long and happy lives.[21] Such at least is the *repugnant conclusion* that a utilitarian ought perforce to sustain, and this is why his overall conception should be judged to be morally defective. Without going so far, Hare asserts that it is better, for an animal, to have a life that is short and in the end fairly mediocre (because it ends on a human's plate) than no life at all.

LIQUIDATION

The jurist Gary Francione reckons that what is wrong with our way of treating animals to be eaten, to be used for research, to keep us company, to work, or to amuse is the fact that we accord them the status of property.[22]

According to him, "our moral and legal acceptance of the importance of sentience has not resulted in any paradigm shift in our treatment of non-humans."[23]

We admit, he says, that animals can suffer and, from this point of view, the contribution of the utilitarians is of inestimable value.

But if the utilitarians have shown that nonhuman beings deserve to be accorded the same consideration as human beings because they are, as much as humans, liable to suffer, they have not furnished any argument serving to abrogate the legislative provisions entitling us to sell, buy, hire, or destroy them.[24]

Now, it is their *status as property* that is at the origin of a great number of shocking treatments we inflict upon animals.

This is why, Francione asserts, "the efforts of animal advocates ought to be directed at promoting veganism and the incremental eradication of the property status of nonhumans."[25]

In the end, he formulates the following radical claim: "If we took animals seriously and if we recognised the obligation we were under not to treat them as things, we would cease to produce domestic animals but also to facilitate their production. It would then be up to us to take care of those we have today, but we would cease to breed them for human consumption and we would leave domestic animals in peace. We would stop eating animals, making clothes out of them or using products of animal origin. We would consider vegetalism (veganism) to be beyond dispute the fundamental principle of morality."[26] But this proposition, the logic of which is impeccable, would have the disadvantage of causing the complete disappearance of all animals, with the exception of wild animals. Pets would have no future if it were impossible to get hold of them.

Francione is not content simply to recognize this implication of his argument. He *embraces* it. For him, it is not a question of simply letting domestic animals reproduce by themselves: "We should quite simply sterilise all living domestic animals, in order to ensure that every last one disappears: the only means of putting an end to their slavery. The extinction of domestic animals—with no distinction made between species serving as pets and those used for food—would be the sole remedy for our crimes."[27] That is a state of affairs which we might well hesitate to promote. We should not forget that, if we can talk of progress in our moral relationship with animals, it is not simply because more and more humans today think that we should treat animals far better than we are treating them at present. It is also because we have stopped trying to treat them as humans, as responsible beings, answerable for their actions.

Apart from certain characters in *Monty Python*, no one seems any longer to regret the fact that nowadays we no longer stage grand trials of animals charged with breaches of public order, following due legal process and imposing the death penalty should the occasion arise, such as were held in the Middle Ages. This is the same process as has occurred in the case of children, whose interests and needs have been recognized, at the same time as limits have been set on their responsibility.

There are normative reasons for not treating animals as humans, even if, from the moral point of view, it does not seem possible to justify any radical difference.

Is it possible to envisage a certain type of relationship with nonwild animals that would exclude the right to own them, but that would not stop them flourishing?

12

THE UTILITY MONSTER

Is it possible to be a consistent utilitarian?

You think that it is not unjust to conduct experiments on living animals because you reckon that the sum of benefits for humans is greater than the total of animal suffering.

You think that it is not unjust to breed animals to be eaten or to be used to make garments, so long as you do not employ cruel or intensive methods, because the humans obtain a great deal of pleasure from them and the animals do not experience too much suffering, especially if they are killed in a sufficiently painless fashion.

You think that what counts morally is producing the greatest possible sum of well-being in total.

You may request admittance to the utilitarian club!

But if you are in the club, you risk being forced to concede that it would be just to give all the wealth to a few individuals and to leave billions of humans in poverty.

Indeed, this is what you would have to conclude if it is demonstrated, beyond a shadow of a doubt, that the enjoyment of these few individuals is so immense that it very largely compensates for the misery of billions of people who have nothing.

The same reasoning should lead you to deem it just that a single person whose capacities for enjoying are gigantic monopolizes all the goods of the planet, or that all humans sacrifice themselves for him.

This kind of being may be called a utility monster (in the philosophical sense of the word "utility," which signifies the benefit we derive from a thing).[1]

Would you be prepared to remain in the utilitarian club, if these conclusions were inescapable?

13

A VIOLINIST HAS BEEN PLUGGED INTO YOUR BACK

Would you be willing to remain immobile for nine months in bed in order to save the life of an unknown person?

SCENARIO

You wake up one morning with an unknown person in your bed. You realize that a whole network of tubes joins you together at the back, and that fluids are circulating round this network. An unknown person has been plugged into your back while you were asleep![1]

How? Why?

In actual fact, it is the members of a music appreciation society who have organized the whole thing. They have sedated you, kidnapped you, and persuaded some doctors to plug this unknown person into you, having found no better way of saving his life. I should add that the unknown person is a violinist of consummate genius, stricken by a very grave disease of the kidneys. You alone have the blood needed to gradually clean out his kidneys and the tubes are precisely to flush them out.

In order to reassure you, the doctors tell you that you will only have them for nine months. In order to convince you of the importance of this medical procedure, they add that the violinist will die immediately if you unplug him.

You can of course act like a Good Samaritan and sacrifice nine months of your life for this violinist who is unknown to you and whom you did not even decide to save at the outset.

But if you demand to be unplugged, would that be monstrously immoral? Would it not be an act of legitimate self-defense, perfectly acceptable from the moral point of view, with regard to an intrusion that would leave you immobilized for nine months?

If you answer yes, you will also have to answer yes to the question of knowing whether there exists a moral right to interrupt an undesired pregnancy, for we are concerned here with like cases that should be treated alike.

THE MOST RADICAL DEFENSE OF ABORTION

For certain philosophers, if it were possible to prove conclusively that fetuses are persons who have the same rights as newborn infants, the question of knowing whether you can eliminate them would be settled. You would not be able to.

It is this argument that the thought experiment of the violinist plugged into one's back is supposed to challenge. It poses the following problem: even if you grant that fetuses are persons, at any rate potentially, is it not possible, nonetheless, to envisage cases in which it would be legitimate to take steps to counter the threat that they represent to the survival of the mother or to her quality of life?[2]

Think of someone who kidnaps you and sequestrates you for months, while regularly taking your blood and your bone marrow. Would it be morally permissible to put an end to this aggression?

The violinist plugged into one's back has really set the philosophers talking, which is no bad thing, obviously. But the radical implications of this thought experiment regarding the defense of abortion have not obtained unanimous agreement.

In actual fact, everything hinges upon the question of knowing whether the intention to unplug a sick person who has been hooked into one's back and that of terminating an undesired pregnancy are sufficiently similar for us to be under an intellectual obligation to treat them in the same way.

For many philosophers, it is hard to see the fetus as an intrusion, save in cases of rape.[3]

Since the woman's responsibility is involved in the case of a consenting sexual relationship, she must accept its consequences, namely, in certain cases, seeing the pregnancy through to its conclusion.

But it is hard to see why the fact of having consented to a sexual relationship that culminates in a pregnancy should imply an absolute duty to see it through to its conclusion.

It is well known that there is a range of different reasons for accepting an interruption of a pregnancy whose moral validity everyone (or nearly everyone) recognizes.

Philosophers and theologians advocating an absolute prohibition on abortion are rare indeed. With the exception of a few fanatics, they have always held that in cases of rape, incest, significant deformations of the fetus, and grave danger to the mother's life, abortion was permitted.

The argument enabling us to justify such actions is the same in every case. There is no absolute duty to see a pregnancy through to its conclusion. If the cost is too high for the mother, it is morally permissible to interrupt it.[4] Essentially the circumstance is no different from the one that Thomson has attempted to clarify.

The whole question is to discover to whom the right to assess the moral costs belongs. To whom should we leave the decision from the moral point of view?

Like Ronald Dworkin, Judith Jarvis Thomson seems to rule out abortions of convenience, those performed simply in order to avoid postponing a holiday, for example.[5]

Personally, I reckon that pregnant women should be left free to make the decisions they deem appropriate in their own case, exempt from any philosophical inspection of their reasons. If they are free to abort, they should be so whatever their motive may be. I reject, therefore, the position of Thomson and Dworkin.

What about you?

14

FRANKENSTEIN, MINISTER OF HEALTH

What is the value of the argument that says we must not play God or go too far against nature?

SCENARIO 1: POSTHUMAN

If geneticists of genius enable us to enhance to a considerable extent our muscular, perceptual, affective, and cognitive capacities, as well as our size and other aspects of our external form, our present criteria for identifying membership in the human species will necessarily be modified.

If it becomes possible by chemical or mechanical means to instill all manner of beliefs, desires, and sensations in our brains, techniques of surveillance and manipulation of minds could be taken very far: the very notions of personal experience and of the freedom of our inner conscience would not be able to resist.

If the transplanting of natural or artificial organs no longer poses any technical problem, the ideas we form of the sacred, indivisible, and unavailable character of the human body and of its intimate links to our personal identity are destined to change.

If reproductive human cloning becomes possible, we will probably be obliged to renounce the idea that a personal future of which we know almost nothing is constitutive of our identity.

If the aging process is better understood and better controlled, if we live infinitely longer in good health, our conceptions of what a "wasted" or a "successful" life is cannot remain the same.

If it becomes possible to create transhuman, posthuman, or subhuman beings, cyborgs, or chimeras, the ideas we form of the limits of the moral community, that is to say, of the beings we have chosen not to treat as things, goods simply to exploit or to consume, are liable to be profoundly transformed.[1]

It would be absurd to deny that if all these knowledges and techniques became readily applicable and accessible, there would be practical consequences so far as our own lives were concerned.

Would they all be negative? Might they radically modify our conceptions of ethics?

We are still very far from understanding all the implications of the applications of biomedical technologies.

We can envisage the possibility of their rendering certain preconceived ideas concerning human nature obsolete *and modifying our conceptions of the good.*

But why should they affect *our conceptions of justice* and their exigencies, such as the equal access of all to desirable technical innovations?

Do you think that we should ban the realization of these biotechnical projects even if everyone could profit from them equally?

Do you think that we should ban the realization of these biotechnical projects even if it could help to eliminate certain natural inequalities between people?

Do you think that we should ban the realization of these biotechnical projects without taking justice into account, simply because it would jeopardize our conceptions of human identity?

Do you think that we should ban the realization of these biotechnical projects without taking justice into account, simply because it would jeopardize our conceptions of the good?

Do you think that it would be possible to accept certain of these projects but not all of them, or do you think that we should ban all of them without exception, for fear of a *slippery slope* that would lead us inexorably from the most tolerable to the most monstrous?

SCENARIO 2: TOO HUMAN

At the age of forty, women still have on average half of their life ahead of them, and their longevity is set to rise. Assisted by medical advances, they will remain in good health for longer and longer, thereby able to preserve and nurture both their skills and their looks. The possibility of freezing an ovum will allow them to conceive a child belatedly without risks for the child's health, and even to do so after menopause. Equality with men as regards procreation will cease to be a utopia.

However, women seem overwhelmingly inclined to reject such a prospect. It is rejected entirely by 92 percent. Only 8 percent of French-women under the age of forty seem ready to countenance such a possibility. And, within this group, only 3 percent say that if they had the chance, they would "certainly" do it, while 5 percent say that they would "probably" do it![2]

Why?

In their explanations, they say that we must not "go too far against nature." Yet they have largely accepted chemical contraception. Wasn't that a clear goodbye to nature?

What is the value of the argument that says that we must not go "too far against nature"?[3]

Like all very general notions, "nature" has several senses. For John Stuart Mill, there are two main ones:[4]

1. "Nature" means everything that exists and everything that could exist according to physical laws (which excludes miracles but not GMOs).
2. "Nature" means the world as it would be without man's intervention (which excludes, directly or indirectly, everything that exists on the planet).

In the first sense, the idea that man *must* follow nature is absurd, for man can do nothing else but follow nature. Everything that he lives or feels depends upon the laws of nature. Everything that he does, everything that he makes rests upon the laws of nature (even the GMOs).

In the second sense, the idea that man *must* follow nature is irrational and immoral.

Irrational: Every human action amounts to altering the course of nature, and every useful action to improving it. Doing nothing "against nature" would amount to doing nothing at all! One could also say that "taking nature as a model" in the second sense would imply an absolute ban upon every technological innovation, including the hammer.

Immoral: If man did *everything* that nature does, we would find him absolutely monstrous: "In sober truth, nearly all the things which men are hanged or imprisoned for doing to one another are nature's every-day performances. . . . Nature impales men, breaks them as if on the wheel, casts them to be devoured by wild beasts, burns them to death, crushes them with stones like the first Christian martyr, starves them with hunger, freezes them with cold, poisons them by the quick or slow venom of her exhalations, and has hundreds of other hideous deaths in reserve, such as the ingenious cruelty of a Nabis or a Domitian never surpassed."[5]

I would add, concurring with Mill (something of a habit of mine), that the duty to follow nature (or the ban on going against nature) *in both senses* flouts several elementary rules of moral reasoning.

To say that man *must* follow nature (or not go against nature) violates the rule: *it is pointless to oblige people to do what they do necessarily.*

Indeed if man can do nothing else but follow nature (in the first sense), what is the point of hammering away at the notion that it is his duty to do so? What is the point of recommending that he do what he is already doing?

Furthermore, appeals to nature in the second sense, in order to say what is good or bad, just or unjust, consistently violate the rule: "*one cannot derive an ought from an is.*"

This rule does indeed imply:

1. It is not because something *is* natural that it is good.
2. It is not because something *is not* natural that it is bad.

The appeal to nature leads us, finally, to flout the principle that *like cases must be treated alike*, and to invent all sorts of "slippery slopes."

To say that there is a slippery slope amounts to asserting that, if we tolerate a particular action whose moral value is the object of a controversy (euthanasia, research on embryos, abortion, and the like), we will thereby *necessarily* come to tolerate actions whose morally reprehensible character is not the object of any controversy, such as the wholesale elimination of the poor, the weak, the ugly, and the handicapped or belated infanticide. If we prefer not to end up drawing such inadmissible conclusions, we would do better not to put ourselves on the slippery slope that necessarily leads to them.

The problem raised by this argument is that the reasons for which we should *necessarily* end up with unacceptable conclusions are either hidden or unfounded.

The case of the public debate on cloning is interesting because we can clearly see how the idea that we must not "go too far against nature" or "take ourselves to be God" entails an unconsidered use of the slippery slope argument and other errors of moral reasoning.

1. Cloning techniques could of course be put to malevolent purposes. Yet the same holds for other techniques of artificial procreation also, which is not sufficient reason to justify the banning of them. No one, for example, thinks that we should ban in vitro fertilization outright under the pretext that one day a tyrannical government might compel women to carry frozen embryos in order to repeople a nation whose workforce had been depleted by retirements. Why does cloning cause us to fear the worst? Is this not a groundless fear of a slippery slope?

2. It is fairly easy to understand what could justify a massive demand for cloning for therapeutic purposes, even if we are against its implementation for all sorts of reasons, religious ones among others. But what could really justify a demand for massive reproductive cloning? The rule *it is pointless to ban people from doing what they will not do in any case* is flouted.

3. Cloning is often denounced as a violation of the person because the child born thus would be the product of a purely instrumental project. But if we had to ban every reproductive project that could be judged to be "instrumental," there would not be many left. For centuries we made children so as to be looked after, cared for, and sustained when we grew old or fell ill. We cannot claim that such parental projects were not instrumental, and yet no one seems to think that they were particularly immoral.

In reality, the project of making children is always more or less instrumental. We continue to reproduce in order to guarantee a measure of material or affective security, to give pleasure to our partner or our relatives, and so on.

It is only in the case of cloning that the supposedly instrumental character of reproduction is judged to be immoral or monstrous. Why?

The rule *treat like cases alike* is violated.

From the fact, however, that the majority of the arguments against cloning have to be rejected because they violate the elementary rules of moral reasoning, it does not follow that there are good reasons for promoting it.

A thought experiment could help us to see why.

It is not completely far-fetched to envisage a situation in which men's natural fertility would be threatened by a general and irreversible impoverishment of human sperm. In the circumstances, cloning could represent a reasonable solution, perhaps the only one, to the problem of the survival of the human species.

Can we envisage other cases that could justify a promotion of cloning? If not, why should we promote it?

15

WHO AM I
WITHOUT MY ORGANS?

Who am I if all my cells have been built up again upon an identical pattern or if all my organs have been replaced?

SCENARIO

Imagine a technology that allows all the particles of which you are composed to be copied down to the last detail and to be reconstructed at a distance so that they are absolutely identical. You are transported by means of this technology to another planet. Unfortunately, the operator, a scientific genius, is a little absentminded, like all scientific geniuses. He forgets to destroy the original. There are therefore at the same moment two "you's," wholly identical, particle for particle. Who is the real "you"? The one who stayed on Earth or the perfect copy on another planet?[1] There exists a very ancient version of this kind of problem.

THESEUS'S BOAT

According to the legend, the Athenians were supposed to have preserved Theseus's boat for centuries by replacing its planks one by one as they wore out.[2]

Some asserted that the boat remained the same. But others thought that it no longer had anything to do with the original, that it was a different boat.

Philosophers are still divided over this question, as of course they are over all the others bequeathed to them by the Greeks.

Be this as it may, what should interest us, from the point of view of moral reflection, is the fact that, once it has become technically possible to replace our original organs with other organs, natural or artificial, grafted or prosthetic, an identical problem now arises for us, and in a quite concrete sense.

Is the body of a person whose organs have been replaced by grafts or prostheses still the same?

As our laws are presently constituted, and independently of any metaphysical commitments, we should, according to certain jurists, answer that it is still the same.[3]

The body would thus be an entity that remained identical to itself regardless of any modification of its parts.

A criminal who, prior to his trial, had replaced all his organs (with the exception perhaps of his brain) with grafts and prostheses would nevertheless be liable to the same penalties. He would be the same but with different organs.

In other words, the body as support for identity and personal responsibility is an abstract and unalterable totality, and never a simple sum of its detached parts. It is as such that it is inalienable, that it is the bearer of certain rights even after death, whereas its elements and its products can, for their part, be yielded, exchanged, and replaced.

Insofar as the replacement of parts of the body does not alter identity and personal responsibility, there ought not to be any insurmountable moral or political obstacle to the circulation of elements of the body removed with the actual or presumed consent of its owner. For it would not be a violation of the body itself, which would remain an inalienable moral and juridical entity.

From all of the above, it follows that trading in elements or functions of the body does not at all signify commercializing the body itself.

Various "questions having to do with society" such as the legislation covering sex workers, the remuneration for blood or sperm donorship, and surrogate motherhood could be rendered less inflammatory if this legal distinction were respected.

Furthermore, it could be the case that in the future, through the advances made by medicine, we will end up seeing our organs as things that are somewhat alien to ourselves and that do not determine our identity.

The existence of a trade in organs would then become scarcely any more repugnant than that of a fruit and vegetable market or a market for items of furniture sold as separate units.

Will the moral problems posed for us by the "commodification" of the functions, products, and elements of the human body have disappeared?

Can we reduce to the status of cultural prejudices, destined soon to become obsolete, all the reservations that exist regarding the trade in organs or salaried surrogate mothers?

Do there exist universally and eternally valid moral arguments that could tell us why the trade in the parts and reproductive functions of the human body should be disallowed, even if the partners to such an exchange will it?

A disciple of Kant would say that it is because this trade is contrary to human dignity.

Why? Because every human person has a value and not a price. It is moreover precisely in this that their dignity consists. The human body being the support of the person, it inherits its moral properties. It has a value and not a price. Giving it a price, as is necessary when it is bought or sold, is violating its dignity.

Consequently, for the disciple of Kant, what is wrong in the commodification of the body is not the fact of its contradicting certain cultural norms that have nothing eternal or universal about them, but the fact of its violating this eternal and universal moral principle: the dignity of the human person.

However, does the appeal to human dignity enable us to distinguish in a sufficiently precise fashion between what can legitimately be bought and sold and what cannot in any circumstance?

Is it contrary to human dignity to receive remuneration in return for putting at someone else's disposal our image or our scientific discoveries?

Why would it be contrary to human dignity to sell our skills at giving sexual pleasure or at bearing a child for another, but not to sell our skills as an athlete, our patience, our dexterity, our knowledge, or our intelligence?

It is contrary to the laws and mores of our society to receive remuneration in return for the gift of an organ. But in what respect is it contrary to human dignity?

16
AND IF SEXUALITY WERE FREE?

What would a world in which sexuality were free be like?

We put our capacities to give sexual pleasure at the disposal of others instead of keeping them for ourselves. Why?

The answer is not obvious. Sex is no bed of roses. It is an activity that has a certain psychological, physical, and even economic cost.

It is because these costs of sex are well known that we can very well understand those who prefer to watch a football match on the television or to cut their toenails.

Evolutionists tell us that there exist instinctive causes, tied to the interests of the species, informing our tendency to engage in activities whose individual benefits are not obvious.

But we do not always follow our instincts and, in any case, the question that might come under the competence of the philosopher does not have to do with causes (the province of the biologist) but with reasons.

More precisely, it is the question of knowing whether such reasons are good and legitimate.

What then are the reasons why we put our capacities to give sexual pleasure at the disposal of others instead of keeping them for ourselves?

Sex may follow the logic of exchange, because there is something to be gained in return: love, gratitude, sexual pleasure, admiration for our beauty or our talents in bed, children, a partner for life, money, a helping hand when moving houses or redecorating our apartment, and so on.

But sex may also follow the logic of the gift, and there may therefore be no expectation of anything specific in return, not even sexual pleasure: because we love absolutely just as we can love God or a star, because we wish to give all that we possess, because we have the feeling that it is our duty, because we are completely infatuated physically or morally, and so on.[1]

In sum, there exist an infinity of reasons for putting our capacities for giving sexual pleasure at the disposal of others.

Is it legitimate to hierarchize them, to judge that certain reasons are good and others bad?

Aside from a few cynics, no one denies that love can be a good reason for engaging in a sexual relationship. But it is neither the only reason, nor necessarily the best one. Why sacralize it, as some do? Why accord it such a moral privilege?

Is it really tawdrier to use our sexual capacities to fund a weekend in Capri?

What would happen in a world in which sexuality was truly free?

In such a world, the reasons for putting our capacities for giving sexual pleasure at the disposal of others would no longer be hierarchized. We would cease to think that some are noble and others ignoble.

Sexual activities would escape not only penal repression (we would do what we wished with our sexual life so long as we caused no harm to others) but also moral intervention (there would no longer be any bad reasons for putting our sexual capacities to a particular use). It would be a world in which sexuality would at last be freed from moral and political paternalism.

But we could go further still and imagine a world in which there would quite simply no longer be a reason to make use of our sexual capacities. It would be a world completely liberated from sexuality.

In such a world, the obsession with sex would completely disappear. We would no more think about it than we would about God in the most secularized of societies.

Sex would no longer be of any practical interest. It would no longer be a resource in our dealings with our fellows.

There would no longer be any interest in the reproductive aspect. Recourse to medically assisted procreation in all its forms (cloning and artificial uteruses included) would become the general rule.

There would no longer be any interest in the scientific aspect. No one would any longer seek to explain conduct in terms of its sexual antecedents.

It is not hard to understand why we might like to live in a world in which sexuality was finally liberated completely from moral and political paternalism.

But it is harder to grasp why we might like to live in a world completely liberated from sexuality, unless we were really very puritanical . . . or very tired!

17

IT IS HARDER TO DO GOOD INTENTIONALLY THAN IT IS TO DO EVIL

If we judge a human action to be bad, we will tend to think that it is intentional even if it is not.

In the philosophical tradition, the moral value of an act is judged by its intentions. But certain experimental studies show that, spontaneously, we judge intentions by the moral value of actions.

More precisely, our tendency to judge that a person is acting intentionally will be stronger if the results of his action are bad, and weaker if the results of his action are good.

It is Joshua Knobe who came to this startling conclusion, when examining a series of research projects carried out according to the following model.[1]

The subjects of the investigation are asked to judge the behavior of a company boss in two different situations:

1. The company boss doesn't give a damn about destroying the environment or protecting it so long as he increases his profits. If he pursues a policy that destroys the environment, will you say that he has destroyed it intentionally?

2. The company boss doesn't give a damn about destroying the environment or protecting it so long as he increases his profits. If he

pursues a policy that improves the environment, will you say that he has improved it intentionally?

In his investigation, Knobe observes that 82 percent of respondents judge that the company boss who pursues the destructive policy has done it intentionally, and that only 23 percent judge that the company boss who pursues the protective policy has done it intentionally. However, in both cases the company boss acts in exactly the same way so far as his intentions were concerned!

Hence this conclusion, which stresses the importance for the moral evaluation of the action that it be perceived as intentional action: if an action is judged to be bad, we will be more inclined to reckon that it is intentional.[2]

Faced with this kind of experiment, we can level the following objection: it is not obvious that knowledge of the usual methods of attributing intention helps us to better understand the notion of intention itself.

They are two different questions.[3]

18

WE ARE FREE,
EVEN IF EVERYTHING
IS WRITTEN IN ADVANCE

Even if a superpowerful computer predicts, years in advance and with absolute precision, what we are going to do, we will do it freely even so!

Imagine that, a century from now, we know all the laws of nature and we build a supercomputer capable of deducing, on the basis of these laws and the present state of the world, everything that is going to happen.

If it knows the present state of the world down to the last detail, it will be able to predict with absolute precision every action and every event to come.

Imagine that this supercomputer knows the state of the world down to the last detail on March 25, 2150, twenty years before the birth of Charlie. The supercomputer deduces from the state of the world and the laws of nature that Charlie is going to commit a holdup at the Bank of America (which still exists of course) on the street corner, on January 26, 2195, at 6:00 P.M.

The prediction is correct, obviously, and Charlie commits a holdup, on January 26, 2195, at 6:00 P.M.

Do you think that, when Charlie commits the holdup, he is acting freely?

SCENARIO 1

This scenario has been submitted to a group of students who had no training in philosophy.

Of them, 76 percent replied: "Yes, Charlie acts freely."[1]

But we know that our tendency to estimate that a person is responsible for his actions is much stronger when these actions are judged to be immoral.

Two other scenarios have therefore been devised along the lines of the same model but with a moral or neutral ending in order to check if this factor might by itself suffice to explain why liberty was attributed to a person whose actions were known in advance.

SCENARIO 2

The supercomputer predicts that Charlie is going to save a child on January 26, 2195, at 6:00 P.M.

SCENARIO 3

The supercomputer predicts that Charlie is going to go jogging on January 26, 2195, at 6:00 P.M.

Scenarios 2 and 3 have been submitted to other groups with the same general characteristics. What is astonishing is the fact that the results do not vary significantly:

> 68 percent answer that Charlie acts freely when he saves the child exactly as the supercomputer predicted;
>
> 79 percent answer that Charlie acts freely when he goes jogging exactly as the supercomputer predicted.

One can compare these percentages with the first result, where 76 percent answered that Charlie acts freely when he commits the holdup predicted by the supercomputer.

In other words, if we reckon that a person is free even when his actions are known in advance, this is not only in cases where those actions are judged to be immoral.[2]

Professional philosophers have long wondered, without having made much progress, whether it is possible to reconcile what we know of the behavior of humans, subjected, like everything belonging to the natural world, to forces that elude them, and our tendency to judge them as if they were free and responsible for their actions.

How can we set about rendering these somewhat contradictory ideas and attitudes compatible?

The philosophers have proposed different solutions to this conflict. One of the most widely discussed derives from Hobbes. It consists in observing that a free act is not an act that is mad, arbitrary, or without reasons, but an act caused or determined by our own reasons, that is to say, a voluntary act. In reality, "free" would not be the contrary of "caused" or "determined," but merely of "nonvoluntary," "constrained," or "imposed by a threat or by force." It is in this voluntarist sense that liberty and determinism are compatible.

But those who are called "incompatibilists" are more demanding. For them, to be free is not only to act according to our own reasons, but to have, in addition, the power to choose our reasons or to be at their origin. Now, according to them we do not have that power. This is why liberty and determinism are incompatible.[3]

Another way of attempting to resolve the conflict involves saying that our beliefs in determinism and in liberty can happily coexist without contradicting each other, for they come under wholly different aspects of our lives.

On the one hand, we know that there exist reasons for believing that we are subject to forces that elude us or that we cannot act otherwise than we do.

On the other hand, we cannot help having emotional reactions of joy, anger, and indignation toward what we do or what others do—as if we were free. These attitudes express the deep necessities of life in society. It would be absurd to imagine that we could eliminate them.[4]

In other words, our belief in determinism and our belief in liberty reflect different necessities. Each belief has its own independent life. The one has no reciprocal influence upon the other. It is in this sense that they are compatible.

But an "incompatibilist" could always object that our emotional reactions of joy, anger, and indignation toward what we do or what others do are simply irrational and should not influence our judgments.

In short, for certain philosophers, known as "incompatibilists," liberty and determinism are irreconcilable. If determinism is true, we are not free. And if we are not free, all ideas of responsibility or of "deserved" punishment are cruel and irrational human inventions.

For other philosophers, known as "compatibilists," liberty and determinism are reconcilable. Even if determinism is true, we can be free to act and responsible for our actions.

Certain experiments show that, contrary perhaps to what we might expect, the majority of people tend to align themselves with the second group. They are compatibilists.

Thus, as we have seen, a majority has tended to answer that a person acts freely, even if a superpowerful computer predicted years in advance and with absolute precision what he was going to do.[5]

To this kind of experiment, we can level the following objection: There is no obvious answer to the question of knowing why we should take into account people's opinions on this metaphysical question of determinism and liberty. It may be that the majority of people have mistaken views on these difficult questions.

19

MONSTERS AND SAINTS

Is it harder to be a monster or a saint?

COMING TO SOMEONE'S AID

X is making a phone call in a phone booth in a very busy shopping mall. Just as X is coming out of the box, a bystander drops a folder, the contents of which fly about in all directions. The bystander tries to pick up the documents as quickly as possible. Will X come to his aid before the crowd has had time to trample them underfoot?

What do you need to know about X in order to predict what he will do?

You expect the genuine personality of individuals to be revealed in this sort of circumstance. You therefore think that it will suffice to know the "personality" or the "character" of X in order to know what he will do.

If X is generous or compassionate, he will help the bystander.

If X is mean-spirited or selfish, he will not help.

In any case, that is the kind of prediction you should make if you believe in personalities or characters (it is the same thing in this analysis).

The problem is that, in this kind of situation, character is not so determining as you might suppose. This at any rate is what a very large number of experiments on helping behavior (over a thousand between 1962 and 1982!) have shown.[1] Here are a few examples: Some psychologists devised a scenario in which the bystander who dropped his folder was the experimenter's accomplice.[2] The phone booth had been tampered with. Sometimes a coin (worth one Euro) was very much in evidence in the slot that returned the change. Sometimes there was no coin. The results were spectacular:

1. From the group of those who had found a coin in the slot, 87.5 percent helped the bystander.
2. From the group of those who had not found a coin, only 4 percent helped the bystander.

The experimenters therefore advanced the following hypotheses:

It is sufficient for X to have found a coin in the slot for X to behave generously, whether X was mean-spirited or not.

It is sufficient for X not to have found a coin in the slot for X to behave like a "rat," whether X was compassionate or not. It is the *situation* rather than the personality that enables us to predict conduct.

In order to account for the mechanism, they supposed that the determining factor was mood. In fact, according to them, what, in this context, directly motivates us to help is being in a good mood. Apparently a small stroke of good luck suffices to put us in this state.

They chose this hypothesis on account of its very wide scope. There are in fact fairly significant relationships between good mood and good performances in tests on memory, cooperative behavior, and risk-taking, and between good mood and what psychologists call "prosocial" (altruistic, generous) behaviors in general.

The fact of there being relationships between good mood and prosocial behaviors is hardly astonishing; indeed, it is almost a banality.

What is more astonishing is the degree to which the factors triggering a good mood and the associated prosocial behaviors may be *trivial* or *insignificant*.

In order to be good, all that is necessary is to find a coin in the slot in a public phone booth!

The other factors associated with being in a good mood and with generous behaviors are also astonishingly insignificant.

Thus, it has been shown that being exposed to certain pleasant smells has a positive relationship with the fact of behaving in a generous fashion.[3]

The scenario devised was very simple.

One of the experimenter's accomplices asked some people in a shopping mall if they would give change for a dollar.

Those who were just next to a baker's from which emanated the smell of freshly baked bread or Viennese pastries did it willingly; those in a spot smelling of nothing in particular were far more reluctant.[4]

In this kind of experiment too, the hypothesis is advanced that it is a good mood linked to the perception of the agreeable smell that is decisive.

And what is striking is the trivial, insignificant character of the factor that serves as a trigger.

A pleasing smell of warm croissants suffices!

Other factors liable to induce "prosocial" behaviors have been examined: the impact of a group, the influence of philosophical formation, and finally the personality as a control hypothesis.

They are less trivial but also less decisive.

IN ORDER TO GO TO THE AID OF THOSE IN NEED YOU SIMPLY HAVE TO NOT BE TOO HEMMED IN

To judge by certain experiments, there is a greater tendency to help when you are alone with the victim than when you are in society.[5] No one claims that an explanation of this fact (if there is one) is easy to give. The most plausible hypotheses are as follows. When we are in society, two mechanisms may inhibit our propensity to help others:

1. The influence of the apathy of others (if no one lifts a finger, we will not lift a finger either: we believe that apathy is the appropriate attitude).
2. The "diffusion of responsibility"[6] (we feel less guilty about not acting if we say to ourselves that another person could act).

If we are pessimists, we can say that we simply have to be in a group in order to behave like a "creep." If we are optimists, we can say that we simply have to be alone in order to behave like a "good guy." However, being alone is not always sufficient, as the hardly reassuring experiment of the "Good Samaritans" shows.

YOU MERELY HAVE TO NOT BE IN A HURRY IN ORDER TO BE A GOOD SAMARITAN

Some theology students are summoned to a university building in order to take part in a study of religious education and the strength of vocations.[7]

After a rapid presentation of the questionnaire, they are told that they should go to another building to finish the interview, taking their time (one group), rapidly (another group), or in very great haste (the final group).

Between the two buildings the experimenter has stationed an accomplice, who falls down, groaning, as the seminarians are passing.

One might expect all the seminarians (who know the parable of the Good Samaritan by heart!) to stop and help the poor victim. But this is not at all what happened. In actual fact, the only ones tending to stop were those who were not in a hurry;

The results are as follows:

In a great hurry: 10 percent stop to help.
In something of a hurry: 45 percent stop to help.
Not in a hurry: 63 percent stop to help.

Certain seminarians, among those who are most hurried, do not hesitate to trample the victim underfoot if he gets in their way, thus presenting a caricature of human indifference to the suffering of others. We cannot really say that the victim behaves in a threatening fashion, or that the environment is stressful, as it is in large modern cities!

The explanatory hypothesis that springs to mind is that, as good seminarians, they felt under a moral obligation to their experimenter and found themselves caught in a conflict of duties. But this is hardly plausible, given the disproportion between the obligations toward the experimenter (it was not an exam, but an additional, voluntary activity of no real importance) and those they should have had as seminarians toward a person in distress.

One might fancy testing to see whether the same kind of behavior could be observed toward relatives. Would we trample our brother or mother in order to arrive on time at an unimportant meeting?

What is interesting, nonetheless, from the moral point of view is the relationship with unknown people, with strangers. And what we can say, in this regard, if we are pessimists, is that it is enough to be in a hurry to forget the Gospels. But if we are optimists, we can say that it is enough not to be in a hurry to be a Good Samaritan!

What could mitigate this optimistic conclusion are the doubts that there are as to the validity of these results outside of the experimental context, and as to the possibility of drawing generalizing inferences on the basis of research that only concerns specific populations and in small numbers. I will return to this point below.

WHO HELPS MORE: WOMEN OR MEN? THE RICH OR THE POOR?

If we set these generalizations aside, we will retain a few fairly interesting specific results.

We might suppose—above all, if we are sensitive to certain prejudices—that women will have a greater tendency to help than men. But the facts do not lend themselves to this hypothesis.

Sociological studies on "prosocial" behaviors have shown either that there was no significant difference between men and women or that there were more "prosocial" behaviors among men.[8]

And the rich? Are they in general more "prosocial" than the poor? The results resemble those given above. No significant difference, but in both classes there is a greater tendency to help neighbors or members of the same community.[9]

And personality?

The preliminary tests undergone by the seminarians in the experiment lead us to classify them with the compassionate "personalities." But the experiment has shown that these tests predicted behavior badly.

In other cases, however, they have not been in vain. Certain studies have shown that people described as "prudent" will be less inclined to help a bystander whose folder has been dropped than people described as "caring about the esteem of others."

All in all, the "situational" hypothesis, which contests the importance of character in the prediction of conduct, has not been refuted.

This hypothesis does not deny the existence of certain typical traits of behavior at a very high level of generality. It merely states that they do not enable us to predict or to explain conduct.

HARMING OTHERS

Could we behave like Nazis, humiliate or massacre the weakest (those who are handicapped, old people, children, and so on) or those who have personally done nothing to us *simply because we have been given the order to do so*?

A famous test, devised by the psychologist Stanley Milgram, was held to have given us the means to answer this distressing question.[10]

In 1960, he sent out a series of promotional mailings and placed small ads in local papers, inviting the people of New Haven, in the northern United States, to take part in a psychological experiment, for a small fee.

The idea was to subject people of differing ages and social milieux to this experiment. Among those chosen were postmen, teachers, workers, and engineers: around a thousand altogether, for the whole sequence of experiments and some variants, conducted over three years, between 1960 and 1963.

Once on site, the psychologist in charge informed the people selected that the aim of the test was to check whether physical punishments could enhance the capacity to memorize a list of words.

A "teacher" and a "learner" were chosen for each test. But in fact the "learner" never varied, being invariably an accomplice of the psychologist-experimenter, a mature actor particularly skilled at screaming blue murder.

The "learner" was strapped to a chair and electric wires were attached to his body while the "teacher" looked on.

So that the "teacher" could really grasp what a discharge from the machine represented, he was administered a fairly painful shock of 45 volts, and told that he himself would be sending discharges of as much as 450 volts, that is to say, ten times as powerful as the one he had just received.

The "teacher" was then installed in another room, from where he could no longer see the "learner." He was put at the controls of an impressive electric shock machine.

Then the test began.

The "learner" was supposed to memorize lists of paired words. When given one word, he was supposed to say the other.

Each time the "learner" made a mistake, the "teacher" was supposed to administer an electric shock.

The experimenter gave the order to gradually increase the power of the shock, always in a "firm, polite voice" and without expressing the slightest threat, under the pretext of checking to see if that would improve the "learner's" capacity to memorize.

The "teacher" could perceive, through the cries and groans of the "learner," that he was causing a great deal of suffering. The "teacher" was often distressed. The experimenter then urged him to continue, issuing a graded series of orders, ranging from "continue please" to "you have no other choice, you *must* go on."

If the "teacher" expressed concern for the health of the "learner," the experimenter assured him that he was not causing any irreversible harm. After the 150-volt shock, the "learner" screamed and asked for the test to be halted. He was in too much pain: he no longer consented.

It was at this moment that the "teachers" hesitated the most. The experimenter's urgings that they continue were repeated, always in the same firm and polite tone, and always without expressing the slightest threat.

Despite everything, 65 percent of the "teachers" persevered with the experiment to the very end, that is to say, they administered shocks of 450 volts, provoking howls of agony, followed by gasps and by a meaningful silence suggesting that the "learner" really could not any longer be in a good state.

The "teachers" who had persevered to the end were called "obedient," and those who had refused were called "disobedient."

It is very important to specify that none of the "obedient" derived any pleasure from obeying. Milgram had not stumbled by chance upon a bunch of New Haven sadists. All were ill at ease and anxious. All hesitated, sweated, bit their lips, groaned, dug their nails into their flesh.[11]

Some declared, subsequently, that they did not believe that the electric shocks were genuine. But aside from the fact that this was only a minority (80 percent thought that the shocks were real), these distressing attitudes did not give the impression that the "teachers" believed that it was all a hoax.

Although all kinds of ethical considerations have restricted the possibilities of reproducing the experiment (it cannot be said that no harm was caused to those "teachers" who had been most "obedient," and who discovered that they had behaved like monsters!), we are acquainted, however, with a great number of replicas and variants.[12]

What has struck psychologists is the consistency of the results: "two-thirds obedient, everywhere the experiment has been tried, is a fair summary."[13]

Certain psychologists expected that "culture" would have a crucial influence. This is not the case. The same results have been obtained in Jordan (63 percent "obedient") as in the United States (65 percent).[14] And if Germany stands out (85 percent "obedient"), it is for the worse, if I can put it like that.

Others were expecting gender to have a crucial influence. This is not the case. The proportion of "obedient" women is the same as that of men in Milgram's experiments (65 percent for both sexes). And if in certain studies the women are a little more "obedient" than the men, in others they are a little less so.[15]

Finally, certain psychologists predicted that personality would have a crucial influence. Since the most "authoritarian" was supposed to be the most respectful of authority, the proportion of "the obedient" should have been much higher among the "authoritarian."

This is not the case. Milgram has had his test taken by subjects classified as "authoritarian" and as "nonauthoritarian" in personality tests. The experiment has not shown significant differences of behavior between the two groups.

From the point of view of moral philosophy, it is the final result that is the most important. It tends to show that what determines behavior is not character but other factors tied to situation, such as pressure from a group or from an authority.

Another conclusion we can draw is that there is no such thing as a moral or an immoral personality. If this is true, virtue ethics is unlikely to survive intact.

However, the debate surrounding this question is not yet resolved.

Kohlberg defends a stadial theory of moral development, from egoism to autonomy, passing through conformism. According to him, those individuals who have attained the highest stage of moral development should be more numerous among the "disobedient."[16]

This is a hypothesis that concedes that personalities more moral than others do exist. But, in the present state of research, it remains speculative, and all the more so given that Kohlberg's model of "moral development in stages" is far from being unanimously accepted.

When we try to understand the mechanisms that Milgram was seeking to bring to light, we must take into account the fact that the mere introduction of a few variants served to boost the rate of refusals:

1. When the volunteer was accompanied by one or several other accomplices who told him to refuse or who themselves refused when asked to conduct the tests, a sort of coalition against the experimenter was ultimately forged.
2. Furthermore, when the volunteer *saw* the accomplice or had to grab hold of his hand in order to force him to receive an electric shock, the rate of refusals also increased.
3. Finally, when the experimenter did not seem altogether worthy of confidence (stained coat, an overfamiliar way of talking, and so on), the refusals also increased.

This is why, moreover, the extrapolations made on the basis of Milgram's results with a view to explaining the behavior of mass murderers acting under the orders of the Nazis are in part unjustified.[17]

Those mass murderers worked as a team, in direct contact with their victims, without being subjected to an absolute authority.

According to Milgram's theory, a greater number of them should have refused to put to death old people, women, and children who personally had done them no harm.

Among the most widely accepted explanations of the behavior of these mass murderers, certain scholars assert that their principal motivation was to not appear to be "shirkers," to be "weak," to be "weaklings" in the eyes of others. The theory of submission to authority is invoked to support this hypothesis.[18]

This is an error. In actual fact, if these explanations are correct, what motivated the behavior of the mass murderers was conformity with individuals who were their *equals* and not submission to a *higher* authority.

The interpretation of Milgram's results remains open. One of the most interesting, in my view, suggests that the problem for the "teachers" administering the shocks was a problem of justification of the kind involved in slippery slope arguments or in "sorites," logical paradoxes that end up proving that the bald do not exist or that everyone is bald.[19]

If I have agreed to send an electrical discharge of 50 volts, why not 60, since the difference between the two is not huge? If I have agreed to send an electrical discharge of 60 volts, why not 70, since the difference between the two is not huge? And so on, up to 450.

The "teachers" hesitated after the 150-volt shock, that is, at the moment at which the "learner" screamed and asked that the test be halted. But if the "teacher" continued, the same slippage could occur. Why would a powerful shock be acceptable but not a very powerful one?[20]

Can we draw from experiments regarding submission to authority the conclusion that doing good or doing evil depends not upon our own (moral or immoral) convictions, or upon our own (good or bad) character, but absolutely upon the chance that has placed us in such-and-such circumstances?

Milgram's investigation is in the end somewhat paradoxical. He defends the idea that it is situation and not character that determines conduct. If he applied this principle literally, he ought not to draw any general conclusion as regards human conduct on the basis of his experiments. He ought merely to be satisfied with saying that people conduct themselves thus in that particular experimental setup, period. Every conclusion going beyond this would introduce considerations regarding human nature or characters, of a kind that he absolutely excludes on principle.

Yet Stanley Milgram nonetheless wants to say something about human nature. He reckons that he is able to endorse Hannah Arendt's thesis on the banality of evil. Is this not contradictory?

This objection has been leveled fairly frequently. It is not wholly justified.

After all, what Milgram seeks to isolate are the general factors that may have a causal influence upon conduct in other contexts as well, such as dependence upon a scientific authority.

It is a welcome objection nonetheless, inasmuch as it recommends prudence in the philosophical use that may be made of his empirical findings.

WHAT IS THE USE OF THESE EXPERIMENTS IN PHILOSOPHY?

In moral philosophy, the experiments regarding submission to authority have above all served, in recent years, to challenge one of the foundations of every form of virtue ethics since Aristotle: the existence of good, just, or virtuous "personalities," which remain such regardless of pressures or threats from the surrounding environment.

In its most recent versions, virtue ethics rests on the idea that there exist "personalities" so virtuous that they could serve us as moral examples.

In order to know what we must do, we merely have to ask ourselves what X or Y (Socrates or Gandhi rather than a serial killer!) would have done.

But psychological theories known as "situationist" (no relation to Guy Debord's grand theory, also called "situationism") assert that the idea of a "virtuous personality" does not have a very clear meaning.

This way of defining people by their "personality" derives from a somewhat irrational tendency to judge them globally.

In reality, there is neither unity nor significant empirical continuity in attitudes and conduct.

What are the arguments in favor of this nonunified conception of human behavior, which is so much at odds with our ordinary intuitions?

WHAT IS A "CHARACTER" SO FAR AS COMMON SENSE IS CONCERNED?

It is, broadly speaking, a certain way of acting or feeling that is *consistent*, that is, stable over time and unvarying from one situation to the next. When it is said of someone that he is "generous," "honest," "strong," "determined," "brave," "mean," "jealous," "disloyal," "weak," "wicked," or "vicious," we have, it would seem, ideas of this kind in mind.[21]

"Character" is also supposed to explain and predict conduct in an economical fashion. When we have in mind, consciously or unconsciously, the idea of "character," we make predictions such as "he will probably try to recover the jewels that he has offered *because he is mean.*" When we have in mind, consciously or unconsciously, the idea of "character," we make predictions such as "he has returned the briefcase full of euros *because he is honest.*"

The "situationist" psychologists dispute the existence of such dispositions, which are *stable over time, unvarying from one situation to the next,* and relevant to the explication and prediction of real conduct, basing their case upon empirical studies. According to them, no one is "generous," "cruel," or "mean" systematically and invariably every moment of their lives, no matter what situations or people are involved.[22]

What we can conclude from their research is that in reality the existence of "characters" is undemonstrable or unverifiable. What could the *proof* of the existence of a "character" be? Would consistency of conduct suffice?

In actual fact, all behavioral proof of a psychological disposition is open to dispute.[23] Certain people could *be* cruel, but we will not see them in that guise because they will refrain from *acting cruelly* so as not to expose themselves to the anger, contempt, or indignation of others. Certain people could *act bravely* in time of war, for example, but so as to conform to what others are doing or for fear of punishment, that is to say, without *really being* brave.

Besides, how many brave or cruel actions would we have to perform in order to prove beyond all reasonable doubt that we *really* were a brave or cruel person? If a person were to show themselves to be cowardly just once, should their bravery be doubted? If they displayed compassion just once, should their cruelty be doubted? In short, we could not be certain that someone is really cruel or brave if they never showed it, but we would not be any the surer if they were to show it sometimes or often.[24]

These questionings are not philosophical speculations pure and simple. If, in order to assess "character," psychologists have been seeking methodological means aside from observable conduct ("personality tests," for example), it is precisely because such conduct did not furnish reliable proof.[25]

The inconsistency of the ordinary attributes of "character" is itself a startling fact, and one that needs to be taken into account. In our everyday judgments of a person's "character" or "personality," what we know of their *real conduct* does not seem to have any systematic influence.[26]

Finally, we must indeed acknowledge that the "scientific" or "unscientific" attribution of a "character" or of a "personality" depends upon dubious inferences. It resembles the expression of prejudices more than a factual observation.[27]

It expresses a tendency to judge people "globally," and as such it can wreak social havoc when it is *negative*.

Think of the devastating effects of negative global judgments, independent of any considered taking-into-account of real conduct, on "blacks," "Jews," "Asians," "Muslims," "women," "prostitutes," "gypsies," and so on.

It is not even clear that a *positive* global attribution is any more appreciated. A blind love, independent of any considered taking-into-account of real conduct, of "charismatic leaders," "gurus," "stars," and politicians in your own camp can wreak just as much social havoc.

Furthermore, the value of "character" in explaining action is weak or secondary, or indeed null.

If, in order to explain why Charlie has smashed all the crockery in the kitchen, we simply say that he has a "mean (nervous) character," no one will be satisfied.

It will be pointed out to us that we have given an unsatisfactory explanation. We will be asked to provide motives (has his girlfriend betrayed him with his best friend? did she make fun of his ridiculous haircut? was it the crockery of his stepmother, whom he loathes? and so on).

Sometimes, however, we do accept explanations in terms of character, and without inquiring as to any other motives, as in the case of "he returned the briefcase full of euros *because he is honest*."

Are these explanations not inadequate at best, useless and misleading at worst? Must we renounce notions of "character" and "personality" on account of these difficulties? This is what empirical, "situationist" psychologists believe.[28]

But their arguments remain highly controversial.

Other psychologists indeed reckon it false to think that there is no unity or meaningful empirical continuity in the attitudes and conduct of a person. Their arguments go as follows:

1. Perhaps there is no *absolute* unity or continuity. But it would be absurd to deny that there exist *tendencies* or relative (more or less strong) consistencies of character. These tendencies are real and empirically observable. They are not merely "social constructs," "narrative effects," or "illusions" useful to the survival of individuals who, in order to flourish, need to judge others swiftly and globally on the basis of sometimes tenuous scraps of evidence.

2. It is, admittedly, difficult to prove that there are absolutely evil personalities doing their utmost to inflict suffering on anyone, no matter what context. For even if such rivals of Satan exist, they would not dare or would not wish to speak of themselves thus (this was the case with the prominent Nazis), and we would therefore lack subjective proof.

3. Conversely, there are certainly examples of people who are just and good, who remain such whatever the circumstances, and who have been able to bear witness to their feelings. During the Nazi occupation, there were collaborators and informers, and there were those who remained indifferent, but there were also the Righteous, the compassionate and brave people who saved the persecuted, and who have subsequently borne witness to how things went with them.[29]

The existence of the Righteous, even if they were only a very small minority, poses a real problem for the "situationist" psychologists.

First of all, the moral environment was the same for them as it was for their neighbors who remained indifferent or who acted as informers, and yet they, the Righteous, acted differently.

Second, asserting that there are compassionate and brave personalities is not so costly theoretically as presupposing the existence of purely "evil" personalities. When you say to people that they are good, they will not ask you for proof. When you tell them that they are evil, they probably will ask you for it. Generally speaking, we ask for less proof of the existence of compassionate and brave personalities, and we must provide more robust arguments in order to prove that such personalities do not exist.

Finally, "situationist" psychologists find it very difficult to dismiss the case of the Righteous, for there would seem to be no determining sociological factors that could explain why they, and not others, acted as they did. Now, in the absence of such factors, psychological hypotheses appealing to the notion of "personality" can flourish.[30]

Some have said that religion was a crucial factor. This is an error. There were, admittedly, some religious people among the Righteous. But there were also some religious people who were informers or collaborators, or who remained indifferent. It was not enough to be religious to be one of the Righteous.

Many people were on the margins and many individualists were numbered among the Righteous. But there were also marginal people and individualists among the informers, the collaborators, and the indifferent. It was not enough to be marginal or an individualist to be one of the Righteous.

Conversely, some personality traits characteristic of the Righteous are not found in the informers or collaborators or in the indifferent. The Righteous were, according to certain psychologists, people who had an extended sense of responsibility for others, a sense of shared humanity and humanist values.[31] These psychologists have gathered together these traits in order to build an "altruistic personality." This is an idealization on the basis of which they deem it possible to predict behavior. The problem is that such predictions are only confirmed in certain domains.

Thus, Oskar Schindler, the German industrialist who bravely saved the lives of a thousand Jews and whose actions were glorified in a famous film by Steven Spielberg, was considered to be one of the Righteous.

However, there is scant justification for the claim that Schindler had an "altruistic personality." He certainly behaved in an altruistic fashion toward his Jewish workers, and for so acting he may be congratulated.[32] Yet he was not only altruistic. In other areas of his life, in love or in business, he was in fact dreadfully selfish. In short, it can be said that he behaved in an altruistic fashion in a certain context, but not that he had an "altruistic personality." His way of conducting himself was not unified enough for this kind of generalization to be justified.

In order to account for the conduct of the Righteous without referring to unified "altruistic personalities" that are consistent in their behavior, the "situationist" psychologists have sought other, more contingent factors.

Among the situational factors they have highlighted, one of the most interesting is the fact that a direct appeal for protection was made to the Righteous, which they did not wish to or could not refuse. They would perhaps not have become Righteous if nothing had been asked of them.[33]

But the persecuted may perhaps have addressed their appeal to them because they sensed that they were Righteous.

Another interesting factor has been identified. The conduct of the Righteous was often incremental. They began by helping on an ad hoc basis and without running any risks. Subsequently, they felt more and more responsible for the people they shielded, and more and more involved in the mission of saving them. In the end, this mission became the most important thing of all, more important than even their own life.[34]

Such an explanation does not appeal to the idea of an "altruistic personality," and does not in any way detract from the admirable nature of the act in question.

Are the implications of the situational theory for virtue ethics as somber as certain experimental philosophers claim?[35]

The friends of the virtues have tried to block such objections by means of the following two arguments:

1. We can give to the idea of being a good person the value of an ideal that does not need to be realized concretely.
2. Virtue ethics is not reducible to the idea that virtuous personalities exist. Its purpose is simply to justify the proposition that *certain acts* are virtuous (brave, honest, generous, and so on) and that every serious ethical theory must give reasons for promoting this kind of act.[36]

Are these amendments sufficient to save virtue ethics?

Do they not strip virtue ethics of everything that makes it interesting: giving a place to character and to personality in moral evaluation?

PART II
THE INGREDIENTS
OF THE MORAL
"CUISINE"

20
INTUITIONS AND RULES

Let us return to the case of the child who is drowning. It is constructed as follows:[1]

---

1. It would be monstrous to let a child die if he is drowning in a pond before your very eyes, when you could save him by making the most minimal of efforts, with no risk to your own life.
2. If you judge that it would be monstrous to let a child die if he is drowning in a pond before your very eyes, when you could save him by making the most minimal of efforts, with no risk to your own life, you ought also to judge that it is monstrous to let a child die of hunger in a country stricken by drought, when you could save him simply by sending a check for twenty dollars to an organization combating famine.

The first proposition expresses a *moral intuition.*

The second proposition, which is longer and more complicated, appeals to rules of moral reasoning. Completely developed, it would have the following appearance, which could serve to discourage readers allergic to sentences that are a little too abstract (let us hope that they are not all allergic to them): "If you judge it to be monstrous to do A, you should judge it to be monstrous to do B, for A and B are alike, and like cases must be treated alike." In other words, it assumes the plausibility of a comparative judgment (A and B are alike), and the *acknowledgment of a rule of moral reasoning* ("like cases must be treated alike"). The combination of the two allows us to grant moral intuitions a hypothetical status that could be to their advantage.

Peter Singer begins in fact by soliciting the reader's approval by means of the following assertion: "It would be monstrous to let a child drowning in a pond before your very eyes die, when you could save him by making the most minimal effort and without any risk to your own life."

But it is above all else with a view to convincing us that this is exactly how we behave when we refuse to devote a certain part of our income to combating famine.[2]

The issue, for Singer, is not that of knowing if everyone thinks that it would be monstrous to let a child drowning in a pond die when it would be easy to save him, or whether it is only the better educated or those who have received a religious education.

Nor is the issue that of knowing if the reasons why we think that it would be monstrous to let a child drowning in a pond die when it would be easy to save him are skewed by nonrational, psychological factors, such as natural empathy toward persons floundering in icy water. Peter Singer's argument simply says:

"If you judge it to be monstrous to let a child drowning in a pond before your very eyes die, when it would be easy to save him, you should also judge that it would be monstrous not to devote a certain part of your income to combating famine."

It is in this sense that the argument is hypothetical.

Of course, we can go further and wonder as to the validity of the assertion. Is it true that it is *always* monstrous to let a child drowning before your very eyes in a pond die, when it would be easy for you to save him? But that's another story.

On the basis of these examples, we can in any case advance the hypothesis that every conceptual analysis of ethics proceeds by way of the examination of these two ingredients:

1. moral intuitions;
2. rules of moral reasoning.

I have evoked them in an informal fashion. It is time that they were analyzed more systematically.

THE PLACE OF MORAL INTUITIONS
IN THE CONSTRUCTION, JUSTIFICATION,
AND CRITIQUE OF MORAL THEORIES

For philosophers concerned with normative ethics in an analytic perspective, the chief problem nowadays is the place of moral intuitions in the construction, justification, and critique of moral theories.

They have observed that "political and moral philosophers frequently appeal to 'moral intuitions' in their reasonings. They regard moral theories and moral principles as doubtful if they contradict their intuitions. And they have a tendency to mobilize 'intuitions' in the elaboration and defense of their own theories."[3]

They think that, in order to advance in ethical reflection, what we must first of all examine is the value of this Method (with a capital M, to signify its importance in moral philosophy), which was inspired at the outset by John Rawls's idea of "reflective equilibrium," but which since then has taken on a life of its own.[4] The questions raised by the Method are of the following kind: To what extent can we trust our own moral intuitions, if we have them, with a view to knowing what is good or just? How are we to distinguish between the "good" moral intuitions, those we must take into account if we wish to avoid our moral theories being of no relevance to our lives, and the "bad" ones, those we would do better to drop in order to avoid saying any old thing? Can certain of the causes of our moral intuitions be discounted outright? If, for example, we learned that our moral intuitions in favor of the rights of animals have no other cause but our feelings of undeclared love for the character of Bambi, should we take it into account in moral debate?

THE VALUE OF THE RULES OF MORAL REASONING

It is good to take a slightly closer interest, from an analytic perspective, in moral intuitions. But that should not make us forget that a great number of difficult questions are also raised in relation to the *rules of moral reasoning*.

Are they well formed?
Are they redundant?
Are they consistent?

21
A LITTLE METHOD!

We have differentiated between the thought experiments carried out by professional philosophers with their colleagues in mind and the "democratized" thought experiment.

More concretely, a "democratized" thought experiment unfolds as follows:

1. We present to subjects selected according to various criteria deemed to be pertinent (young or adult, boys or girls, educated or not, religious or not, and so on) a range of little fictions that are supposed to arouse their moral perplexity, such as The Killer Trolley. They are either presented in written form as "vignettes" (to use the technical term), or else recounted by the experimenter. They end with questions such as "what would you do?," "what must be done?," "did he do well?," "is it morally permissible?," and so on.

2. We note the spontaneous answers of the people exposed to the narrative.

3. We ask them to justify their spontaneous judgments.

4. We seek to account for the statistical distribution of the answers.

5. We attempt to draw more general conclusions as to the validity of moral theories: consequentialism, deontologism, virtue ethics.

The "democratized" thought experiment, in moral philosophy, consists in this whole sequence: construction of the moral fiction, presentation to the largest possible sample selected according to the most varied criteria, recording of the spontaneous judgments and a discussion of the attempts to justify such judgments, the comparing of the explanations with the causes and the reasons, and theoretical conclusions.

The thought experiment for philosophers skips the second and third stages: presentation to the largest possible sample selected according to the most varied criteria and recording of the spontaneous judgments and a discussion of the attempts to justify such judgments.

All these experiments concern our moral *beliefs*, that is to say, what we find good or bad, desirable or undesirable, just or unjust, whether these beliefs are *spontaneous* or *reflective*.

They enable us to evaluate the validity of consequentialist or deontological intuitions, as well as to rethink one of the most traditional questions in moral philosophy: does there exist an innate, universal "moral sense," a "moral instinct," and exactly what form does it take in our minds?

We have also distinguished between these thought experiments and behavior experiments: helping or destructive behaviors as the case may be.

Experimental moral philosophy has taken a particular interest in laboratory experiments such as that of Stanley Milgram, with a view to putting the idea of a moral or immoral "personality" to the test.

When we are faced with this huge program, one objection may immediately spring to mind. Is it not a particularly naive project, insofar as it seems to place its trust in research that raises methodological and epistemological problems that are far from negligible?

METHODOLOGICAL PROBLEMS

In the majority of works to which moral philosophy refers, the subjects of the investigation are exposed to *imaginary* situations, which they have probably never faced in their lives, at any rate in this simplified form.

These works suffer from the shortcomings characteristic of the genre: the difficulty of evaluating the exact scope of the results outside of the experimental conditions, the tendency to force the subjects' answers into preestablished categories that are perhaps not their own, and so on.

Furthermore, the conclusions of this research are formulated in statistical terms, which raises all manner of problems regarding the number of subjects involved in the experiment (which is sometimes not so numerous), their "representativity," and the thresholds beyond which a result is held to be *meaningful*.[1]

If a piece of research claims to establish that "evil is banal" because 20 percent of thirty students in moral philosophy were prepared to administer painful electric shocks to their peers in the context of a paid experiment, one would not be wrong to mistrust it.

EPISTEMOLOGICAL PROBLEMS

All this research (laboratory experiments and investigations in the field) belongs to the human sciences. Now the possibility (as well as the intrinsic interest) of aligning these disciplines with the natural sciences, by using their methods, with the same *explicatory* and *predictive* ambition, is still highly controversial.

The more skeptical reckon that the project of applying, to human behavior in general and to psychological states in particular, methods that have only been tested in the explication and prediction of physical events has no chance of success.[2]

If the human sciences are not, and never will be, rigorous sciences, explicatory and predictive, even when they imitate the latter's methods, do they amount to anything more than armchair philosophy? What is the point of wasting time in examining them more closely?

One should add that, for a good many philosophers, the vocation of the human sciences is such that the interest of their results, supposing there were any, would be far from evident for moral reflection.

The human sciences seek to inform us about what is. They describe facts. One of the vocations of moral philosophy is to tell us what is good, what we should do. It proposes norms.

Now, say these philosophers, we cannot derive any norm from a simple fact. Thus, from the fact that the majority of people give nothing to organizations combating famine, it does not follow that this is good or what we should do.

These methodological and epistemological objections are well known to philosophers, who have taken the wager of interesting themselves in empirical research. They are generally very aware of methodological problems. The laboratory experiments and field investigations they use are few in number. Such works serve as reference points, having withstood constant methodological criticism since they were first published.[3]

The two epistemological objections appear to be more difficult. But in reality they are not conclusive, given the limited aims of experimental moral philosophy.

In order to determine what is just or unjust, good or evil, moral reflection cannot do without references to the moral intuitions of each and every one of us, any more than it can do without references to typically human "capacities" or "needs."[4]

In order to analyze moral judgments or behaviors, moral reflection does indeed have to refer to peoples' "motivations," "intentions," "emotions," "character," and "personality."

In other words, moral reflection is never wholly independent of certain facts, in the sense that it invariably uses concepts whose characterization is linked to certain facts (the moral intuitions *of each and every one of us*, *typically human* needs, *peoples'* motivation and character, and so on).

"Experimental" philosophers only intervene when these concepts are deployed in their colleagues' arguments.

They question the privilege that certain philosophers accord themselves of thinking that they know more than anyone else about such concepts, without having taken the trouble to go and look at them.

But this does not mean that "experimental" philosophers wholly reject the idea that the passage from facts to norms poses problems, or that they naively disregard the limits of the human sciences.

22

WHAT REMAINS OF OUR MORAL INTUITIONS?

One principle of general epistemology tells us: "Hypotheses consistently contradicted by the facts should be rejected."

Certain philosophers would wish there to be a correspondence between this general principle and a specific principle of moral epistemology: moral principles consistently contradicted by our moral intuitions should be rejected.[1]

It is in the name of this last principle that utilitarianism is presumed to have long been refuted. In actual fact, almost all thought experiments seem to show that utilitarian principles are counterintuitive. The experiments of The Utility Monster and of The Furious Crowd were even specially invented to prove it. Yet utilitarianism still flourishes. Is it because there are some particularly stupid moral philosophers? This is a hypothesis that we cannot obviously dismiss out of hand, but I do not believe that the resistance of philosophers to antiutilitarian intuitions would provide a proof of it.

We must first of all say to ourselves that, if it seems irrational to preserve empirical hypotheses that have been systematically belied by the facts, it does not seem at all irrational to retain moral principles that have been consistently contradicted by our moral intuitions.[2]

This is an asymmetry that speaks in favor of the utilitarians. They could perfectly well maintain that where there is a conflict between their principles and ordinary intuitions, it is the intuitions that should be rejected. But we must not conclude from this that the utilitarians care nothing for intuitions. In reality, they only reject the intuitions that place them at a disadvantage. They do not complain when they find *intuitions that speak up for their point of view*. There are in fact enough moral intuitions to satisfy everyone. Thus, the following intuitions speak in favor of utilitarianism:

1. People have a tendency to seek pleasure and to avoid pain.
2. If we have a choice between two actions, we must choose the one that maximizes the good or minimizes the evil.
3. It is irrational, and even immoral, to cling fanatically to principles when their consequences are disastrous.

The deontologists proceed in exactly the same fashion. They reject the intuitions that place them at a disadvantage. But they do not complain when they find intuitions that speak up for their point of view, such as the one that would debar us from thinking it permissible to push a fat man onto a track in order to stop a runaway trolley.

What, moreover, thought experiments show is that every moral intuition is liable to be interpreted in several different ways: the utilitarian is never automatically excluded.

Hence the pair of spontaneous judgments passed by the majority of people:

1. "It is morally permissible for a trolley driver who is about to crush five trolley workers to divert it onto a loop upon which just one trolley worker is working."
2. "It is not morally permissible to push a fat man onto the track with the same aim in mind."

The philosophers offer three different interpretations of these judgments:

1. People spontaneously apply the *deontological* principle so as not to treat a person simply as a means.
2. People spontaneously apply the *deontological* doctrine of respect for fundamental rights.

3. People suffer because they remain intellectually loyal to their utilitarian line and are *emotionally* led to neutralize it.

What strikes me as really important from an epistemological point of view is the imperative never to confuse an intuition, the justification for this intuition, and its interpretation by psychologists and philosophers.

In the thought experiment of The Killer Trolley, this classification corresponds to the following data:

WHAT IS INTUITION?

It is the (raw) fact that people spontaneously produce when answering "it is morally permissible to throw the points lever" and "it is not morally permissible to push the fat man."

WHAT IS JUSTIFICATION?

It is the answers given by the subjects of the investigation to the psychologists and the philosophers who ask them to justify their spontaneous judgments. It is of the sort "we should not take ourselves for God and decide who is to live and who is to die," or "diverting a threat to five trolley workers and creating a new threat to the fat man are not the same thing," or, more often, "I cannot explain why!"

WHAT IS INTERPRETATION?

It is the explications of the intuitions and justifications advanced by psychologists or philosophers: "people spontaneously apply the principle of double effect" or "irrational emotional reactions inhibit rational consequentialist judgments."

We completely change our point of view when we pass from intuitions and justifications to interpretations. We pass from the gaze of the agent to that of the interpreter.

When psychologists or philosophers say that people have "deontological intuitions" or "consequentialist intuitions," they are expressing themselves in a clumsy or inappropriate fashion.

The "it is not morally permissible to push the fat man" intuition is a raw fact, which is neither deontological nor consequentialist. It is not delivered to us with its deontological or consequentialist interpretation. It is the interpretation of the psychologists or the philosophers that allows us to stick this sort of label on it.

If a Kantian says that "it is not morally permissible to push the fat man" is a *deontological intuition,* this is an abuse of language. He should say, "My interpretation of the intuition is deontological."

If a consequentialist asserts that "it is not morally permissible to push the fat man" shows that our *consequentialist intuitions* are inhibited by irrational emotions, this is an abuse of language. He should say, "My interpretation of the intuition is consequentialist."

We must therefore be careful not to confuse the intuition with its interpretation, if we wish not to commit this kind of abuse.

But respecting this distinction can pose a serious problem for those who seek to justify their moral conceptions or to refute a moral conception by appealing to intuitions.

These intuitions do not by themselves say anything. For them to acquire this function of refutation or of justification, they have to be interpreted. Since we can interpret them in several different ways, we should not be astonished by their capacity to endorse different theories.

A deontologist can perfectly well interpret the pair of judgments "it is morally permissible to throw the points lever" and "it is not morally permissible to push the fat man" in such a way as will allow him to assert that they refute consequentialism.

A consequentialist can certainly interpret the pair of judgments "it is morally permissible to throw the points lever" and "it is not morally permissible to push the fat man" in such a way as will allow him to assert that they refute deontology.

Given these conditions, how could intuitions help us to decide between these two great rival moral theories?

23

WHERE HAS THE
MORAL INSTINCT GONE?

How does it come about that we tend to judge the actions of others in terms of good and evil, just and unjust, when, very often, they do not directly concern us?

How are we to explain the fact that our altruistic, benevolent, or generous actions are in no wise exceptional when our species is supposed to be composed of fundamentally selfish individuals, preoccupied above all with their own material well-being?

Among the traditional answers to these questions, some refer to the impact of a social apprenticeship proceeding by means of rewards and punishments, and others to the existence of an "innate moral sense" or of a "moral instinct."[1]

LEARNED MORALITY

If we judge others in moral terms, and if we happen to act morally, it is merely because we have been trained to do so since our early childhood, and because there exist institutions that have the means to constrain us to act thus subsequently.[2]

INNATE MORALITY

If we judge others in moral terms and if we happen to act morally, it is because we are naturally equipped with certain moral capacities that express themselves very soon after birth. It is as if we were *programmed*, so to speak, to judge others in moral terms and, for our part, to behave fairly frequently in an altruistic or benevolent fashion, perhaps on account of the advantages such conduct has for our species.[3]

This second hypothesis, known as "naturalist" (as opposed to "culturalist"), is the one most widely debated today.

We must admit that theories of social conditioning through rewards and punishments, known as "behaviorist," have become somewhat obsolete in every domain of the human sciences.

It is in linguistics that the assault on these theories has been most effective. Many linguists have admitted that our apprenticeship in our mother tongue poses a problem. Indeed, a child ends up mastering his mother tongue without ever having been taught it systematically. He is capable of composing in this language an incalculable number of well-formed sentences that he has never heard.

The best possible explanation of this phenomenon seems to be that all humans are equipped with innate linguistic capacities that enable them to reconstruct their language in its entirety on the basis of the very rudimentary information that they receive.

This is a hypothesis of the same kind that appears to be gaining ground in the moral domain.

Just as there would seem to exist innate linguistic capacities enabling us to speak a language that we have never systematically learned, so too we would seem to have innate moral capacities enabling us to know what is good or evil, just or unjust, without anyone ever having systematically taught us it.[4]

The fact that even babies react with distress to the sight of pain inflicted upon others, or that the reactions of children to injustice are similar irrespective of the education received, would lend support to this hypothesis.[5]

This so-called theory of a moral sense (earlier defended by the Scottish philosophers of the eighteenth century) does not say that humans are naturally good. It can certainly admit that alongside these benevolent or "prosocial" tendencies there are other ones that are destructive and "antisocial" and that are likewise innate.[6]

It merely asserts that humans are inclined to apply moral judgments to the actions of others without having learned how to do so, and their so-called prosocial or moral (altruistic, generous, and the like) actions are in no way exceptional. This is all that the idea that humans are "naturally moral" would mean.

Certain researchers reckon that the so-called theory of the modularity of the human mind could supply a firm scientific foundation to the idea of a natural moral sense.

This is not the view of Jerry Fodor, who has strived to give a sufficiently precise content to the notion of module.[7] According to him, the notion of a moral module is simply a metaphor, appealing but of no scientific interest.

Why?

WHAT EXACTLY IS A MODULE?

According to Fodor, a module is a highly specialized psychological mechanism, organized so as to deal with certain wholly specific problems in the most effective manner possible: recognizing forms, sounds, smells, colors, the texture or taste of things, cutting up a flow of sound into words and sentences, and so on.[8]

A module functions like a reflex: automatically, rapidly, independently of our consciousness and of our will. We can clearly identify its physical foundation: a module stops working when this foundation is destroyed (think of sight). It is impermeable to beliefs and knowledges. This at any rate is what we can conclude from the existence of certain perceptual illusions. Even if we *know* that two lines are the same length, we will *see* one as longer than the other if they end in angles going in opposite directions (the so-called Müller-Lyer illusion).

For Fodor, the only genuinely modular mechanisms, the only ones answering to *all* these criteria, are *perceptual*. We are concerned here by and large with our five senses and with systems for the automatic decoding of language.

Thought, for its part, is not and cannot be organized in modules, for in order to think we must put our beliefs into relation rather than isolate them. This is a process that is not necessarily rapid, that has nothing automatic about it, and that has no clearly localized inscription in the brain. This is why, according to Fodor, there are no cognitive modules in the strict sense. The work of thought pertains to a sort of general intelligence that traverses all manner of domains, and not to idiotic modules with a specific goal, which stupidly perform the task for which they have been programmed.[9]

All in all, Fodor categorically rejects the theory of "massive modularity," a conception of the human mind defended by Dan Sperber, among others, who admits the existence of an infinity of modules, which are in countless different forms and which possess all manner of functions, perceptual, cognitive, moral, or otherwise.[10]

Fodor very explicitly disallows the idea that there could be moral modules when he pokes fun at the idea that "special, domain-specific, modular mechanisms for cheater detection" might exist.[11]

Do we really have in our heads a moral module for "detecting cheaters"?[12]

On the basis of certain experimental studies, the psychologist Leda Cosmides and the anthropologist John Tooby draw the conclusion that our mind is naturally equipped with a system that enables us to detect in a rapid, automatic, and almost unconscious fashion those who in social cooperation do not merit our trust. This is what they call the "module for detecting cheaters."[13]

Their point of departure is a famous psychology experiment known as the "card selection task," proposed by Peter Wason in 1966.[14]

The aim of this experiment is in fact not very clear. But it has become customary to say that it serves to test mastery of conditional reasoning in the form "if P then Q," or our Popperian capacities to select the best hypotheses.[15]

The experiment, put to supposedly "intelligent" people (first-year university students, for example), goes as follows.

There are 4 cards, each with a number on one side and a letter on the other.

D F 3 7

The subjects are told:

"In front of you there are 4 cards, each with a number on one side and a letter on the other. *If one card has a "D" on one side, it will have a "3" on the other.* What cards must you turn over in order to discover if this rule is true?"

An amateur logician would be able to point out that you only have to know the truth table for the conditional connective "if . . . then" to succeed. Indeed, the task consists of asking yourself: is "if D then 3" true of this set of cards? This is an application of the general case in which you ask yourself if such-and-such reasoning respects the truth table of the conditional connective "if . . . then." This table shows that the conditional is false in *one case only*: when the antecedent is true and the consequent false (that is to say, when you have P true and Q false in the table).

Here is the truth table for the conditional connective "if . . . then" (symbolized here by "→"

P	Q	P→Q
True	True	True
True	False	False
False	True	True
False	False	True

In order to obtain a concrete idea of the accuracy of this table, consider the following example. My friend tells me: "if you pass a tobacconist, buy me some cigarettes." I agree to do so.

1. If I pass a tobacconist (P true) and I buy some cigarettes (Q true), everything is fine.
2. If I do not pass a tobacconist (P false) and I do not buy some cigarettes (Q false), there's no problem either.
3. If I do not pass a tobacconist (P false) but I buy some cigarettes all the same (Q true), my friend is not going to reproach me for it!
4. But suppose now that I pass a tobacconist (P true) and *I do not buy cigarettes* (Q false). My friend will quite rightly point out that I have not complied with the rule that I had agreed to. "You passed a tobacconist and you did not buy cigarettes. Why?"

In reality, it is the only case from the four in which my friend could reasonably complain about my actions and in which I would be obliged to find some excuse.

Let us return to the task of selecting the cards.

The amateur logician ought to say to himself: "In order to know whether the rule 'if P then Q' is respected, one merely has to verify that there is no case in which P is true (there is a D) and Q is false (there isn't a 3). It is therefore pointless to pick up the card where there is a 3 (Q is true) and pointless to pick up the card where there is an F (P is false). One merely has to pick up the card D and the card 7. If D does not have 3 on the back, or if 7 has D, the set of cards will then not verify 'if D then 3.'"

It all seems so simple!

But the results of the experiment are catastrophic. The failure rate is very high.[16]

The subjects, even if they are logicians, almost all tend to choose either card D, or cards D and 3, when they should choose D and 7. We might think that the results would be better if the task was presented in a more concrete guise, with more familiar examples. In actual fact a more concrete formulation does not alter the results at all. We find the same failure rates with statements of the type "go to the Yankee Stadium" and "take the train."

However, performances are considerably enhanced when the task is formulated in terms of *permission* or *prohibition*. The task of selecting from the following cards, for example, yields good results:

"We wish to know whether, in this café, the rule stating that you are not allowed to drink beer if you are under eighteen is respected."

The first card has "twenty-five years old," the second "Coca Cola," the third "sixteen years old," the fourth "beer."

In almost 75 percent of cases, the subjects choose the right cards: "sixteen years old" (to verify whether it has "beer" on the back) and "beer" (to verify whether it has "sixteen years old" on the back).[17]

Finally, the results are also good when the task is formulated in terms of *promise* or *social exchange*: "If you give me a good idea for my article on massive modularity, I will offer you a Big Mac."[18]

In short, the subjects are terrible when the task is formulated in *descriptive* terms and good when it is formulated in *deontic* terms.

How are we to account for this result? For Leda Cosmides the answer is obvious. It is evolutionary psychology that holds the key: we have a module for the detection of "cheaters," that is to say, those who want to profit from the fruits of social cooperation without making any personal contribution themselves (think of a picnic at which you must try to avoid having guests who come empty-handed and who nonetheless polish off all the sandwiches).[19] It is because we have such a module that we are so adept, so quick at carrying out the task, of selecting cards when it is *deontic*. And if we possess this module today, it is, so the theory goes, because it was very useful to our ancestors, who needed to rapidly identify those upon whom it was better not to rely in social cooperation.

This explanation calls for at least two observations:

1. In order to suppose that our mastery of deontic conditionals proves that we possess a so-called module for the detection of cheaters, we would have to admit, for parity's sake, that, since we do not have mastery of descriptive conditionals, we do not possess a "module for classical logic." The mind would therefore not be entirely modular. There would be Fodorian "central" systems. This is exactly what the friends of massive modularity would wish to deny.

2. According to Fodor, a peripheral system only works rapidly and automatically because it is sensitive solely to a certain class of stimuli (the sounds of a language, for the module concerned with cutting up sentences in the flow of sound, for example). In the case of the module for the detection of cheaters, what would the stimulus be? It ought to involve a social exchange. But a filter does indeed seem to be necessary to select from the entirety of observable human actions those that can fall within the class of social exchanges. Is this filter itself a module? If it is not a module, the process of detecting cheaters will not be purely modular or modular all the way through. Now this filter by definition cannot be modular, for its task is general: it consists in *selecting* raw information according to a holistic process, and not in *producing* such information.[20]

IS THE DEBATE CONCERNING MODULARITY NOTHING BUT A VERBAL DISPUTE?

To the best of my knowledge, no psychologist gives a strong sense to the idea of massive modularity. Its accredited champions think that a certain degree of specialization is sufficient for it to be reasonable to speak of "modules."[21] What they propose, generally speaking, is to *weaken* the criteria of identification for Fodor's modules, which they find far too exacting.

But if it is not necessary to satisfy *all* of Fodor's criteria in order to be a module, if a certain degree of specialization suffices for it to be reasonable to speak of "modules," then, of course, all manner of things could be considered to be modules, though Fodor would never have been prepared to speak of them thus!

In the absence of common criteria for the identification of modules, I do not see very well how the differences of opinion between the champions and the opponents of massive modularity could ever be resolved.

Essentially, a large part of the dispute over modularity arises from the fact of Fodor's opponents oscillating between two contradictory attitudes toward his criteria for the identification of modules.

Sometimes they recognize Fodor's criteria and maintain that certain parts, at any rate, of the central systems are modular according to his criteria. At other times they contest these same criteria and are content to say that the central systems are modular, but in a weak sense of the term "modular."

GOODBYE TO THE MORAL INSTINCT?

Among the researchers who seek to rehabilitate the theory of the moral sense by justifying it through the existence of moral modules, Jonathan Haidt is one of the most combative.[22] He rejects the strict or stringent conception of modules. He thinks that it is not necessary for a psychological mechanism to feature absolutely all the characteristics that Fodor attributes to modules for it to be a module.

Personally, I have nothing against this none too stringent conception of modules. But it seems to me that in endorsing it, after the manner of Jonathan Haidt, it is hard to preserve, as he seeks to do, the strict distinction between the part that can be called "spontaneous" and the learned or reflexive part of moral reactions.

According to the less stringent conception of modules, in fact, we can perfectly well conceive of mechanisms that would not be as impermeable to beliefs or knowledges as the perceptual mechanisms, but that would be sufficiently specialized in their functioning to be regarded as modules.

Does so unstringent a conception of modules still enable us to distinguish, in our moral reactions, what concerns the intuitive moral reflex from what is the product of organized moral thought?

If these moral modules do not function as perceptual modules, that is to say, in an automatic fashion and altogether independently of beliefs or reasons, how could we isolate, in a reaction presumed to be moral, the intuitive part and the part depending upon an apprenticeship and upon reflection?

And if it is impossible to isolate these two aspects of moral judgment, how could we prove that certain of our moral reactions are natural, innate, or instinctive?

24

A PHILOSOPHER AWARE OF THE LIMITS OF HIS MORAL INTUITIONS IS WORTH TWO OTHERS, INDEED MORE

Experimental moral philosophy seeks to understand the mechanisms governing the formation, in peoples' heads, of moral ideas. But it is with a view to drawing certain conclusions as regards their trustworthiness as means of moral knowledge.[1] It does not merely seek to *describe* moral beliefs and to explain their social or psychological *causes*. It tries to understand whether the fact of our moral ideas having such-and-such causes does not prevent them from being just.

It is in this sense that experimental moral philosophy is a *philosophical* endeavor, and not a purely sociological or psychological one.

At any rate, it is one thing to suppose that the hypotheses of psychologists, ethnographers, sociologists, and specialists in the neurosciences might be of some interest in moral philosophy, but it is quite another to assert that what they say is incontestably true, and that the last word goes to them whatever question has been posed.

Deeply engaged with empirical research though experimental moral philosophy may be, *it does not allow it the last word*, either from the methodological or from the moral or political point of view.

Its recurrent question is the following one: If, at the origin of our so-called moral judgments, there are always negative judgments like hatred or resentment, purely selfish interests, or *psychological mechanisms that have nothing to do with ethics*, such as a preference for one's own relatives, does this not entirely discredit them as authentically *moral* judgments?[2] How could we trust them to tell us what is good or just?

What we know of the judgments of each and every one of us in domains other than ethics does not inspire optimism.

Thus, the way in which a public health program is presented strongly influences our approval or disapproval of it.

Suppose we imagine an epidemic that threatens the lives of six hundred people.

The minister of health proposes two different programs:

1. At worst two hundred people are saved, at best everyone is saved.
2. At worst four hundred people die, at best no one dies.

The people to whom this choice is put tend to reject the second program, even though it is the same as the first.[3]

In order to account for this phenomenon of apparently irrational resistance, thinkers have invoked the existence of a psychological mechanism that leads us to be disposed to take more risks in order to not lose something than to win the same thing.[4]

Why would our spontaneous moral judgments not be affected by mechanisms of the same kind?

If this were the case, would it not be irrational to trust them to know what is just or good?

ARE EMOTIONAL REACTIONS NECESSARILY IRRATIONAL?

Posing the question is important. But the answers are not given in advance.

For certain psychologists, the fact that our judgments are affected by emotional factors suffices to render them irrational.

This is how Greene discredits deontological judgments. Brandishing images of the brain obtained by MRI scans, he asserts that the formation of such judgments can be correlated with intense emotional activity.[5] They are therefore irrational.

The claim is debatable. Proving that a belief is correlated with emotions does not give us the right to assert that it is false or irrational. All that we can say, strictly speaking, is that it is difficult to *justify* by appealing to this sentiment purely and simply, without further specifications as to its conditions of appearance. But that does not absolutely prevent us from thinking that our emotions can enable us to *know certain properties of the world*. It is not absurd to reckon that the fear of a bear running toward you salivating and howling when you have no means of protection directly detects, without going by way of reflection, a real property of this bear, namely, its dangerousness.

One thought experiment, often examined, asks that we envisage our reactions to the sight of *a bunch of louts setting fire to a live cat for their own amusement.*[6]

It could serve to establish a parallel between the perception of non-moral properties such as danger and that of moral properties such as goodness or wickedness. If you experienced anger or disgust when faced with such a sight, it would not be in error. It is, it could be said, because you have detected directly, without going by way of reflection, one of the real properties of this act, namely, its cruelty.[7]

In short, just as it is legitimate to think that our sensations enable us to know if it is raining or if the weather is fine, we can envisage the possibility that our emotions could enable us to know, in certain favorable conditions, certain properties of the world around us, such as being dangerous or being cruel. The emotions would not necessarily be causes of error. They could be sources of knowledge.[8]

25

UNDERSTAND THE ELEMENTARY RULES OF MORAL REASONING

Those who believe in moral intuitions never offer an exhaustive list of them. They are right. They could be quite numerous. We can only make an inventory of the most widely discussed:

1. There exists a certain form of moral wisdom that recommends that we not "play around too much with nature."
2. Everyone prefers real pleasures caused by real things or people to artificial pleasures induced by a machine or by pills.
3. Everyone knows how to distinguish between a life worth living and another life that is entirely without interest.
4. No one is capable of imagining a moral world completely different from our own, in which it would be good, just, or admirable to inflict gratuitous suffering on others.
5. Intentions count in morality, which is not always the case in other domains, for example, in etiquette, where respect for rules is strict and admits no exception for good intentions.
6. No one gives the impression of seriously believing that there is nothing objective or universal in morality.
7. We tend to believe that, even if we are not really free to act otherwise than we do, this does not suffice to absolve us of responsibility for our actions and to render illegitimate the indignation of others at actions of ours that cause them harm.

8. Certain things have a moral importance (pursuing a politics of the Left or of the Right) and others do not (driving on the right or on the left).
9. Certain things are morally unworthy (behaving in a servile manner toward the powerful), and others are not (putting ourselves wholly at the service of those who are in urgent need of us).

The spontaneous, unthinking, nonlearned, universal, or innate character of these intuitions remains highly controversial, as does their precise meaning. Certain experimental studies show that people do not exactly have the intuitions that philosophers attribute to them. Others teach us that the predictions of certain philosophers regarding these intuitions are accurate. But the list of intuitions to be discussed is obviously not closed.

We can, on the other hand, fairly easily identify some elementary rules of moral reasoning, even if, of course, we cannot rule out the possibility that others may be discovered or that analysis may lead us to eliminate one of them because it is redundant or incoherent.

And as no one wonders (for the time being) if such rules are innate or learned, we are spared one more controversy in regard to them.[1]

The three best-known elementary rules of moral reasoning are: "ought implies can" (or "no one has to do the impossible"); "one cannot derive an ought from an is" (or "you must not confuse judgments of fact and judgments of value"); and finally, "like cases must be treated alike" (or "it is unjust to weigh two different weights using two different measures").

We can certainly add a fourth rule, one that is a little less known but that is hard to do without when analyzing norms of permission, obligation, or prohibition: *it is pointless to oblige people to do what they will necessarily do of their own accord; it is pointless to prohibit people from doing what they will not willingly do in any case.*

In all, there are therefore four elementary rules of moral reasoning, at least.

In order to introduce a little order into the debate concerning them, I will refer to each by means of a letter, and I will rank them. The ranking is not intended to imply any precedence, however.

R1: *One cannot derive an ought from an is.*
R2: *Ought implies can.*

R3: *Like cases must be treated alike.*

R4: *It is pointless to oblige people to do what they will necessarily do of their own accord; it is pointless to prohibit people from doing what they will not willingly do in any case.*

R1: ONE CANNOT DERIVE AN OUGHT FROM AN IS

There are reasons for believing that people often act in a selfish, greedy, xenophobic, or sexist fashion. Let us admit that we are concerned here with an indisputable *fact*. Would it be logical to draw from it the conclusion that it is *good* to be selfish, greedy, xenophobic, or sexist, or that we *ought to be*?

No, and no one moreover seems to reason thus. Even the selfish, the greedy, the xenophobic, and the sexist look for other reasons (which will probably not be any better) to justify their attitudes. They too seem to apply the most famous of the rules of moral reasoning: "One cannot derive an ought from an is."

In actual fact, "one cannot derive an ought from an is" is a more general rule. It places certain limits upon all reasoning in which it is a question of *permission*, *obligation*, or *prohibition*, and which for this reason is called "normative" or "deontic" (from the Greek *deon*, "ought"). It therefore also concerns juridical or epistemological reasoning.

It is sometimes called "Hume's law" or "Hume's guillotine," for it is Hume who proposed the first rigorous formulation of it. Yet certain liberties have thereby been taken with the text in which he evokes the passage from certain factual assertions to moral injunctions.[2]

Indeed, in this text, Hume does not exclude every passage from what is to what ought to be. He simply observes that this intellectual movement should be explained, whereas it generally is not.[3] Now this passage has to be explained, for otherwise it remains irrational. In order to be faithful to Hume, we should therefore write: "one cannot derive an ought from an is, or at any rate not without further argument."[4]

There exist other formulations of the rule "one cannot derive an ought from an is."

For example: "We must carefully distinguish judgments of fact—it is true, it is false—and judgments of value—it is good, it is bad—and avoid deriving the second from the first."

But Hume does not speak about the passage from judgments of fact to judgments of *value*. What poses a problem for him is the passage from facts to *norms* of obligation or prohibition.

Karl Popper has proposed an epistemological formulation of the rule "one cannot derive an ought from an is." According to him, we can perfectly well agree as to the facts and continue to disagree over the norms. Hence the idea that the norms do not necessarily flow from the facts:

> That most people agree with the norm "Thou shalt not steal" is a socio-logical fact. But the norm "Thou shalt not steal" is not a fact, and can never be inferred from sentences describing facts. This will be seen most clearly when we remember that there are always various and even opposite decisions possible with respect to a certain relevant fact. For instance, in face of the sociological fact that most people adopt the norm "Thou shalt not steal," it is still possible to decide either to adopt this norm, or to oppose its adoption; it is possible to encourage those who have adopted the norm, or to discourage them, and to persuade them to adopt another norm. To sum up, *it is impossible to derive a sentence stating a norm or a decision or, say, a proposal for a policy from a sentence stating a fact.*[5]

Another formulation is due to Poincaré: "we cannot derive a normative conclusion from nonnormative premises."[6]

It is in this *logical* formulation that the rule "from what is, we cannot derive what ought to be" has proved of most interest to philosophers, and it is in this same formulation that it has been the most fiercely contested.

Thus, John Searle has maintained that, from a factual statement such as "Smith has said to Jones 'I promise to give you twenty dollars,'" it is possible *logically* to derive the normative statement "Smith ought to give twenty dollars to Jones."[7]

But the whole question is that of knowing if the premise of the reasoning "Smith has said to Jones 'I promise to give you twenty dollars'" is *purely* factual or descriptive.

We might suppose, among other considerations, that this promise is only a promise if it has not been extorted and if it does not conceal a threat.[8]

Compare it with "Smith has *promised* Jones that he will steal his DVD collection from him at the first available opportunity." Can we derive from it "Smith *ought to* steal Jones's DVD collection"?

It is not sufficient to promise something for an obligation to flow from it. It is necessary that the promise be valid, that it not conceal a threat, that we see clearly the good it contains, and so on.

If we grant that the concept of promise contains some normative aspects of this kind, inseparable from its descriptive aspects, we could no longer say that the statement "Smith has said to Jones 'I promise to give you twenty euros'" is purely descriptive. And Searle would no longer be able to assert that he has derived this normative statement from a purely descriptive statement.

Supposing, however, that Searle is in the right, and that his argument allows us to think that from *certain* descriptive statements we can draw normative conclusions, could we generalize this result?

Could we maintain that from every descriptive statement we can derive a normative conclusion? This does not seem to be the case.

Let us return to the argument rejected by Popper: "most people believe that one should not steal," therefore "one must not steal."

To argue thus is to commit what is called in informal logic the "paralogism of popularity," that is to say, a mistake we encounter each time an argument concludes "from the popularity of a view . . . its truth."[9]

In reality, from the fact of everyone believing that P, it does not follow that P is true, and from the fact that no one believes that P, it does not follow that P is false.

In the same way, in order to justify a statement asserting that such an institution is good or just, other arguments are needed besides "this is what everyone believes." If this argument were well founded, the philosophers of Antiquity would have been right to assert that slavery was not immoral, since it was what everyone believed.

Those who accept the rule "one cannot derive an ought from an is" certainly do not think that we should avoid invoking the slightest detail relating to life in society in order to justify normative statements such as "you must not steal" or "you must always keep your promises." But they will all tend, I believe, to judge that, from the fact of everyone acting in a certain way or believing it is good to act in this way, it does not follow that it is good to act thus or that it is our moral duty to do it. They will reckon, probably, that if this were the case, we should say goodbye to every moral critique, and let the clichés and the prejudices prevail.

R2: OUGHT IMPLIES CAN

According to the second rule, it is absurd to demand of someone that they do impossible things, such as being in two different places at the very same time.

It is generally formulated as follows: "ought implies can," or in more popular versions "no one is held to the impossible."[10]

It is the awareness of the existence of such a rule that causes us to find scandalous certain demands addressed to foreigners wishing to regularize their situation. In order to have employment, you need a place of residence, but in order to have a place of residence, you need employment, and so on. What is appalling about this kind of norm is the fact of its seeming to oblige us to do the impossible.

However, every in-depth discussion of the rule "ought implies can" requires that its principal terms, "ought" and "can," be specified, and it is there that the difficulties begin.

Thus "ought" has at least two totally different meanings: probability ("it should rain," "it should already be there") and obligation ("you must pay me back what you have borrowed"). In "ought implies can," "ought" must obviously be taken in the sense of the deontic modality of *obligation*. But it can involve an absolute duty or a duty that admits exceptions, a categorical duty that imposes itself irrespective of the aims of the agent or a hypothetical duty, with respect to certain aims of the agent.

The term "can" is likewise difficult to define. We may have in mind logical or physical possibilities, but also psychological possibilities. None is easy to identify. Thus, we may wonder whether the physical or psychological possibilities to which reference is made are those of a species or of an individual. What is possible for a particular individual is not so for other members of the same species. It is not impossible for human beings to run one hundred meters in under ten seconds, above all if they are drugged up on amphetamines. But it would be personally impossible for me to do it even with the most sophisticated products. I do not even know if I am still capable of running more than 20 meters without stopping.

These difficulties do not prevent the rule "ought implies can" and its popular equivalent, "no one is held to the impossible," being of some use in the selection of obligations that have a meaning. It enables us to assert that it would be absurd to oblige people to run more quickly than the capacities of the species to which they belong allow. It could also justify the idea that it is absurd to oblige people to run more quickly than is personally possible for them.

R3: LIKE CASES MUST BE TREATED ALIKE

Among the thought experiments presented here, certain of them would not be so striking if "like cases must be treated alike" did not have the status of an elementary rule of moral reasoning.

Consider The Child Who Is Drowning in a Pond and A Violinist Has Been Plugged Into Your Back.

1. If you judge it to be monstrous to let a child die in order to preserve your new shoes and to avoid being under some pressure at work, you should also judge it to be monstrous to let children from poor countries die of hunger, when you would merely have to devote a tiny part of your income to saving them, for we are concerned here with like cases requiring a like response.[11]

2. If you judge it to be morally acceptable to rid yourself of an intruder who wishes to immobilize you for nine months, you should also judge it to be morally acceptable to interrupt an unwanted pregnancy, for it is a matter of like cases having to be treated alike.[12]

We may of course ask ourselves whether like cases—or merely analogous ones—are involved.[13]

We may ask ourselves whether similarity implies an *absolute identity* or a sufficient one, an identity in certain aspects (moral, for example) or in every aspect (such as the exact age of the child or the child's color in the case of The Child Who Is Drowning in a Pond), which would be absurd.

But that takes nothing away from the value of rule R3, which is hypothetical and demands that we treat these cases alike if and only if there are reasons for thinking that they *are* alike in certain relevant respects.

R4: IT IS POINTLESS TO OBLIGE PEOPLE TO DO WHAT THEY WILL NECESSARILY DO OF THEIR OWN ACCORD; IT IS POINTLESS TO PROHIBIT PEOPLE FROM DOING WHAT THEY WILL NOT WILLINGLY DO IN ANY CASE

1. You are in the act of shutting the door when a person, who sees you doing this, nonetheless orders: "Shut the door!" At first sight, this order is redundant, absurd. What is the point of obliging you to do what you were in the process of doing?

2. You have decided to spend the whole day in bed because you feel that you have the flu. Let us suppose that a person *forbids* you from getting out of your bed when they know that you have neither the intention nor the means to leave it. At first sight, this ban is redundant, absurd. What is the point of forbidding you to do what you did not wish to do?

The examples could be multiplied. Our lives can be ruined by pointless obligations or prohibitions. Happily, philosophical reflection offers us some tools with which to rid ourselves of them. It is possible, indeed, to construct principles that serve to filter the norms of permission, obligation, and prohibition, to know which of them are coherent, intelligent, and valid and which are redundant, contradictory, and pointless.

Thus, a principle of normative parsimony, formulated by Kant, renders null and void the norms that oblige us to do what each of us would do naturally of our own accord (such as being in good health and happy).

This principle plays a very important role in his critique of the moralities of happiness. For Kant moral prescriptions that demand that we be happy would be ridiculous, for it is a goal that we inevitably aim at of our own accord.[14]

We could say that this same principle of normative parsimony renders null and void the norms that prohibit us from doing what we would not do willingly in any case (such as being ill or unhappy).

We would therefore have two rules of normative parsimony, which we could baptize *Kant's razor*, in homage to his argument against the moralities of happiness, and with reference to the famous Occam's razor.[15]

We could formulate them as follows:

1. It is pointless to oblige people to do what they do necessarily of their own accord.
2. It is pointless to prohibit people from doing what they will not do willingly in any case.

These rules could play an extremely important role in the critique of the so-called naturalist theories of the moral sense, those that posit the existence of an innate moral faculty.

If people were equipped with an innate "moral sense," how would we account for the unbelievable quantity of moral obligations and prohibitions in all known human societies?

26

DARE TO CRITICIZE
THE ELEMENTARY RULES
OF MORAL ARGUMENT

For many philosophers these four rules are unassailable. In reality, each can be contested, and their overall coherence placed in doubt.

There exists an abundant literature in which R1 ("one cannot derive an ought from an is") is rejected in the name of R2 ("ought implies can").[1]

R3 ("like cases must be treated alike") is a purely formal rule that could oblige us to endorse a whole series of morally repugnant judgments. It shares certain characteristics with a more than dubious argument, the one known as the slippery slope. These are two reasons, among others, to use it with caution.

Finally R4 ("It is pointless to oblige people to do what they will necessarily do of their own accord" and "It is pointless to prohibit people from doing what they will not do voluntarily in any case") seems to contradict certain habits, such as those that consist in encouraging those who are already in the act of doing what they have been asked to do ("Go on, continue!").[2]

Let us consider this more closely.

QUESTIONS WITH REGARD TO R1:
"ONE CANNOT DERIVE AN OUGHT FROM AN IS"

Despite its superior position as the mother of all rules of moral reasoning, "one cannot derive an ought from an is" is by no means a principle that must be respected at all costs if we aspire to produce a coherent overall philosophical conception. Valid theories can be constructed without respecting it.

1. Those philosophers who are the most radically subjectivist where morality is concerned are certainly prepared to concede that what is good morally, or what it is fitting to do, is nothing else than what everyone approves, everywhere or else in a particular society.[3] From what is (what everyone approves), they derive what ought to be (what is good or what we must do).

2. Bertrand Russell denounces utilitarianism because, according to him, it is a doctrine that derives the desirable (pleasure must be maximized) from what is desired (we naturally seek to maximize pleasure), that is to say, the norm from the fact.[4] But that has not stopped utilitarianism from flourishing.

3. The naturalists inspired by Aristotle have proposed all manner of examples tending to show that the rule "one cannot derive an ought from an is" is a modern invention that distances us more and more each day from true morality, which would be founded upon the nature of each being and their needs. When we say, "you must water the green plants," we spontaneously draw a normative conclusion ("you must") from a fact relating to the natural needs of plants (absorbing water, among other things). It is, admittedly, a hypothetical "you must," a conditional duty, which depends upon a desire for preservation on the part of these plants, wherever it may come from. But the idea that there could be other moral duties, "categorical imperatives," unconditional, absolute, completely detached from the desires, needs, or interests of concrete beings—is it not completely harebrained, a philosophical fantasy of no real importance?[5]

4. For almost the whole of the last half-century, normative research in law, in ethics, and in politics has found quite solid epistemological foundations, with, among others, the development of John Rawls's so-called method of reflective equilibrium.[6] This is a method that renounces the attempt to "found" ethics. It merely proposes to bring face to face the spontaneous moral beliefs of competent judges, our moral principles, and our systematic philosophical theories in order to construct, little by little, a sufficiently coherent overall moral conception.

In certain of its versions, this method rejects the idea that our moral beliefs and our nonmoral beliefs could be justified separately, as if there were absolutely no relation between the two. One then speaks of a "wide" reflective equilibrium.[7]

5. Experimental moral and political philosophy is a new area of study that mobilizes very high-level researchers nearly everywhere in the world.[8] The idea informing this program is that a normative quest completely independent of the empirical facts generally culminates in unrealistic, weak, or pointless conclusions. They are unrealistic due to their not taking into account certain empirical data relating to mental architecture or to social organization. They are weak, given that they consist in bringing back certain vague and general principles like "human dignity" and that they disregard the particular maxims followed by people when going about their business. Finally, they are of very limited interest as regards the orientation of the agents in question, for they take no account of their opinions and of their concrete concerns.

The subjectivists, the utilitarians, the naturalists, the "coherentists" in the broad sense, and the experimental moral philosophers do not at all seem to think that it is completely illegitimate to establish links of all kinds between what is and what ought to be.

That amounts to many philosophers all told, and they cannot all be bad!

QUESTIONS REGARDING R2:
"OUGHT IMPLIES CAN"

Certain thought experiments could lead us to doubt the clarity of this rule.

Romeo lives thirty kilometers from the center of Rome. He arranges a date with Juliet, one Thursday, at 8:00 P.M., in Rome, in the Piazza Navona. By arranging this date, Romeo has made Juliet a promise, placing him under an obligation or making it his *duty* to be in Rome, on that Thursday, at 8:00 P.M., and in the Piazza Navona.

But on the day of the date, Romeo dines too lavishly. He decides to have a siesta. He does not hear the alarm clock, needless to say. He wakes suddenly at 7:59 P.M. Too late! He *cannot* be in the Piazza Navona at 8:00 P.M.

Does it follow that his *duty* is annulled? No, from the fact that he *cannot* keep the date, it does not follow that he *ought* not to. Would it be *contradictory* to say that Romeo has a *duty* to keep his date even if he does not have the *capacity*? No.

This is indeed why Juliet does not seem to be behaving wholly irrationally when she reproaches Romeo for having failed (as usual, we should say) in his obligations.

On the other hand, it does indeed seem that Romeo's duty would have been annulled if he had been kidnapped during his siesta or if he had died of a stroke due to his lavish meal. Finally, this thought experiment risks leading us to two contradictory conclusions:

1. "Ought implies can" is true: Romeo *ought* to keep his date with Juliet if and only if he *can* be there.
2. "Ought implies can" is false: Romeo *ought* to keep his date with Juliet even if he *cannot* be there.[9]

Thus, valid philosophical theories can be constructed without respecting the rule R1, "one cannot derive an ought from an is." And, to the question of knowing whether the rule R2, "ought implies can," is true, there is no definite answer.

Furthermore, R1 and R2 could contradict each other.

CONFLICTS BETWEEN R1 ("ONE CANNOT DERIVE AN OUGHT FROM AN IS") AND R2 ("OUGHT IMPLIES CAN")

The rule R2 ("ought implies can") can be specified as follows: "Charlie *ought* only to go to the moon if he *can* go there." From this formula we can logically derive another:

"If Charlie *cannot* go to the moon, he cannot then be obliged to go there: he *ought* not to go there."

But this new formulation poses a problem for all those who admit R1 in the logical version "we cannot derive a normative conclusion from nonnormative premises."

Indeed, "if Charlie *cannot* go to the moon, then he *ought* not to go there" well and truly violates R1 in its logical version, since a normative conclusion ("Charlie *ought* not to go there") is derived from a nonnormative premise ("Charlie *cannot* go there")![10]

Thus R2 seems to contradict R1.

If this conflict is real, we must choose between the two rules, or amend both of them so as to render them compatible.

The subjectivists, the utilitarians, the naturalists, the "coherentists" (in the broad sense), and the experimental moral philosophers take the liberty of disregarding the rule R1: "one cannot derive an ought from an is."

Are there arguments for doing without R2, "ought implies can," or for amending it?

Yes. It is a rule that seems to have absurd implications. It should lead us to think the following:

1. A ruined debtor does not have a duty to pay his debts, since he does not have the capacity to do so.
2. A kleptomaniac does not have a duty not to steal, since he cannot not steal.
3. A sadist and a psychopath do not have a duty not to massacre their victims, since they do not have the capacity to do otherwise.[11]

Besides, the rule "ought implies can" seems to exclude moral conflicts. If we reckon that moral conflicts do not exist, the rule is not threatened. But if we believe in moral conflicts, it is.

I *ought to* jump into the water in order to try to save a child to my right who is drowning in a lake.

But this child's twin is drowning in the same lake, to my left, and at a distance such that I cannot save both twins at once.

By virtue of the principle of impartiality, which demands that like cases be treated alike, if it is true that I should try to save the one, it is also true that I should try to save the other. In other words, I *ought to* try to save both. But it is, obviously, a thing that I *cannot* do. This kind of case enables us to envisage the possibility that "ought" does not necessarily imply "can."[12]

What these examples show is simply that there is no *logical* link between ought and can, and not that the rule "ought implies can" has no justification.

On the basis of these examples, it does not seem illegitimate, indeed, to conclude that, in our world at any rate, it is *logically possible* to demand the impossible.[13]

But, supposing that it is, indeed, logically possible to demand the impossible, the question would then be that of knowing why we *should*.

What indeed would a world in which we could demand the impossible be like? Would we like to live in such a world?

QUESTIONS REGARDING R3

The rule R3 "treat like cases alike" poses a very general problem. It is a rule of formal consistency that demands that we *persist* in our moral judgments without explaining what justifies them.

But let us suppose that, through completely failing to understand what the moral vocabulary signifies, we have sincerely judged Hitler to be a fine fellow. According to the rule "treat like cases alike," we ought to assert that all those who behave like Hitler are fine people!

The principal moral question is that of knowing why we have been so stupid as to formulate the initial judgment "Hitler is a fine fellow."

In reality, the rule R3, "treat like cases alike," only has a secondary moral importance: its moral value depends upon the quality of the initial judgment.

In this particular case, it would be better not to follow the rule.

An identical problem is posed by the moral requirement of impartiality, of which the rule R3 is one expression. We can be perfectly impartial by treating everyone equally badly.

Besides, the rule R3, "treat like cases alike," presents certain characteristics that it has in common with an argument that is often employed in moral debate but whose validity is doubtful: the slippery slope argument.[14]

It is a less embarrassing objection, for it is possible in part to refute it.

THE SLIPPERY SLOPE ARGUMENT

It is not hard to illustrate this argument, so frequently deployed in public debate.[15]

Those who are more liberal say: "We begin by limiting late abortion, and we will end up banning contraception. Why will sexual relationships whose purpose is not procreation not then be banned?"

The more conservative will reply: "We begin by permitting abortion, and we will end up allowing infanticide. Why will we not decriminalize voluntary homicide?"

The more liberal say: "We begin by banning actively assisting those who beg to die, and we will end up prohibiting suicide, as in former times."

The more conservative retort: "We begin by permitting assisted suicide, and we will end up allowing the elimination of the old, the poor, and the handicapped. Why not then allow it for any other category within the general population whose life is deemed not worth living?"

The philosophers have sought, of course, to formalize these common arguments in order to evaluate them.

According to Bernard Williams, for there to be a slippery slope, two conditions are necessary:[16]

1. The outcome we end up with should be indisputably horrible (legal permission to eliminate children at an early age or the handicapped and so on).

2. What causes us to slip toward this horrible outcome is not a logical or conceptual necessity but a *natural* progression due to social, psychological, or biological factors. In other words, the slippery slope argument must not be confused with what are known in logic as "sorites," those paradoxes that can cause us to doubt the existence of the bald, of heaps, or of dwarfs.[17]

Now, it often happens that these two conditions are not met.

It can be asserted that an outcome would be horrible without demonstrating it, as in the following example:

Slippery slope: If cloning for therapeutic purposes is permitted, we will end up legalizing reproductive cloning. Since reproductive cloning is horrible, let us ban cloning for therapeutic purposes.

Objection: We have not proved that reproductive cloning is horrible. We have merely *asserted* that it is.

It can be asserted that there exists a necessity to pass from the tolerable to the horrible, without specifying the nature of this necessity, as in the following example:

Slippery slope: If cloning for therapeutic purposes is permitted, we will end up with legalizing reproductive cloning, and then the instrumentalization of the body of the clone: it will serve as a storehouse of health products, of limbs and organs for the benefit of the progenitors. It will be a moral catastrophe.

Objection: Why should we necessarily pass from the first stage, controversial but tolerable, to the last, which everyone should find horrible? Why should the usual repressive mechanisms not suffice to avoid the slide from the tolerable to the horrible? If we vote for a total ban on cloning, it is because we reckon that it will be respected. Why do we not have the same confidence in a more limited prohibition, which would only exclude the monstrous treatment of clones?

In short, where do we get the idea that a limited ban or a strict legal framework for this biotechnical innovation would not be respected?

Is it based upon the psychological hypothesis that the desire to dominate or to exploit our fellows has no bounds?

Is it based upon the metaphysical hypothesis that humans have a propensity to always do the worst?

Is it based upon the sociological hypothesis that we are subject to crazed rules of competition, which oblige us to go ever further in technical innovation without heeding the human harm?

In the public debate, this is not spelled out. Nor is it among the philosophers who take an interest in cloning.

CAN WE DEFEND THE RULE "LIKE CASES MUST BE TREATED ALIKE" WITHOUT SUCCUMBING TO THE SLIPPERY SLOPE ARGUMENT?

At first glance, it is logically impossible to defend the rule R3, "like cases must be treated alike," without conceding the slippery slope argument.

Indeed, defending "like cases must be treated alike" amounts to not taking into account certain differences that are not morally meaningful. It is this that justifies the passage from one case to another. Thus, we can consider that there is no morally meaningful difference between the fact of ridding yourself of an intruder who wishes to immobilize you for nine months and certain forms of voluntary interruption of pregnancy. We will conclude, according to rule R3, that the two cases should, from a moral point of view, be treated in the same way.[18]

Now, this is also what we seem to do when we deploy the slippery slope argument. We assert that the legislation covering assisted suicide is akin to permission to exterminate the poorest people in our hospitals, and that we will *necessarily* pass onto the second once the first is accepted.

But, in reality, no defender of "treat like cases alike" suggests that we pass, *in fact*, necessarily, from one similar case to another. The comparison is purely conceptual. It is never a question of a "natural progression."

Asserting, for example, that there is no meaningful moral difference between a masseur and a sex worker absolutely does not suggest that, if you start out as a masseur in a physiotherapist's consulting room, you will necessarily end up doing tricks in Central Park!

The rule "treat like cases alike" is conceptual. It has nothing to do with the slippery slope argument, which envisages a "natural progression."

QUESTIONS REGARDING R4

When you are ordered to shut the door even though you are in the very act of shutting it, and no one giving you the order knows it, this order is redundant from the conceptual point of view, and *intellectually pointless*. It is stupid, in a certain sense.

When you are forbidden to leave your bedroom even though you have absolutely no intention of doing so because you have the flu, and no one forbidding you knows it, this prohibition is redundant from the conceptual point of view, and *intellectually pointless*. It is stupid, in a certain sense.

But that does not mean that this order and this prohibition *express nothing*, that they have no practical function.

Ordering someone to do what they are in the very act of doing can sometimes serve to mark approbation or express support, as when we yell at a boxer in the act of finishing off his opponent: "Finish him off!"[19]

Prohibiting someone from doing what he did not wish to do can have the same positive function of support or approbation, as when someone says to you, "don't go out, you've got the flu," when you had absolutely no intention of going out.

But, in many cases, ordering someone to do what he is in the very act of doing or prohibiting him from doing what he did not wish to do can have a less sympathetic function. It may involve an act that humiliates and thus underlines a certain state of domination or subordination.

Is not ordering someone to do what he was in the very act of doing a way of telling him that his will counts for nothing?

Is not prohibiting someone from doing what he did not wish to do a way of telling him that his will counts for nothing?

CONCLUSION

MORALITY WITHOUT "FOUNDATIONS"

The majority of philosophers will tell you that, if you are concerned with moral thought, you must begin by reading and rereading the great texts in the history of ideas in order to have "firm foundations."

But it is not obvious that the best means of inviting the reader to undertake ethical reflection is to give him the feeling that he can calmly rest upon the doctrines elaborated by the "giants of thought."

This is why it seems to me that it would be more logical for him to be directly confronted with the difficulties of moral thought, by submitting to his perspicacity a certain number of problems, dilemmas, and paradoxes, and by exposing him to the results of scientific studies that run counter to certain received ideas within the philosophical tradition.

1. Utterly harebrained thought experiments (invisible criminals, mad doctors, killer trolleys, experience machines, and the like) submitted to huge samples, whose conclusions lead us to doubt the robustness or universality of our moral intuitions.
2. Laboratory experiments regarding human generosity or cruelty, whose results place in question the idea of there existing exemplary moral personalities.

3. Investigations into the causes of moral beliefs that lead us to doubt their moral character.
4. Psychological research into the morality of children, showing to what extent the idea that there exists a "moral instinct" or an "innate moral sense" is muddled.
5. Comparative anthropological studies of moral systems leaving us with the impression that morality is not always very clearly distinguished from religion or from social conventions.

These materials now form the "corpus" of experimental moral philosophy, a set of works that associate philosophical reflections and empirical research, such that we obviously do not know in advance where they will take us.

It seemed to me, at the outset, that we should not decide in advance that these works absolutely cannot clarify questions of moral philosophy, under the pretext that they are concerned with facts and not with norms or values, and that there exists an impassable abyss between the two kinds of investigation.

A deeper examination of these works has shown, I believe, that this initial stance was not unjustified.

Thus, experimental moral philosophy has already helped us to understand the following:

1. Virtue ethics rests upon a confused notion, that of the "moral personality."
2. The existence of a moral instinct is far from having been proved.
3. The boundaries between the moral, the social, and the religious are not obvious.
4. The standard method used to justify moral theories by appealing to moral intuitions is not reliable.

What experimental moral philosophy can allow us to recognize is the fact that *nothing* in the concepts and methods of moral philosophy is immune from challenge and revision. This is a result that cannot leave those concerned with the possibility of authentic research in moral philosophy indifferent.

It allows us to think that moral debate is not completely irrational, and that it can advance through conceptual critique, the questioning of prejudices, and the exchange of arguments that are logical and that respect the facts.

VIRTUES AND MORAL INSTINCT

Two ancient theories are making a spectacular comeback in present-day debates: virtue ethics of an Aristotelian inspiration and the theories of the moral sense, according to which there exists an innate moral instinct that is peculiar to our own species and to a few other animal species.

These two theories are not obviously compatible.

Virtue ethics asserts that it is possible to acquire an exemplary moral personality through education, observation, and imitation. What is important from the moral point of view is not that virtue is natural, but that it becomes a sort of "second nature," a set of habits of thinking and acting that no longer even need to be pondered.

For their part, the theories of a moral sense posit the existence of innate moral capacities, while at the same time conceding that these capacities require some time and a favorable milieu in order to pass from the potential to the actual.

These two conceptions of moral development are not necessarily contradictory. They can nevertheless become so, if the friends of virtue ethics reckon that it is not at all necessary to entertain the hypothesis that we have innate moral capacities in order to explain the acquisition of our "moral habits."

Nothing, indeed, in virtue ethics excludes the idea that these habits could be inscribed on a "blank page," that is to say, on a highly malleable mind, lacking in any "natural" predisposition toward good or evil, thanks to the work of competent educators, skilled in wielding the carrot and the stick.

Another question that experimental moral philosophy helps us to answer is: do the basic hypotheses of these theories have a foundation?

Virtue ethics rests upon the idea that there exist exemplary moral personalities. But according to certain psychologists, who are practitioners of a "situational" psychology, the very idea of "personality" is dubious.

According to them, no one is funny, generous, or brave in every context. Defining people through a "character" and explaining their conduct through its manifestations arise from a tendency to judge people *globally*. This "global" approach has nothing particularly rational about it, since it is also encountered in racist, sexist, and xenophobic judgments. Can the virtue ethics that is founded upon the notion of "personality" withstand these objections? It has to try in any case, if it is to retain the esteem that it has earned in recent decades.

For their part, moral sense theories have not managed to give a clear answer to the question that they themselves were raising. What part do the learned and the innate play in our moral judgments and behaviors? Do we have the methodological and conceptual means to rule out altogether the idea that our moral judgments and behaviors are entirely the product of an apprenticeship conducted through rewards and punishments? We have not really got there yet.

THE MORAL, THE SOCIAL, THE RELIGIOUS

One of the most recent and best-constructed theories of moral development maintains that we establish very early on the distinction between three domains:

1. the *domain of morality*, whereby we universally exclude actions consisting in doing harm to others;
2. the *domain of the conventions*, whereby we exclude certain actions in which the wrong done to others is not obvious, such as eating pork or dressing in pink to attend a funeral. These rules are only valid for the community and are justified or guaranteed by a sacred text or the word of an authority;
3. the *personal domain*, which is supposed to concern only our own selves, and which has to do with individual appraisal (it may, for example, concern a taste for such-and-such a sport or for such-and-such a bodily decoration).

This distinction between three domains may be refined in the course of moral development from childhood to the entry into adulthood, but it exists from the earliest age.

What is important is the fact that, according to this same distinction, the early moral sense is expressed in negative reactions toward actions that cause harm to others. Children are naturally "minimalist," in the sense that, for them, ethics is reduced to the concern not to harm others.

A large part of current research consists in testing the validity of this construction. A diametrically opposed "maximalist" hypothesis has been devised and subjected to empirical testing.

It states that we develop very early on a tendency to judge as immoral all manner of actions that do not directly harm others: blasphemy, suicide, consuming impure food, ways of dressing or treating our own bodies that are deemed to be scandalous, and so on.

Furthermore, the majority of sexual prohibitions (the prohibition of incest between consenting adults included) and dietary prohibitions (not eating pork, shellfish, and the like) are considered by those who abide by them to be *universal* prohibitions and obligations, that is to say, moral norms. The same applies to obligations toward ourselves (shaving our heads, letting our beards grow, not drinking alcohol or taking drugs, and so on) and the dead (not burying them or burying them on the bare ground and so on).

To summarize the debate, we can say that it involves a confrontation between two camps, the *maximalists* and the *minimalists*.

For the maximalists, our basic morality is very rich. We develop very early a tendency to judge all manner of "victimless crimes" as immoral. We do not clearly separate the moral, the social, and the religious.

For the minimalists, our basic morality is much poorer. It only excludes those actions that deliberately cause harm to others. It clearly and universally separates the moral, the social, and the religious.

In order to discover what is the best theory from the normative point of view, the philosophers are in principle very well equipped. But they have every interest in taking account in their arguments of this empirical controversy, if only to gain some idea of the efforts that would have to be made in order to arrange things so that the norms they advocate could be implemented.

If our basic morality is poor or minimal, considerable social labor would be required to turn us into moralizers who are intolerant of styles of life differing from our own, and who are always tempted to poke our noses into other people's affairs.

If our basic morality is rich or maximal, considerable social labor would be required to turn us into liberals who are tolerant of styles of life differing from our own, and who are ever respectful of other people's privacy.

MORAL INTUITIONS

The method used to justify the great moral theories abides by the following protocol:

1. Construct bizarre thought experiments in order to reveal our moral intuitions.
2. Assert that the theories that are not to our liking are false because they contradict these moral intuitions.

It seems to me that we can doubt the trustworthiness of this method on account of its *epistemological limits*:

1. Intuitions are raw facts to which we can give all manner of interpretations. It is always possible to find an interpretation that leaves the theory we are defending intact.
2. Two theories can be incompatible with each other and yet compatible with the same intuitions, once the latter have been placed in a certain perspective. The appeal to intuitions does not enable us to know which is the best.

These epistemological limits in no way prevent us from seeking other means of refutation, such as the bringing out of internal contradictions or other criteria of justification, such as simplicity or coherence. But they do imply that it will be impossible to decide between two equally simple and coherent rival theories by appealing to intuitions.

In my opinion, this result should not discourage us and lead us into radical skepticism toward moral thought.

The epistemological limits of the appeal to intuitions should rather open our minds to pluralism, that is to say, to the idea that there exist several equally reasonable overarching moral conceptions, the permanent confrontation of which does not only have disadvantages. The positive aspect of this confrontation is that it prevents us from lapsing into a moral simple-mindedness. Thanks to it, each theory can become progressively more complex, more subtle, more aware of its own limits and also of its domain of legitimate intervention.

Obviously, we would find it hard to cheerfully accept this perspective, if we yearn to *furnish foundations for morality*, for example, to propose a single, ultimate, unshakeable, and unalterable principle, upon which the disparate ensemble of our moral beliefs could rest and be entirely secure intellectually.

But why should we seek to "furnish foundations for morality"? Why should we think that we should do more, or that we could do more, than try to somewhat ameliorate our moral beliefs through philosophical criticism, by eliminating the most absurd and the most exaggerated of our prejudices?

GLOSSARY

Applied Ethics

Its program consists, by and large, of evaluating, from the moral point of view, the arguments employed in public debates relating to certain specific domains of action (relations with nature and with animals, biomedicine, sexual relationships, global justice, and so on). It may proceed to this evaluation by adopting as criteria the principles of the existing moral theories (utilitarian, Kantian, or others). But this is not necessary. In applied ethics, a respect for general principles of coherence and a profound understanding of the specific domain (in issues of health or the environment, for example) are tools that certain philosophers prefer to the blind application of general principles. Research in applied ethics sometimes even leads to these principles being placed in question.

Compatibilism-Incompatibilism

Is it possible to reconcile what we know of the behavior of humans, subject, like everything belonging to the natural world, to forces that escape them, and our tendency to judge them as if they were free and responsible for their actions? How are we to render these two contradictory ideas "compatible": we are free and at the same time subject to the determinism of nature?

One of the ways of demonstrating that liberty and determinism are not incompatible consists in pointing out that a free action is not an action that is mad, arbitrary, and without reasons, but an action caused or determined by our own reasons, that is to say, a voluntary reason. But the "incompatibilists" answer that to be free is not only to act according to one's own reasons but also to have the power to choose one's own reasons. According to them, we do not have that power.

Another way of attempting to resolve the conflict amounts to saying that our beliefs in determinism and liberty can perfectly well coexist without contradicting each other, for they relate to completely different aspects of our lives. Even if reason tells us that we are subject to forces that escape us, we cannot help having emotional reactions of joy, anger, and indignation toward what we are doing or what others are doing, as if we and they were free. It would be absurd to think that such reactions could be eliminated.

But an "incompatibilist" could always object that our emotional reactions of joy, anger, and indignation toward what we are doing or what others are doing are simply irrational and should not influence our judgments.

Consequentialism

For the consequentialist what counts morally is not blindly respecting certain absolute constraints upon action, such as those that would prohibit our treating someone simply as a means, but rather acting in such a way that there is, in total, the most good or the least evil possible in the universe. And if it is necessary, in order to get there, to free ourselves from such constraints, we must do so. Consequentialism does not however impose any definition of the good. We may in fact distinguish between several different consequentialist conceptions in terms of their definition of it. The most famous is utilitarianism. For it, the good is pleasure, or the satisfaction of the preferences of each. But a consequentialist may also recommend that friendship or fundamental rights be promoted. Can all these goods, however, be the object of this kind of calculation? What does it mean to act in such a way that there is "the most friendship possible in the universe"? Would it be morally recommended to sacrifice a few friends in order to have more in total? Furthermore, our

fundamental rights have the property of being untouchable and inviolable. Can consequentialism really make a place for them in its system?

Deontologism

For the deontologist (from the Greek *deon*, "duty"), there exist absolute
constraints upon our actions, things that one should never do: "do not
lie" and "do not treat a person simply as a means" are examples of this
kind of constraint.

Kantian morality is the model for strict deontological moralities. But
there are less exacting deontological moralities, which concede some
exemptions from the constraints upon action in order to avoid infringe-
ments upon the well-being of all that are too grave. Is this not proof that
rigid respect of these constraints, without interrogating their contribution to the well-being of all, has something irrational about it?

Doctrine of Double Effect

This moral doctrine, whose original formulation is attributed to Thomas
Aquinas, designates two effects, one good and the other bad, of an action
that, considered in itself, is good, or neither good nor bad.

One might think of the bombardment of a bunker in which is hidden
the high command of a cruel army waging an unjust war, and in which
there are also civilians. One of these effects is good (eliminating unjust
aggressors). This is the purpose of the action, what its authors intend. The
other is bad (killing innocent civilians). It is anticipated by the authors
of the action. It is an inevitable "collateral effect." But it is not this effect
that is intended by the action or desired by its authors. It is not even conceived to be a means of arriving at the result intended. According to the
doctrine of double effect, this kind of action with two effects is morally
permissible under these conditions (the bad effect is not intended, it is
not a means), to which we must add that the harm caused (in terms of
innocent victims, for example) is not disproportionate.

But the doctrine still remains just as controversial. For the consequentialists, it is false: there is no meaningful moral difference between massacring civilians as the anticipated collateral effect of an action whose
intention is good, massacring civilians as a means to achieve a certain

goal, and massacring civilians tout court. For the deontologists, this doctrine is muddled: it is simpler to say that we should never treat a person simply as a means. For the friends of the virtues, we are too wary of causing a harm for the motive of coming to the assistance of someone to accept the doctrine of double effect in its current form.

Ethics and Morality

This is a division that is judged to be fundamental in nonanalytic moral philosophy, but not in analytic moral philosophy, where one sets out rather from a distinction between metaethics, normative ethics, and applied ethics (see the entries in this glossary). It must be said that the opposition between ethics and morality lacks clarity. Sometimes ethics concerns the relation to self and morality the relation to the other. Sometimes ethics is on the side of the desirable, and morality on the side of the prohibited or the obligatory. Sometimes ethics is on the side of critique and invention, and morality on the side of conformity. But what sort of ethics would it be that was in no way concerned with the relation to others, or that dispensed entirely with the notions of prohibition and obligation? What sort of morality would it be that had no creative and critical dimension or that had nothing desirable about it?

Facts and Norms

The majority of philosophers reject the idea that it is intellectually legitimate to pass, without any additional argument, from a factual statement (which tells us what people think or do) to a normative statement (which tells us what we should think or do). Thus the statement "from the fact that slavery exists and has always existed, it follows that it ought to exist" is completely illogical and ill formed. But in many cases, we reckon that we can pass from factual statements to normative statements. The fact that slavery is incapable of satisfying the most basic human needs is a sufficient reason for thinking that we must abolish it absolutely and universally. Furthermore, the rule "no one is obliged to do what is impossible" (or, in technical terms, cannot implies ought not), which everyone seems to accept, posits that we can pass from a fact (we cannot) to a norm (we ought not to).

Internalism-Externalism

The word "internalism" refers to two different ideas in moral philosophy. The internalism of the judgment asserts that an authentic moral judgment is necessarily accompanied by a certain motivation to act in accordance with its requirements. If I sincerely assert that "it is wrong to let children from the poorest countries die of hunger," it is obvious, for the internalist, that I am committing myself, in some way, to doing everything in my power to change this state of affairs.

The externalist rejects the idea that there exists a necessary link between our moral judgments and motivation. For him, the sentence "I know that it is good, but I have no wish to do it" is perfectly intelligible. It is, according to him, borne out daily by cases of depression (I have kept my moral beliefs but I have lost the motivation to act in accordance with them) and of amoralism (I know what is good, but I don't give a damn). The whole question is that of knowing whether amoralism really exists. Does someone who does not do what he knows is good really know that it's good? Is it authentic knowledge?

The internalism of existence tells us that there cannot be reasons for acting that are completely external to the whole formed by the most characteristic beliefs, desires, and emotions of people, that is to say, by their "motivational system." But if this conception were true, the reason would have no reason to act in a tolerant fashion. Such reasons would be completely external to his "motivational system."

Metaethics

Metaethics has the ambition to describe the moral judgments of each and every one of us and to identify their most meaningful properties from a philosophical point of view. It poses semantic, ontological, epistemological, and psychological questions. The most debated ones are the following.

What do the words "good" and "just" mean? Can we derive judgments of value from judgments of fact? How are we to justify our moral judgments? Can our moral statements be true or false? Do our moral judgments necessarily contain a motive for acting? Do there exist "moral facts" that are as objective as physical or mathematical facts? What is the value of the different "foundations" that have been given to morality: God, nature, reason, feelings, society? Does morality need "foundations"? To what extent can we reply to these questions without taking into account two other branches of moral philosophy, normative ethics and applied ethics? Is the distinction between the three so obvious?

Moral Intuitions

These are spontaneous moral judgments, which are not derived through an argument from general principles or from moral theories. According to another conception, they are basic moral judgments that are obvious to all and that have no need to be justified by principles or theories. Do we have the means, however, to distinguish clearly, on the inside of our moral judgments, between the spontaneous and the reasoned part?

Moral Modules

A module is a highly specialized psychological mechanism, organized in order to treat in the most effective manner certain wholly specific problems: recognizing forms, sounds, smells, colors, and the texture or the taste of things; cutting up a flow of sound into words and sentences; and so on. A module functions like a reflex: automatically, rapidly, independently of our conscience and of our will. The most important thing is the fact of its being impermeable to our beliefs and our knowledges. Thus, even if we know that two lines are the same length, we will see one as longer than the other if they end in angles going in opposite directions (the so-called Müller-Lyer illusion).

According to a less exacting conception of modules, it is not necessary for a psychological mechanism to present absolutely all of these characteristics to be a module. We can perfectly well conceive of mechanisms that would not be as impermeable to beliefs and knowledges as perceptual mechanisms, but that would be sufficiently specialized in their functioning to be considered modules. It seems that we can only speak of moral modules in the sense of the least exacting conception of modularity.

Saying that there exist "moral modules" amounts to supposing that we have certain "moral reflexes" that can, however, be modified by thought.

Does so unexacting a conception of modules still allow us to distinguish in our moral reactions what relates to the "intuitive"?

Normative Ethics

The vocation of normative ethics is prescriptive. It asks itself what we must do, what is good or bad, just or unjust. It revolves today around a huge debate concerning the exact form and the value of three great theories: deontologism, consequentialism, and virtue ethics. It may be summarized through a handful of questions: What is a moral theory? Do we really need a moral theory in order to make a correct moral judgment and act in a way that is fitting? And if we do need one, which is best? What methods do we have available in order to know? What is a moral reflex and what is the product of organized moral thought?

Reflective Equilibrium

How are we to justify rationally a moral judgment such as "slavery is an evil"? The principal threat in such attempts at justification is infinite regress. We have to justify the justification and so on to infinity.

The foundationalist reckons that the threat can be contained, either by invoking great basic principles that are self-evident ("all men are born equal in right," for example) or by appealing to elementary experiences of a perceptual or emotional kind (anger, indignation at slavery, and so on).

The coherentist disputes the validity of this method. According to him, the idea of an "ultimate" justification is illusory because the notion of intellectual evidence is vague, and because elementary experiences can never by themselves justify moral judgments. We must at least add some normative reasons for thinking that these experiences can fulfill this justificatory function.

For the coherentist, the only reasonable way of attempting to justify our moral judgments consists in showing that they can belong to a set of judgments that are sufficiently coherent among themselves. But the foundationalist may object that coherentism is threatened by circularity or systematic falsity. There is no shortage of perfectly coherent and sys tematically false narratives (reports of spies, fairy stories, and so on). The method known as "reflective equilibrium," which we owe to John Rawls, proceeds through the reciprocal adjustment of the spontaneous judgments of rational and reasonable persons and reflections on the great political or moral principles. It is coherentist. It therefore inherits the advantages, as well as the shortcomings, of this conception of the justification of moral ideas.

Slippery Slope

Saying that there is a "slippery slope" amounts to asserting that, if we tolerate a certain action whose moral value is the object of a controversy (euthanasia, research into embryos, abortion, and the like), we will necessarily come to tolerate actions whose morally repugnant character is not the object of any controversy, such as the wholesale elimination of the poor, the weak, the ugly, and the handicapped and belated infanticide. If we do not wish to end up at these inadmissible conclusions, it is better not to place ourselves on the slippery slope that leads necessarily to it. The problem posed by this argument is that the reasons for which one should necessarily end up with these conclusions that no one should accept are either well hidden or else unfounded.

Utilitarianism

Consequentialism asks us to promote the good, but it does not pronounce upon the nature of the good to be promoted. Utilitarianism is a specification of consequentialism, in the sense that it proposes a certain definition of the good to be promoted. What we must do, so far as utilitarianism is concerned, is work for the greatest pleasure (or for the greatest well-being or for the satisfaction of preferences) of the greatest number. This objective may be pursued in two different ways:

1. By evaluating through a calculation the contribution of each act to the promotion of the greatest good for the greatest number (act utilitarianism).
2. By following, without calculation, certain general rules such as "do not torture" and "do not lie," of which there is every reason to think that, if everyone followed them, one would help to promote the greatest good of the greatest number (rule utilitarianism).

It is supposed that the advantage of utilitarian thought over other moral conceptions is its giving us the means to approach moral questions in a rational fashion and without too many prejudices.

But is act utilitarianism so rational? It asks us to carry out a calculation of the positive and negative effects of each action that we get ready to perform. Is such a calculation not impossible or too costly? Rule utilitarianism, for its part, asks that we respect rules of common sense that have always worked. Is it really up to helping us to rid ourselves of our prejudices?

Victimless Crimes

These are actions that are regarded as crimes but that have caused no unconsenting harm to a concrete person. The category covers personal relationships between consenting adults (incest, homosexuality, prostitution), violations of abstract entities (blasphemy against gods or ancestors), actions directed against oneself (suicide, cleanliness, control of hair, sexual secretions).

Virtue Ethics

Virtue ethics takes its inspiration to a greater or lesser degree from Aristotle. It is sometimes called "aretist" (from the Greek *arête*, "excellence"). It asserts that the only thing that matters morally is personal perfection: being someone good, a person of good character, generous, affectionate, brave, and so on. The rest—that is to say, respecting great principles or working for the greater good of the greater number—is secondary. The question is to know in what respect it is a moral doctrine, inasmuch as it does not tell us what we must do or what we must aim at. In order to withstand this objection, the modern versions of virtue ethics assert that what we must do is imitate "exemplary" moral personalities. But aside from the fact that this kind of conception no longer has anything to do with Aristotle, who never said that a good action consisted in imitating such-and-such a person, it poses an internal logical problem. According to which criteria will we choose these personalities and decide that they are "morally" exemplary? Must we choose Gandhi or Napoleon, like a character in Dostoyevsky? Do we not already have to know what is moral in order to make the right decision?

NOTES

PREFACE: AN ANTIMANUAL OF ETHICS

1. I could have written "to ethics or morality," two terms that I use indiscriminately, for I do not think that it is useful to give too much weight to this distinction. For an explanation, see the entry "Ethics and Morality" in the glossary.

2. A large part of modern normative ethics, taking its inspiration from John Rawls, rests upon a coherentist or antifoundationalist epistemology. See Norman Daniels, ed., *Reading Rawls: Critical Studies on Rawls' "A Theory of Justice"* (Stanford: Stanford University Press, 1989); see also the entry "reflective equilibrium" in the glossary. And the irreducible heterogeneity of moral doctrines is defended in, among others, Charles Larmore, "L'hétérogénéité de la morale," in *Modernité et morale* (Paris: Presses Universitaires de France, 1993), chap. 4; and Thomas Nagel, "War and Massacre," in *Mortal Questions* (Cambridge: Cambridge University Press, 1979), 53–74.

3. Peter Singer, *The Life You Can Save: Acting Now to End World Poverty* (New York: Random House, 2009), 4–5.

4. Ibid., 4–12.

5. Kwame Anthony Appiah, *Experiments in Ethics* (Cambridge, Mass.: Harvard University Press, 2008).

6. John M. Doris and Jesse J. Prinz, review of Kwame Anthony Appiah, *Experiments in Ethics*, *Notre Dame Philosophical Reviews*, October 3,

2009. Like every research program involving more than two research-ers, experimental moral philosophy is divided into several different cur-rents. My way of presenting this program is by no means orthodox, and I would not advise a student to use it in an exam (though there is little risk of there being one—in France, at any rate).

7.   This, according to Appiah, was the method of Hobbes, Descartes, Locke and Hume: Appiah, *Experiments in Ethics*, 7–11.

8.   Hilary Putnam, *The Collapse of the Fact/Value Dichotomy, and Other Essays* (Cambridge, Mass.: Harvard University Press, 2002).

INTRODUCTION: WHAT IS THE POINT
OF THOUGHT EXPERIMENTS?

1.   Tom Regan, "The Dog in the Lifeboat: An Exchange," *New York Review of Books*, April 25, 1985.

2.   Claudia Wallis, "Baby Fae Stuns the World," *Time*, November 12, 1984; Claudia Wallis, "Baby Fae Loses the Battle," *Time*, November 26, 1984.

3.   Martha Nussbaum, *Love's Knowledge: Essays on Philosophy and Litera-ture* (New York: Oxford University Press, 1990), 46–47.

4.   Kathleen V. Wilkes, *Real People: Personal Identity Without Thought Experiments* (Oxford: Clarendon Press, 1988).

5.   It is in these terms that Martha Nussbaum characterizes the moral value of literature: "As James says, 'The picture of the exposed and entangled state is what is required.'" Nussbaum, *Love's Knowledge*, 46.

6.   Jeremy Waldron, "Right and Wrong: Psychologists vs. Philosophers," *New York Review of Books*, October 8, 2009; Wilkes, *Real People*.

7.   Jacques Bouveresse, "Les expériences de pensée en littérature et en phi-losophie morale: Mach-Wittgenstein-Platon-Cora Diamond," in *La con-naissance de l'écrivain, sur la littérature, la vérité et la vie*, ed. J. Bouveresse (Marseilles: Agone, 2008), 115–22; Cora Diamond, "What If X Isn't the Number of Sheep? Wittgenstein and Thought-Experiments in Ethics," *Philosophical Papers* 31, no. 3 (November 2002): 227–50.

8.   This does not prevent us from being prepared, or so it would seem, to enter through the imagination into every kind of physical world very far removed from our own (worlds in which one can become invisible or shrink at will), whereas we are less ready to enter through the imagi-nation into moral worlds very far removed from our own (worlds in which it is good to hang children for pleasure or to kill one's baby if it

is a girl): Tamar Szabo Gendler, "The Puzzle of Imaginative Resistance," *Journal of Philosophy* 97, no. 2 (February 2000): 55–81.

9. Plato, *The Republic*, bk. II, 359c–362c.

10. Diamond, "What If X Isn't the Number of Sheep?"

11. Wilkes, *Real People*.

12. Samuel Scheffler, ed., *Consequentialism and Its Critics* (Oxford: Oxford University Press, 1988).

13. Robert Nozick, *Anarchy, State and Utopia* (Oxford: Basil Blackwell, 1974); Thomas Nagel, "War and Massacre," in *Mortal Questions* (Cambridge: Cambridge University Press, 1979).

14. Scheffler, *Consequentialism and Its Critics*.

15. Roger Crisp and Michael Slote, eds., *Virtue Ethics* (Oxford: Oxford University Press, 1997); Marcia W. Baron, Philip Pettit, and Michael Slote, *Three Methods of Ethics* (London: Blackwell, 1997).

16. The descriptions of the three great moral theories I have given are designed to allow the reader to grasp what essentially differentiates them. But there exist almost as many ramifications of these theories as there are philosophers defending or contesting them. There are forms of deontologism that do not acknowledge absolute constraints upon actions and that incline to consequentialism. There are forms of consequentialism that attempt to give ground to certain firm constraints upon our actions, and thus approach deontologism. As for virtue ethics, it now exists in several different forms, some of which are hard to distinguish from consequentialism and from deontologism. All the same, this book is not devoted to an in-depth examination of the three great moral theories and of their resources, but to an analysis of the place of intuitions in the justification of any moral theory. I therefore do not propose to enter into too much detail about such theories. I have attempted, with Christine Tappolet, to present as complete a picture as possible of the different versions of consequentialism and of deontologism, and to analyze the resources of each, in *Les concepts de l'éthique: Faut-il être conséquentialiste?* (Paris: Hermann, 2009). See also, for a detailed account of the present state of these moral theories, the essays contained in Scheffler, *Consequentialism and Its Critics*.

17. Immanuel Kant, "On a Supposed Right to Lie from Altruistic Motives," in *Critique of Practical Reason, and Other Writings in Moral Philosophy*, ed. Lewis Beck (Chicago: University of Chicago Press, 1949), 346–50.

18. Kwame Anthony Appiah, *Experiments in Ethics* (Cambridge, Mass.: Harvard University Press, 2008), 78–82.

19. T. M. Scanlon, "Rawls on Justification," in *The Cambridge Companion to Rawls*, ed. Samuel Freeman (Cambridge: Cambridge University Press, 2003), 140.

20. It extends from the philosopher-king of Plato to the rational and reasonable judge of John Rawls: David Copp, "Experiments, Intuitions, and Methodology in Moral and Political Theory," text presented to the Molyneux Spring Seminar on Intuitions, University of California, Davis, 2010, 1–49, and to the ANCO-CERSES seminar at Paris 5-René Descartes in June 2010. One can also view this elitist tradition as a long history of *exclusion* of persons judged to be unsuited to sustaining a well-formed moral judgment: women, the poor, the young, non-Westerners, non-Whites, and so on.

21. Scanlon, "Rawls on Justification."

22. Appiah, *Experiments in Ethics*, 80.

23. Some of these experiments have been conducted upon thousands of persons through the Internet: Steven Pinker, "The Moral Instinct," *New York Times*, January 13, 2008.

24. Appiah, *Experiments in Ethics*; Joshua Knobe and Shaun Nichols, eds., *Experimental Philosophy* (Oxford: Oxford University Press, 2008).

25. According to Peter Unger, *Living High and Letting Die* (Oxford: Oxford University Press, 1996).

26. He is reputed to have actually tested it on his sisters, which today might perhaps have led to him being charged with mental cruelty: Louis Ernest Borowski, Reinhold Berhnard Jachmann, and Ehrgott André Wasianski, *Kant intime*, ed. and trans. Jean Mistler (Paris: Grasset, 1985).

27. Owen Flanagan, *Varieties of Moral Personality: Ethics and Psychological Realism* (Cambridge, Mass.: Harvard University Press, 1991); Vanessa Nurock, *Sommes-nous naturellement moraux?* (Paris: Presses Universitaires de France, 2011).

28. John M. Doris, *Lack of Character: Personality and Moral Behaviour* (Cambridge: Cambridge University Press, 2002).

PART I. PROBLEMS, DILEMMAS, AND PARADOXES: NINETEEN MORAL PUZZLES

1. C. Haney, W. Banks, and P. Zimbardo, "Interpersonal Dynamics of a Simulated Prison," *International Journal of Criminology and Penology* 1 (1973): 69–97.

2.   Kwame Anthony Appiah, *Experiments in Ethics* (Cambridge, Mass.: Harvard University Press, 2008), 89–101.

1. EMERGENCIES

1.   After a case devised in Philippa Foot, "Killing and Letting Die," in *Abortion: Moral and Legal Perspectives*, eds. J. Garfield and P. Hennessy (Amherst: University of Massachusetts Press, 1984), 177–85.
2.   The analysis that follows is taken from Ruwen Ogien, *La vie, la mort, l'État: Le débat bioéthique* (Paris: Grasset, 2009). For other approaches to the same problem, see Martin Provencher, *Petit cours d'éthique et politique* (Montréal: Chenelière Education, 2008), 59–63, which features an extract from the classic essay by James Rachels, "Killing and Letting Die," in *Encyclopedia of Ethics*, 2nd ed., eds. Lawrence Becker and Charlotte Becker (New York: Routledge, 2001), 2: 947–50.
3.   Judith Jarvis Thomson, "Physician-Assisted Suicide: Two Moral Arguments," *Ethics*, special issue, "Symposium on Physician-Assisted Suicide," 109 (April 3, 1999): 497–518.
4.   What follows is a variant of an example given in James Rachels, "Active and Passive Euthanasia," *New England Journal of Medicine* 292 (1975): 78–80.
5.   Tim Mulgan, *The Demands of Consequentialism* (Oxford: Oxford University Press, 2001).
6.   Thomson, "Physician-Assisted Suicide."

2. THE CHILD WHO IS DROWNING IN A POND

1.   The case was devised in Peter Singer, *The Life You Can Save: Acting Now to End World Poverty* (New York: Random House, 2009), 4–12, discussed in James Rachels, "Killing and Letting Die," in *Encyclopedia of Ethics*, 2nd ed., eds. Lawrence Becker and Charlotte Becker (New York: Routledge, 2001), 2: 947–50. See also Peter K. Unger, *Living High and Letting Die: Our Illusion of Innocence* (New York: Oxford University Press, 1996).
2.   Singer, *The Life You Can Save*; Rachels, "Killing and Letting Die."
3.   Immanuel Kant, "On a Supposed Right to Lie from Altruistic Motives," in *Critique of Practical Reason, and Other Writings in Moral Philosophy*, trans. Lewis White Beck (Chicago: University of Chicago Press, 1949), 346–50.

3. A TRANSPLANT GONE MAD

1. The scenario was devised in Judith Jarvis Thomson, "The Trolley Problem," *Yale Law Journal* 94, no. 6 (May 1985): 1395–415.

4. CONFRONTING A FURIOUS CROWD

1. This scenario was devised in Philippa Foot, "The Problem of Abortion and the Doctrine of Double Effect," *Oxford Review* 5 (1967): 5–15. See also Robert Nozick, *Anarchy, State and Utopia* (Oxford: Blackwell, 1974), 28–29.
2. Foot, "The Problem of Abortion."
3. Nozick, *Anarchy, State and Utopia*, 28–51.
4. Ibid.
5. Jean-Cassien Billier, *Introduction à l'éthique* (Paris: Presses Universitaires de France, 2010); Ruwen Ogien and Christine Tappolet, *Les concepts de l'éthique: Faut-il être conséquentialiste?* (Paris: Hermann, 2008).
6. Nozick, *Anarchy, State and Utopia*, 28–29.
7. G. E. M. Anscombe, "Modern Moral Philosophy," in *Ethics, Religion and Politics: Collected Philosophical Papers*, vol. 3 (Oxford: Basil Blackwell, 1981), 26–42. Anscombe wholly rejects this way of seeing the human world through the calculating glasses of consequentialism. But that does not mean that, so far as she is concerned, one should never take the consequences of our actions into account. One could say, I believe, that she distinguishes consequentialism as a general theory fixing *in advance* what is morally relevant (a conception she rejects) and as attention to consequences in particular cases (an attitude she allows). She grants that a prudent estimating of consequences can perfectly well be associated with a strong awareness of absolute prohibitions (she cites the Christian prohibitions on murder, adultery, and apostasy). It is, in her opinion, this association that is at the root of the doctrine of the so-called double effect (see the thought experiment of The Killer Trolley and the glossary). It is a doctrine that she upholds, while at the same time denouncing its abuse: Anscombe, "War and Murder," in *Ethics, Religion and Politics*, 58–59. I would like to thank Cora Diamond and Bernard Baertschi for having enabled me to arrive at a clearer understanding of Anscombe's approach to consequences.
8. Anscombe, "Modern Moral Philosophy," 40.

9. Cora Diamond, "What If X Isn't the Number of Sheep? Wittgenstein and Thought-Experiments in Ethics," *Philosophical Papers* 31 (2002): 227–50.

10. Jonathan Glover, *Causing Death and Saving Lives* (Harmondsworth, UK: Penguin, 1977), 208.

11. Anscombe, "War and Murder," esp. note 19.

12. Anscombe, "Modern Moral Philosophy," 40.

13. Diamond, "What If X Isn't the Number of Sheep?," 247.

14. Glover, *Causing Death and Saving Lives*, 208.

15. Diamond, "What If X Isn't the Number of Sheep?," 245.

16. Ibid., 238.

17. Kaiping Peng, John Doris, Shaun Nichols, and Stephen Sich, unpublished typescript, described by John Doris and Alexandra Plakias, "How to Argue About Disagreement: Evaluative Diversity and Moral Realism," in *Moral Psychology*, vol. 2, *The Cognitive Science of Morality: Intuition and Diversity*, ed. Walter Sinnott-Armstrong (Cambridge, Mass: MIT Press, 2008), 303–31, 322–27.

5. THE KILLER TROLLEY

1. After a scenario devised in Philippa Foot, "The Problem of Abortion and the Doctrine of Double Effect," *Oxford Review* 5 (1967): 160.

2. Ibid.

3. Ibid., 158.

4. Judith Jarvis Thomson, "The Trolley Problem," *Yale Law Journal* 94, no. 6 (May 1985): 1395–415. An earlier version: Thomson, "Killing, Letting Die, and the Trolley Problem," in *Rights, Restitution, and Risk: Essays in Moral Theory*, ed. William Parent (Cambridge, Mass.: Harvard University Press, 1986), 78–93. A later version: Thomson, "Turning the Trolley," *Philosophy and Public Affairs* 36 (2008): 359–74.

5. Marc Hauser, Fiery Cushman, Liane Young, R. Kang-Sing Jin, and John Mikhail, "A Dissociation Between Moral Judgements and Justifications," *Mind and Language* 22 (February 2007): 1–21.

6. There were also control scenarios to check that the respondents had a minimal grasp of the problem posed. Those respondents who judged that it was not permissible to divert the train onto a secondary track, even if no one was there, were eliminated from the investigation.

7. Foot, "The Problem of Abortion," 156–59; Anscombe, "War and Murder," in *Ethics, Religion and Politics: Collected Philosophical Papers*, vol. 3

(Oxford: Basil Blackwell, 1981); Jean-Yves Goffi, "Le principe des actions à double effet," in *Hare et la philosophie morale*, ed. Jean-Yves Goffi, *Recherches sur la philosophie et le langage* 23 (2004): 237; Bernard Baertschi, *La valeur de la vie humaine et l'intégrité de la personne* (Paris: Presses Universitaires de France, 1995), 97–101.

8.   Immanuel Kant, *Groundwork of the Metaphysic of Morals*, trans. H. J. Paton (New York: Harper and Row, 1964), 96.

9.   Hauser et al., "A Dissociation Between Moral Judgements and Justifications," 5. In the appendix, and for reasons that escape me, it is 85 percent and 12 percent, respectively.

10.   Marc Hauser has been suspected of having taken some liberties with his data, so that they support his arguments. This said, the presumption of innocence should of course be respected.

11.   Joshua D. Greene, R. Brian Somerville, Leigh E. Nystrom, John M. Darley, and Jonathan D. Cohen, "An fMRI Investigation of Emotional Engagement in Moral Judgement," *Science* 293, no. 5537 (September 2001): 2105–108. Greene also exploits this hypothesis in order to account for the contrast between our indifference to the fate of children dying of hunger far away from us, with whom we have no physical contact, and our sensitivity to the wretchedness displayed before our very eyes: Joshua D. Greene, "From Neural 'Is' to Moral 'Ought': What Are the Implications of Neuroscientific Moral Psychology?," *Nature Reviews: Neuroscience* 4 (October 2003): 847–50. Florian Cova (personal communication) tells me that Greene has not always distinguished between personal and impersonal actions in terms of the criterion of direct physical contact. He has at times regarded personal action as action in which we treat someone as a means. But I prefer to retain this definition of the personal-impersonal opposition in terms of direct and violent physical contact, in order not to render the debate too confused. If all consequentialists are, have been, or could be deontologists, and vice versa, how are we ever to find our way?

12.   Greene et al., "An fMRI Investigation."

13.   Ibid.

14.   Perhaps by neutralizing the emotional reactions, as Luc Faucher suggests (personal communication). Bernard Baertschi, "Le dilemme du wagon fou nous apprend-il quelque chose de notre vie morale?" (unpublished manuscript).

15.   I prefer to refer the reader to a very lucid text: Bernard Baertschi, *La neuroéthique: Ce que les neurosciences font à nos conceptions morales* (Paris: La Découverte, 2009).

16. Yet more arguments in support of this position are now to be found in the philosophy of the emotions: see Christine Tappolet, *Émotions et valeurs* (Paris: Presses Universitaires de France, 2000).

17. As I pointed out at the outset, the variants were presented at the same time to the respondents. It seemed to me preferable to describe these two variants after a first round of discussion of the first two, so that the part they played in the debate is more in evidence (and also because they are so complicated that it is better to be somewhat prepared in order to understand them).

18. These conclusions may, however, leave us perplexed. Whereas 11 percent only reckon that it is permissible to push the fat man, there are nonetheless 56 percent who think that it is permissible to use him as a means when there is no direct physical contact. It seems to me difficult to conclude on the basis of these results that physical contact is a factor that is not involved! There is perhaps here a tendency to force the data, to get them to speak in favor of the hypothesis one has privileged, which is not peculiar, of course, to this research. Hauser has moreover been reproached for this before.

19. Hauser et al., "A Dissociation Between Moral Judgements and Justifications," 5, 7.

20. Nicolas Baumard, *Comment nous sommes devenus moraux: Une histoire naturelle du bien et du mal* (Paris: Odile Jacob, 2010), 122–25.

21. If we are philosophers (and have read too much Kant), we will be readily convinced that the *worst thing* that can happen to someone is their being treated simply as a means. But what the thought experiment of the trapdoor will serve to show (I extrapolate a little) is that it is not obvious that it is the worst thing. If we are used without violence, it is perhaps not so important. But the best thing, of course, is to be left in peace.

22. I owe thanks to Stéphane Lemaire for suggesting that I spell out the reasons why the consequentialists are still in the running.

23. Kwame Anthony Appiah, *Experiments in Ethics* (Cambridge, Mass.: Harvard University Press, 2008), 73–120; Edouard Machery, "The Bleak Implications of Moral Psychology," *Neuroethics* 3, no. 3 (2010): 223–31.

24. Thomson, "The Trolley Problem."

25. Machery, "The Bleak Implications of Moral Psychology"; Jennifer Zamzow and Shaun Nichols, "Variations in Ethical Intuitions," *Philosophical Issues* 19 (2009): 368–88.

26. Peter K. Unger, *Living High and Letting Die: Our Illusion of Innocence* (Oxford: Oxford University Press, 1996).

27. Ibid.

28. Appiah, *Experiments in Ethics.*

29. Baertschi, "Le dilemme du wagon fou nous apprend-il quelque chose de notre vie morale."

30. Ibid.; Walter Sinnott-Armstrong, "Framing Moral Intuitions," in *Moral Psychology*, vol. 2, *The Cognitive Science of Morality: Intuition and Diversity*, ed. Walter Sinnott-Armstrong (Cambridge, Mass.: MIT Press, 2008), 47–76.

31. Machery, "The Bleak Implications of Moral Psychology."

32. Nagel, "War and Massacre," in *Mortal Questions* (Cambridge: Cambridge University Press, 1979), 53–74.

33. Philip Kitcher, "Biology and Ethics," in *The Oxford Handbook of Ethical Theory*, ed. David Copp (New York: Oxford University Press, 2005).

34. Subsequently Thomson appears to have abandoned an interpretation in terms of rights in favor of another, phrased in terms of "hypothetical consent."

6. INCEST IN ALL INNOCENCE

1. After a scenario devised in Jonathan Haidt, "The Emotional Dog and Its Rational Tail: A Social Intuitionist Approach to Moral Judgment," *Psychological Review* 108 (2001): 814–34.

2. Ibid.

3. Ibid.

4. This, broadly speaking, is the argument in Claude Lévi-Strauss, *The Elementary Structures of Kinship*, trans. James Harle Bell, John Richard von Sturmer, and Rodney Needham (Boston: Beacon Press, 1969).

5. Jesse J. Prinz, *The Emotional Construction of Morals* (Oxford: Oxford University Press, 2007); Luc Faucher, "Les émotions morales à la lumière de la psychologie évolutionniste: Le dégout et l'évitement de l'inceste," in *Morale et évolution biologique*, ed. Christine Clavien (Lausanne: Presses Polytechniques Universitaires Romandes, 2007).

6. Dan Sperber, "Remarques anthropologiques sur le relativisme moral," in *Les fondements naturels de l'éthique*, ed. Jean-Pierre Changeux (Paris: Odile Jacob, 1991), 319–34.

7. See Ruwen Ogien, "Que fait la police morale?," *Terrain* 48 (2007): 31–48.

8. I prefer to give a list of what in this debate are called "victimless crimes" rather than a general definition that would risk raising too many ques-

tions. Thus, as Florian Cova has pointed out to me, attempted murders that come to nothing should not be morally problematic for those who reckon that there is no victimless crime. In order to reject the objection, one would have to distinguish between criminal thoughts (which are, in fact, victimless crimes) and the initial attempts to perform such an act (which are crimes that have not produced victims because they have been averted and so on).

9.   See Ruwen Ogien, *L'éthique aujourd'hui: Maximalistes et minimalistes* (Paris: Gallimard, 2007).

10. Elliot Turiel, *The Development of Social Knowledge: Morality and Convention* (Cambridge: Cambridge University Press, 1983); Elliot Turiel, "Nature et fondements du raisonnement social dans l'enfance," in *Les fondements naturels de l'éthique*, ed. Jean-Pierre Changeux (Paris: Odile Jacob, 1991), 301–17; Elliot Turiel, *The Culture of Morality* (Cambridge: Cambridge University Press, 2002), 113–14. See also the experimental studies analyzed by Vanessa Nurock, *Sommes-nous naturellement moraux?* (Paris: Presses Universitaires de France, 2011), and the original theory of "core morality" that she tries to develop on the basis of them.

11. Larry Nucci, *Education in the Moral Domain* (Cambridge: Cambridge University Press, 2001).

12. Turiel, *The Culture of Morality*, 114, a case drawn from research by Larry Nucci.

13. Without going into technical details, one can say that it contradicts in certain respects the classic theories of Piaget and Kohlberg, according to which understanding of the distinction between the conventional and the moral arises later. Lawrence Kohlberg, "My Personal Search for Universal Morality," *Moral Education Forum* 11, no. 1 (1986): 4–10; Jean Piaget, *The Moral Judgement of the Child* (Harmondsworth, UK: Penguin, 1977); Nurock, *Sommes-nous naturellement moraux?*

14. Jonathan Haidt, S. H. Koller, and M. G. Dias, "Affect, Culture and Morality, or Is It Wrong to Eat Your Dog?," *Journal of Personality and Social Psychology* 5, no. 4 (1993): 613–28.

15. The Kisses and Chicken vignettes were not presented to the youngest individuals, a fact that no one seems to have regretted, although it would perhaps have been interesting to know their reactions, given that it was a study concerned with "innate" or "natural" moral tendencies (at any rate, let us say, for Kisses, if one considers that the youngest might find it difficult to comprehend the act of masturbating in a chicken prior to putting it in the oven).

16. Jonathan Haidt and F. Bjorklund, "Social Intuitionists Answer Six Questions About Moral Psychology," in *Moral Psychology*, vol. 2, *The Cognitive Science of Morality: Intuition and Diversity*, ed. W. Sinnott-Armstrong (Cambridge, Mass.: MIT Press, 2008), 181–217.

17. R. A. Schweder, "The Psychology of Practice and the Practice of the Three Psychologies," *Asian Journal of Social Psychology* 3 (2000): 207–22.

18. Haidt and Bjorklund, "Social Intuitionists Answer Six Questions."

19. This is Fodor's critique of a "modularity gone mad": Jerry Fodor, "Modules, Frames, Fridgeons, Sleeping Dogs and the Music of the Spheres," in *Modularity in Knowledge Representation and Natural Language Understanding*, ed. Jay Garfield (Cambridge, Mass.: MIT Press, 1987).

20. An example scrutinized by Nicolas Baumard, *Comment nous sommes devenus moraux: Une histoire naturelle du bien et du mal* (Paris: Odile Jacob, 2010), 156.

21. John Stuart Mill, *On Liberty* (London: Penguin, 2010), chap. 4, p. 124.

7. THE AMORALIST

1. After a scenario devised in Thomas Nagel, *What Does It All Mean? A Very Short Introduction to Philosophy* (New York: Oxford University Press, 1987).

2. Plato, *The Republic*, bk. 2.

3. The most famous of them are the Thrasymachus of Plato, *The Republic*, bks. 2–4, 8–9, and the Fool of Hobbes, *Leviathan*, bk. 15, 72. To vary such references, one could add the conman in *House of Games*, a film by David Mamet.

4. Elliot Turiel, *The Culture of Morality* (Cambridge: Cambridge University Press, 2002).

5. Ibid.

6. Ibid.

7. Alan Gibbard, *Wise Choices, Apt Feelings: A Theory of Normative Judgement* (Oxford: Clarendon Press, 1990).

8. Nagel, "War and Massacre," in *Mortal Questions* (Cambridge: Cambridge University Press, 1979), 53–74.

9. An amoralist is not an immoralist who openly defies the moral rules with which he is very well acquainted, but rather a person who is indifferent to such rules, owing to a lack either of interest or of motivation:

Joseph Raz, "The Amoralist," in *Ethics and Practical Reason*, eds. Garrett Cullity and Berys Gaut (Oxford: Clarendon Press, 1997), 369–98.

10. Immanuel Kant, *Groundwork of the Metaphysic of Morals*, trans. H. J. Paton (New York: Harper and Row, 1964).

11. To these inconsistencies in thought, Kant adds contradictions in the will. He says that a rule stating that we must never come to the aid of others could not serve as a universal law. It would be a *contradiction in the will*. No one, in fact, can *will* that we never come to the aid of others, since in case of need everyone would be tempted to *will* that we came to his aid: Kant, *Groundwork of the Metaphysics of Morals*. I merely wish to stress the fact that neither the inconsistencies of thought nor the contradictions of the will can be assimilated to practical consequences akin to those that the statement "and if everyone were to do the same thing?" predicts.

12. Bernard Williams, "The Amoralist," in *An Introduction to Ethics* (Cambridge: Cambridge University Press, 1993), 3–13.

13. It is this kind of situation that the so-called prisoner's dilemma experiments are designed to formalize: Robert Nadeau, *Vocabulaire technique et analytique de l'épistémologie* (Paris: Presses Universitaires de France, 1999). Suppose the police suspect you of having committed armed robbery with an accomplice. A seasoned police superintendent would like to extract a confession, for he knows that he lacks the proof needed to take you to court. He therefore proposes the following deal: "If you confess and denounce your accomplice, you'll be free and your accomplice will serve ten years in prison. If you both keep silent, you'll do two years each. If both of you confess, you'll do six years each." You know that the superintendent will make the same offer to your accomplice. At first glance, it seems preferable for you to confess. If you confess and the other does not, you walk free. If you confess and the other does too, you'll serve six years each. But if you do not confess and the other does, you will do ten years, the maximum sentence. The same reasoning can apply to the accomplice: he too would be tempted to confess. All in all, it would be rational for the two accomplices to confess. However, this outcome is not optimal. It is neither the one that gives the best overall result (indeed, it is the worst: twelve years in prison in total instead of four—if no one confesses—and ten if just one person confesses) nor even the one that guarantees the best personal outcome (six years each instead of two if no one confesses).

14. Williams, "The Amoralist," 3–13.

15. Harry J. Gensler, *Ethics: A Contemporary Introduction* (London: Routledge, 1998), 89–90.
16. Ibid.
17. Ibid., 81–96.
18. Ibid., 83.
19. Nagel, *What Does It All Mean?*
20. In moral philosophy we call "externalists" those who grant that we can have reasons for acting without having the corresponding motivation, as opposed to "internalists," who hold that if we do not have the motivation, it is because we do not really have a reason. The possibility of amoralism is often presented as an argument in favor of externalism: David O. Brink, *Moral Realism and the Foundations of Ethics* (Cambridge: Cambridge University Press, 1989), 46–50, and the glossary, for a fuller account.
21. In his examination of *akrasia*, or weakness of will, Aristotle presented this argument with his characteristic use of images, by quoting the proverb "when water chokes, what should a man drink then?" Aristotle, *Nicomachean Ethics*, bk. 7, 1146b.
22. The novel, adapted for the screen by Stanley Kubrick in 1971, features a young, ultraviolent criminal, incarcerated for a long spell, who accepts a terrible reconditioning therapy designed to curb his drives and thus to earn an earlier release from prison.

8. THE EXPERIENCE MACHINE

1. After a scenario devised in Robert Nozick, *Anarchy, State and Utopia* (Oxford: Basil Blackwell, 1974), 42–45.
2. Felipe de Brigard, "If You Like It, Does It Matter If It's Real?," *Philosophical Psychology* 23, no. 1 (2010): 43–57.
3. Ibid.

9. IS A SHORT AND MEDIOCRE LIFE PREFERABLE TO NO LIFE AT ALL?

1. After a scenario devised in Derek Parfit, *Reasons and Persons* (Oxford: Oxford University Press, 1984), 367.

2. Peter Singer, *Practical Ethics*, 2nd ed. (Cambridge: Cambridge University Press, 1993), 184.

10. I WOULD HAVE PREFERRED NEVER TO HAVE BEEN BORN

1. Case discussed in Bernard Williams, "Resenting One's Own Existence," in *Making Sense of Humanity* (Cambridge: Cambridge University Press, 1995), 237.
2. Saul Smilansky, *Ten Moral Paradoxes* (Oxford: Blackwell, 2007), 101.
3. Ibid.
4. Ibid.
5. I am indebted to Valérie Gateau for this hypothesis.
6. I am indebted to Patrick Savidan for this hypothesis.
7. I am indebted to Jocelyn Benoist for this hypothesis.

11. MUST WE ELIMINATE ANIMALS IN ORDER TO LIBERATE THEM?

1. Jean-Luc Guichet, "Questions contemporaines d'anthropologie et d'éthique animale: L'argument antispéciste des cas marginaux" (unpublished manuscript).
2. The mere fact of having entertained it led to Peter Singer being banned from speaking in public in Germany, for reasons that may all too readily be understood.
3. Jeremy Bentham, *Introduction to the Principles of Morals and Legislation*, eds. J. H. Burns and H. L. A. Hart (London: Athlone Press, 1970), chap. 17, p. 283, note b.
4. Luc Ferry, *Le nouvel ordre écologique: L'arbre, l'animal et l'homme* (Paris: Livre de Poche, 1992), 86.
5. Ibid., 84.
6. There are many instance of mutual aid between different animal species: shrimps that clean predators' mouths at the sources of the Nile, birds that protect crocodile eggs, and so on. Such cases are presented in the documentary by Nicolas Gabriel, *L'entraide animale* (Saint Thomas Productions, 1998).

7. Alberto Bondolfi, *L'homme et l'animal: Dimensions éthiques de leurs relations* (Freiburg: Éditions universitaires Fribourg Suisse, 1995), 39.

8. Ibid.

9. Guichet, "Questions contemporaines d'anthropologie et d'éthique animale."

10. These are the conclusions arrived at in particular by the utilitarian philosopher Richard Hare and the jurist Gary Francione: Hare, "Why I Am Only a Demi-Vegetarian," in *Singer and His Critics*, ed. Dale Jamieson (London: Blackwell, 1999), 233–46; Francione, "Taking Sentience Seriously," in *Animals as Persons: Essays on the Abolition of Animal Exploitation* (New York: Columbia University Press, 2008), 129–47.

11. Bentham, *Introduction to the Principles*, 283, note b; J. S. Mill, "Whewell on Moral Philosophy" (1853), in *Utilitarianism, and Other Essays*, by John Stuart Mill and Jeremy Bentham, ed. Alan Ryan (Harmondsworth, UK: Penguin, 1987), 251–52; Peter Singer, *Animal Liberation* (London: Cape, 1990), 7–8.

12. Bentham, *Introduction to the Principles*, 283, note b.

13. See Ruwen Ogien, *L'éthique aujourd'hui: Maximalistes et minimalistes* (Paris: Gallimard, 2007), 81–84, referring to Axel Gosseries, *Penser la justice entre les générations: De l'affaire Perruche à la réforme des retraites* (Paris: Aubier, 2004), 52–53.

14. The majority concede that abortion is permissible in cases of rape or where the mother's life is at risk, whereas they would probably not allow the wounding or mutilation of a baby in good health, for this kind of reason or indeed for others.

15. Hare, "Why I Am Only a Demi-Vegetarian."

16. Ibid., 245.

17. Derek Parfit, *Reasons and Persons* (Oxford: Oxford University Press, 1984), 387–90.

18. Bentham, quoted in Francione, "Taking Sentience Seriously," 192.

19. Ibid., 195.

20. Hare, "Why I Am Only a Demi-Vegetarian," 240.

21. Parfit, *Reasons and Persons*.

22. Francione, "Taking Sentience Seriously."

23. Ibid., 136.

24. Ibid., 134–35.

25. Ibid., 147.

26. Quoted by Kari Weil, "Liberté éhontée," trans. Thierry Hoquet, in *Libérer les animaux?*, *Critique*, August-September 2009, 665–66. The passage is

from an unpublished lecture by Francione delivered at Yale University Interdisciplinary Center for Bioethics, on December 4, 2008.

27. Ibid., 666.

12. THE UTILITY MONSTER

1. After a case proposed in Nozick, *Anarchy, State and Utopia* (Oxford: Basil Blackwell, 1974), 41.

13. A VIOLINIST HAS BEEN PLUGGED INTO YOUR BACK

1. After a case proposed in Judith Jarvis Thomson, "A Defense of Abortion," *Philosophy and Public Affairs* 1, no. 1 (1971): 47–66.
2. Ibid. Thomson invokes the legitimate defense argument in the case in which the mother's life is threatened by the state of the fetus. She therefore grants that there can be a legitimate defense even against an innocent threat, which Bernard Baertschi contests (personal communication).
3. David Boonin, *A Defense of Abortion* (Cambridge: Cambridge University Press, 2003), 133–276.
4. This argument is evoked in Nicolas Baumard, *Comment nous sommes devenus moraux: Une histoire naturelle du bien et du mal* (Paris: Odile Jacob, 2010), 113–14.
5. Ronald Dworkin, *Life's Dominion: An Argument About Abortion, Euthanasia and Individual Freedom* (New York: Vintage, 1994), 33–34.

14. FRANKENSTEIN, MINISTER OF HEALTH

1. Smilansky, *Ten Moral Paradoxes* (Oxford: Blackwell, 2007), 134–37.
2. IPSOS, *Enquête maternité*, 2009.
3. Ibid.
4. John Stuart Mill, "Nature," in *Essays on Ethics, Religion and Society*, ed. J. M. Robson (London: Routledge and Kegan Paul; Toronto: University of Toronto Press, 1969), 375.
5. Ibid., 385.

15. WHO AM I WITHOUT MY ORGANS?

1. After a case proposed in Derek Parfit, *Reasons and Persons* (Oxford: Oxford University Press, 1984).
2. I presented the following analysis in Ogien, *Le corps et l'argent* (Paris: La Musardine, 2010), 46–48.
3. Marcela Iacub, "Le législateur et son scalpel: Le corps humain dans les lois bioéthiques," in *Le crime était presque sexuel et autres essais de casuistique juridique* (Paris: Champs-Flammarion, 2003).

16. AND IF SEXUALITY WERE FREE?

1. On these logics, see Norbert Campagna, *Prostitution et dignité* (Paris: La Musardine, 2008).

17. IT IS HARDER TO DO GOOD INTENTIONALLY THAN IT IS TO DO EVIL

1. After Joshua Knobe, "The Concept of Intentional Action: A Case Study in the Uses of Folk Psychology," in *Experimental Philosophy*, eds. Joshua Knobe and Shaun Nichols (Oxford: Oxford University Press, 2008), 129–47.
2. This point of view has also been defended for conceptual reasons by Gilbert Ryle, *The Concept of Mind* (London: Hutchinson, 1949).
3. To learn more about the contribution of experimental philosophy to the classification of these questions and of many others in general philosophy, the best approach would be to refer to a book that is both brilliant and funny (no harm in that!) by Florian Cova, *Qu'en pensez-vous? Introduction à la philosophie expérimentale* (Paris: Germina, 2011).

18. WE ARE FREE, EVEN IF EVERYTHING IS WRITTEN IN ADVANCE

1. After Eddy Nahmias, Stephen G. Morris, Thomas Nadelhoffer, and Jason Turner, "Is Incompatibilism Intuitive?," in *Experimental Philosophy*, eds. Joshua Knobe and Shaun Nichols (Oxford: Oxford University Press, 2008), 81–104.

2. I obviously do not propose to give details of all the other experiments that were supposed to render this result convincing. Interested readers should refer to Nahmias et al., "Is Incompatibilism Intuitive?," 81–104.

3. Ted Honderich, "Compatibilism and Incompatibilism," in *How Free Are You? The Determinism Problem* (Oxford: Oxford University Press, 1993), 95–106.

4. Peter Strawson, *Freedom and Resentment, and Other Essays* (London: Methuen, 1974).

5. Nahmias et al., "Is Incompatibilism Intuitive?"; Peter Strawson, *Freedom and Resentment.*

19. MONSTERS AND SAINTS

1. John M. Doris, *Lack of Character: Personality and Moral Behavior* (Cambridge: Cambridge University Press, 2002), 34.

2. A. M. Isen and P. F. Levin, "Effect of Feeling Good on Helping; Cookies and Kindness," *Journal of Personality and Social Psychology* 21 (1972): 384–88.

3. R. A. Baron, "The Sweet Smell of . . . Helping: Effects of Pleasant Ambient Fragrance on Prosocial Behavior in Shopping Malls," *Personality and Social Psychology Bulletin* 23 (1997): 498–503.

4. Doris, *Lack of Character.*

5. Ibid.

6. B. Latané and J. M. Darley, *The Unresponsive Bystander: Why Doesn't He Help?* (New York: Appleton Century-Crofts, 1970); Doris, *Lack of Character*, 33.

7. J. M. Darley and C. D. Batson, "From Jerusalem to Jericho: A Study in Situational and Dispositional Variables in Helping Behavior," *Journal of Personality and Social Psychology* 27 (1973): 100–108.

8. Doris, *Lack of Character*, 37.

9. Ibid.

10. Stanley Milgram, *Obedience to Authority: An Experimental View* (New York: Harper and Row, 1974).

11. Doris, *Lack of Character.*

12. The experiment best adapted to today's problems brings face to face a seeker after purely fictitious employment and an unemployment official who has to say humiliating things such as "You're garbage. You'd do better to look for another job," following a scenario devised by the

experimenter: W. H. J. Meeus and Q. A. W. Raaijmakers, "Obedience in Modern Societies: The Utrecht Studies," *Journal of Social Issues* 51 (1995): 155–75.

13. R. Brown, *Social Psychology*, 2nd ed. (New York: MacMillan, 1986), 4.

14. M. E. Shaub and K. A. Yahia, "A Cross-Cultural Study of Obedience," *Bulletin of Psychonomic Society* 11 (1978): 267–69.

15. Doris, *Lack of Character*, 47.

16. Lawrence Kohlberg, "My Personal Search for Universal Morality," *Moral Education Forum* 11, no. 1 (1986).

17. Christopher R. Browning, *Ordinary Men: Reserve Police Battalion 101 and the Final Solution in Poland* (New York: Harper Collins, 1992).

18. Ibid.

19. Jiri Benovsky, *Le puzzle philosophique* (Paris: Éditions d'Ithaque, 2010), 31–33.

20. Doris, *Lack of Character*, 50.

21. Ibid., 24–27.

22. Ibid.

23. Gilbert Ryle, *The Concept of Mind* (London: Hutchinson, 1949).

24. See Ruwen Ogien, *L'éthique aujourd'hui: Maximalistes et minimalistes* (Paris: Gallimard, 2007), 63–66.

25. Doris, *Lack of Character*, 26. But the weak correlation between these personality tests and real behavior affects the credibility of these measures as well, according to Doris.

26. Ibid., 93–97.

27. Ibid.

28. Ibid.

29. Ibid.

30. Samuel P. Oliner and Pearl M. Oliner, *The Altruistic Personality: Rescuers of Jews in Nazi Germany* (London: Collier MacMillan, 1988).

31. E. Fogelman, *Conscience and Courage: Rescuers of Jews During the Holocaust* (New York: Doubleday, 1994); K. R. Monroe, *The Heart of Altruism: Perceptions of a Common Humanity* (Princeton: Princeton University Press, 1996).

32. N. Tec, *When Light Pierced the Darkness: Christian Rescue of Jews in Nazi Occupied Poland* (Oxford: Oxford University Press, 1986).

33. Oliner and Oliner, *The Altruistic Personality*.

34. F. Rochat and A. Modigliani, "The Ordinary Quality of Resistance: From Milgram's Laboratory to the Village of Le Chambon," *Journal of Social Issues* 51 (1995): 195–210.

35. Machery, "The Bleak Implications of Moral Psychology," *Neuroethics* 3, no. 3 (2010): 223–31.

36. Kwame Anthony Appiah, *Experiments in Ethics* (Cambridge, Mass.: Harvard University Press, 2008). John M. Doris and Jesse J. Prinz, review of Kwame Anthony Appiah, *Experiments in Ethics*, *Notre Dame Philosophical Reviews*, October 3, 2009.

20. INTENTIONS AND RULES

1. Peter Singer, *The Life You Can Save: Acting Now to End World Poverty* (New York: Random House, 2009).

2. Ibid., 4–12.

3. David Copp, "Experiments, Intuitions, and Methodology in Moral and Political Theory," text presented to the Molyneux Spring Seminar on Intuitions, University of California, Davis, 2010, 1–49.

4. Ibid.; John Rawls, *A Theory of Justice* (Cambridge, Mass.: Belknap Press of Harvard University Press, 1971). On the place of intuitions in the Rawls method, see Jon Mandle, *Rawls's "A Theory of Justice": An Introduction* (Cambridge: Cambridge University Press, 2009), 8–9. On reflective equilibrium, see the glossary.

21. A LITTLE METHOD!

1. John M. Doris, *Lack of Character: Personality and Moral Behavior* (Cambridge: Cambridge University Press, 2002), 1–14.

2. Donald Davidson, *Essays on Actions and Events* (New York: Oxford University Press, 1980).

3. Doris, *Lack of Character*, 1–14.

4. Bernard Williams, "Must a Concern for the Environment be Centred on Human Beings?," in *Making Sense of Humanity* (Cambridge: Cambridge University Press, 1995), 233–40.

22. WHAT REMAINS OF OUR MORAL INTUITIONS?

1. Kwame Anthony Appiah, *Experiments in Ethics* (Cambridge, Mass.: Harvard University Press, 2008).

2. Saying that it is irrational to retain empirical hypotheses that have been systematically belied by the facts obviously does not mean that the facts can completely refute a scientific theory. We never know what part of the theory they refute in reality and we must sometimes retain a theory in the face of the facts just as we retain a moral theory in the face of the intuitions: W. V. O. Quine, *Theories and Things* (Cambridge, Mass.: Harvard University Press, 1981).

23. WHERE HAS THE MORAL INSTINCT GONE?

1. Vanessa Nurock, *Sommes-nous naturellement moraux?* (Paris: Presses Universitaires de France, 2011).
2. Jesse J. Prinz, "Is Morality Innate?," in *Moral Psychology*, vol. 1, *The Evolution of Morality: Adaptations and Innateness*, ed. Walter Sinnott-Armstrong (Cambridge, Mass.: MIT Press, 2008), 367–408.
3. Haidt and Bjorklund, "Social Intuitionists Answer Six Questions About Moral Psychology," in *Moral Psychology*, vol. 2, *The Cognitive Science of Morality: Intuition and Diversity*, ed. W. Sinnott-Armstrong (Cambridge, Mass.: MIT Press, 2008), 181–217.
4. Jesse J. Prinz, "Resisting the Linguistic Analogy: A Commentary on Hauser, Young and Cushman," *Moral Psychology* 2:157–79.
5. Nurock, *Sommes-nous naturellement moraux?*; John M. Doris, *Lack of Character: Personality and Moral Behavior* (Cambridge: Cambridge University Press, 2002).
6. Doris, *Lack of Character*.
7. Jerry Fodor, *Modularity of Mind: An Essay on Faculty Psychology* (Cambridge, Mass.: MIT Press, 1983).
8. Ibid.
9. Jay Garfield, "Modularity," in *A Companion to the Philosophy of Mind*, ed. Samuel Guttenplan (Oxford: Basil Blackwell, 1994), 441–48.
10. Dan Sperber, "Défense de la modularité massive," in *Les languages du cerveau*, ed. E. Dupoux (Paris: Odile Jacob, 2002), 55–64.
11. Jerry Fodor, "Why We Are So Good at Catching Cheaters," in *The Mind Doesn't Work That Way: The Scope and Limits of Computational Psychology* (Cambridge, Mass.: MIT Press, 2000), 101.
12. The analysis that follows is drawn from Ruwen Ogien, "Ils voient des modules partout," in *Le rasoir de Kant et autres essais de philosophie pratique* (Paris: Éditions de l'Éclat, 2003), 161–87.

13. Leda Cosmides, "The Logic of Social Exchange," *Cognition* 31 (1989): 187–276; Leda Cosmides and John Tooby, "Cognitive Adaptation for Social Exchange," in *The Adapted Mind*, eds. J. Barkow, L. Cosmides, and J. Tooby (Oxford: Oxford University Press, 1992), 163–228.

14. George Botterill and Peter Carruthers, *The Philosophy of Psychology* (Cambridge: Cambridge University Press, 1999), 109–11.

15. Ibid., 110.

16. From 90 percent to 95 percent, according to Steven Pinker, *How the Mind Works* (New York: Norton, 1997), 336–37; from 75 percent to 90 percent according to Botterill and Carruthers, *The Philosophy of Psychology*, 109.

17. R. A. Griggs and J. R. Cox, "The Elusive Thematic-Materials Effect in Wason's Selection Task," *British Journal of Psychology* 73 (1982): 407–20.

18. Cosmides, "The Logic of Social Exchange."

19. Ibid.; Cosmides and Tooby, "Cognitive Adaptation for Social Exchange."

20. Fodor, "Why We Are So Good at Catching Cheaters."

21. Lawrence A. Hirschfeld, introduction to *Mapping the Mind: Domain Specificity in Culture and Cognition*, eds. L. A. Hirschfeld and Susan A. Gelman (Cambridge: Cambridge University Press, 1994).

22. Jonathan Haidt and Craig Joseph, "The Moral Mind: How Five Sets of Innate Intuitions Guide the Development of Many Culture-Specific Virtues and Perhaps Even Modules," in *The Innate Mind*, vol. 3, eds. Peter Carruthers, Stephen Laurence, and Stephen P. Stich (Oxford: Oxford University Press, 2007).

24. A PHILOSOPHER AWARE OF THE LIMITS OF HIS MORAL INTUITIONS IS WORTH TWO OTHERS, INDEED MORE

1. Joshua Knobe and Shaun Nichols, *Experimental Philosophy* (Oxford: Oxford University Press, 2008), 8.

2. For Knobe and Nichols, this hypothesis has some famous antecedents, in Marx, Nietzsche, Feuerbach, and so on: ibid., 7–8.

3. See Kwame Anthony Appiah, *Experiments in Ethics* (Cambridge, Mass.: Harvard University Press, 2008), 82–88, referring to the article by Amos Tversky and Daniel Kahneman, "The Framing of Decisions and the Psychology of Choice," *Science* 221 (1981): 453–58.

4. Ibid; F. M. Kamm, "Moral Intuitions, Cognitive Psychology, and the Harming-Versus-Not-Aiding Distinctions," *Ethics* 108, no. 3 (April

1998): 463–88, at 476; Warren Quinn, "Actions, Intentions and Consequences: The Doctrine of Doing and Allowing," in *Morality and Action* (New York: Cambridge University Press, 1993), 149–74.

5.   Greene et al., "An fMRI Investigation of Emotional Engagement in Moral Judgement," *Science* 293, no. 5537 (September 2001): 2105–108.

6.   We owe this thought experiment to Gilbert Harmann, *The Nature of Morality* (New York: Oxford University Press, 1977), 4.

7.   However Gilbert Harmann, the inventor of this thought experiment, uses it to criticize the objectivist conceptions of ethics. For him, cruelty is not a property that could exist independently of our judgments. It is in our own heads. It is "projected" onto actions, which give us the illusion that a real property of the action is involved.

8.   I obviously cannot enter here into an extended discussion of the basic epistemological distinctions between "truth" and "justification" or "belief" and "knowledge," or of the very lively debates between those who think that we must take account of the causal history of beliefs in order to know if knowledges are involved and those who do not think so. Or between those who think that the emotions can play, in moral knowledge, the same role as perception in physical knowledge and those who wholly disagree. On these questions of general epistemology and of moral epistemology, the best work, in moral philosophy, is the study by Christine Tappolet, *Émotions et valeurs* (Paris: Presses Universitaires de France, 2000). She says far more, and says it far more eloquently, than I ever could.

25. UNDERSTAND THE ELEMENTARY RULES
OF MORAL REASONING

1.   In what follows I have modified in certain respects and greatly expanded the analysis of the four elementary rules proposed in Ruwen Ogien, *La morale a-t-elle un avenir?* (Nantes: Pleins Feux, 2006).

2.   David Hume, *A Treatise of Human Nature* (1739–40), ed. L. A. Selby-Bigge (Oxford: Clarendon Press, 1896), 455–70.

3.   I am indebted to Vanessa Nurock for this clarification.

4.   I have added "without further argument" to the usual presentation of Hume's formula in order to stay close to what he says in the text. But in what follows I shall employ the shortened formula, given that it has become a philosophical commonplace.

5.   Karl Popper, *The Open Society and Its Enemies*, vol. 1, *The Ascendancy of Plato* (London: Routledge, 2003), 66.

6.   Henri Poincaré, *Dernières pensées* (Paris: Flammarion, 1913), 33.

7.   John Searle, *Speech Acts: An Essay in the Philosophy of Language* (Cambridge: Cambridge University Press, 1970), 175–98.

8.   I am indebted to Florian Cova for this observation.

9.   John Woods and Douglas Walton, *Fallacies: Selected Papers, 1972–1982* (1989; London: King's College, 2007), 212.

10. For an overview of the debate, see Ruwen Ogien, "Le rasoir de Kant," in *Le rasoir de Kant et autres essais de philosophie pratique* (Paris: Éditions de l'Éclat, 2003), 81–90 and 195–96 for a bibliography.

11. Peter Singer, *The Life You Can Save: Acting Now to End World Poverty* (New York: Random House, 2009).

12. Judith Jarvis Thomson, "A Defense of Abortion," *Philosophy and Public Affairs* 1, no. 1 (1971): 47–66.

13. This is a question that is consistently posed when we ask ourselves whether we can extend to the fetus the attitude we adopt toward unwelcome intruders: David Boonin, *A Defense of Abortion* (Cambridge: Cambridge University Press, 2003), 133–276.

14. Immanuel Kant, *Critique of Practical Reason*, trans. and ed. Lewis White Beck (Chicago: University of Chicago Press, 1949), 60.

15. Occam was a medieval philosopher and theologian who recommended that we not multiply beings and principles of explanation unnecessarily. See Ogien, *Le rasoir de Kant et autres essais de philosophie pratique*, 76.

26. DARE TO CRITICIZE THE ELEMENTARY RULES OF MORAL ARGUMENT

1.   K. E. Traney, "'Ought' Implies 'Can': A Bridge from Fact to Norm: Part 1," *Ratio* 14 (1972): 116–30.

2.   Vanessa Nurock, *Sommes-nous naturellement moraux?* (Paris: Presses Universitaires de France, 2011).

3.   Harry J. Gensler, *Ethics: A Contemporary Introduction* (London: Routledge, 1998), 89–90.

4.   Bertrand Russell, *A History of Western Philosophy* (London: Routledge, 2004).

5.   Philippa Foot, "Morality as a System of Hypothetical Imperatives," *Philosophical Review* 81, no. 3 (July 1972): 305–16.

6. T. M. Scanlon " Rawls on Justification," *The Cambridge Companion to Rawls*, ed. Samuel Freeman (Cambridge: Cambridge University Press, 2003). See "reflective equilibrium" in the glossary.

7. Norman Daniels, "Reflective Equilibrium," *Stanford Encyclopedia of Philosophy*, http://plato.stanford.edu/entries/reflective-equilibrium/.

8. Kwame Anthony Appiah, *Experiments in Ethics* (Cambridge, Mass.: Harvard University Press, 2008).

9. I have presented the argument in full in Ruwen Ogien, *Le rasoir de Kant et autres essais de philosophie pratique* (Paris: Éditions de l'Éclat, 2003), 81–90.

10. One can try to reject this result by maintaining either that the first premise ("Charlie cannot") is not genuinely descriptive or that the conclusion ("Charlie ought not to") is not genuinely normative. But it is not a foregone conclusion. See ibid., 82–85.

11. Michael Stocker, *Plural and Conflicting Values* (Oxford: Clarendon Press, 1990), 96.

12. An example inspired by Ruth Barcan Marcus, "Moral Dilemmas and Consistency," *Journal of Philosophy* 77, no. 3 (1980): 121–36.

13. Traney, "'Ought' implies 'Can,'" 122.

14. For a very clear presentation of the argument, see Jean-Yves Goffi, *Penser l'euthanasie* (Paris: Presses Universitaires de France, 2004), 29–42.

15. See Ruwen Ogien, *La vie, la mort, l'État: Le débat bioéthique* (Paris: Grasset, 2009), chap. 2.

16. Bernard Williams, "Which Slopes Are Slippery?" in *Making Sense of Humanity* (Cambridge: Cambridge University Press, 1995), 213–23.

17. The traditional example of a "sorites" is that of the heap of wheat. If one grain of wheat does not make a heap, then two do not either, for two grains of wheat are not sufficiently distinct from one grain of wheat. Likewise, if two grains of wheat do not make a heap, then three do not either, for three grains of wheat are not sufficiently distinct from two grains of wheat, and so on. Finally, heaps of wheat do not exist! Jean-Yves Goffi proposes a new version of the same argument, but with grains being replaced by dwarves. A typical dwarf measures 28 inches. Suppose we have an individual measuring 28 + 5 inches. Should we regard him as a dwarf also? Yes, of course, for he does not differ *significantly* from an individual of 28 inches. But if an individual measuring 28 + 5 inches is a dwarf, what about another individual who measures just 5 inches more? Should he also be regarded as a dwarf? Yes, of course, for he does not differ *significantly* from an individual of 28 + 5 inches.

If we continue thus, by adding 5 inches a great number of times, we will end up with the conclusion that an individual of 8 feet tall is a dwarf. Goffi, *Penser l'euthanasie*, 33.

18. Judith Jarvis Thomson, "A Defense of Abortion," *Philosophy and Public Affairs* 1, no. 1 (1971): 47–66.

19. Nurock, *Sommes-nous naturellement moraux?*

INDEX

abortion, radical defense of, 92–93

absolute identity, 160

"altruistic personalities," 127

amoralist, 63–64, 202n9

The Amoralist thought experiment: about, 2, 56–57; changing amoralists, 63–64; law of talion, 62; morally flawed actions, 60–62; morally neutral actions, 60; reasons for being moral, 57–59; universalization, 59–60

And If Sexuality Were Free? thought experiment, 104–6

anger module, 52

Anscombe, Elizabeth, 20–21, 196n7

applied ethics, defined, 181

Aquinas, Thomas, 28

aretists, xix, 8–10, 189, 304

Aristotle, xix, 164, 204n21

autonomy, ethics of, 51

"Baby Fae" affair, xi–xiv

Baertschi, Bernard, 196n7, 207n2

"behaviorist," 143

behaviors, experiments on, xxii–xxiii, 3–5

Bentham, Jeremy, 81–82, 85

bodily form, social belonging and, 79–81

Bondolfi, Alberto, 79

Burgess, Anthony, 63

"character," 123–24

The Child Who Is Drowning in a Pond thought experiment: about, 1, 160; intuition, 12–13; moral questions, 13; negative responsibility, 13; rule, 13; scenarios, 11–12

A Clockwork Orange (Burgess), 63

cloning, 98–99

community, ethics of, 51

compassion module, 52

compatibilism-incompatibilism, defined, 181–82

conceptual consistency, 60

conceptual problem, defined, xviii

Confronting a Furious Crowd
    thought experiment: explained, 1;
    scenarios, 17–23
consequentialism: defined, 182–83;
    explained, xix–xx
consequentialist intuitions, 32–33,
    140–41
consequentialists, deontologists
    and, 36
construction of moral theories,
    moral intuitions in, 133
continuist, 77–78
conventions, domain of, 47, 176–78
Cosmides, Leda, 145
Cova, Florian, 198n11, 201n8, 208n3
critique of moral theories, moral
    intuitions in, 133

"democratized" thought experi-
    ment, 134–35
deontological intuitions, 34, 140–41
deontologism: defined, 183;
    explained, xix–xx
deontologists: consequentialists
    and, 36; on killing and letting die,
    8–10
Diamond, Cora, 196n7
disgust module, 52
divinity, ethics of, 51–53
doctrine of double effect, 28–29, 35,
    183–84
domain of conventions, 47, 176–78
domain of morality, 47, 176–78
double effect, doctrine of, 28–29, 35,
    183–84
Dworkin, Ronald, 93

Emergencies thought experiment:
    explained, 1; scenarios, 7–8

emotional reactions, irrationality of,
    152–53
emotions, role of, 33
epistemological limits, 136–37, 178
ethics: applied, 181; of autonomy,
    51; of community, 51; of divinity,
    51–53; morality and, 184; norma-
    tive, 187; virtue, 3–4, 189
The Experience Machine thought
    experiment: about, 2, 65–70; sce-
    narios, 67–70; tendency towards
    inertia, 67
experimental moral philosophy:
    about, 151–52; explained, x; irra-
    tionality of emotional reactions,
    152–53
"experimental" philosophers, 137
experiments: on behaviors, xxii–
    xxiii, 3–5; "Life Raft," 2
"externalists," 185, 204n20
extinction, 85

facts, norms and, 184
Failure to Render Assistance to a
    Person in Danger scenario, 7
Faucher, Luc, 198n14
female genital mutilation, 53–55
Ferry, Luc, 78
Fodor, Jerry Alan, 144–45, 148, 149
Foot, Philippa, 25, 27–28
Francione, Gary, 86–87, 206n10
Frankenstein, Minister of Health
    thought experiment: explained,
    3; scenarios, 94–99
A Furious Crowd scenario, 17

Goffi, Jean-Yves, 216n17
golden rule, 62
Greene, Joshua, 152, 198n11

Groundwork of the Metaphysics of Morals (Kant), 203n11
Guichet, Jean-Luc, 80

Haidt, Jonathan, 48, 49, 50, 51–53
Hare, Richard, 85, 86, 206n10
harm, injuries and, 82–84
Harmann, Gilbert, 214n7
Hauser, Marc, 27, 31–32, 34, 35, 36
"human nature," xxiii
Hume, David, 157, 214n4
"Hume's guillotine." *See* R1: One Cannot Derive an Ought from an Is
"Hume's law." *See* R1: One Cannot Derive an Ought from an Is
hypothesis: explained, xvii; justification of, xvii–xix

Incest in All Innocence thought experiment: ethics of autonomy, 51–53; ethics of community, 51–53; explained, 2; female genital mutilation, 53–55; maximalism, 47–49; minimalism, 45–47; naturalization of "minimalism" *versus* "maximalism" debate, 50; scenarios, 42–44; 'victimless moral crimes,' 44
incompatibilism, 181–82
"incompatibilist," 111–12
individuals, species and, 79
inertia, tendency towards, 67
injuries, harm and, 82–84
innate morality, 142–44
instincts. *See* moral instincts
internalism-externalism, defined, 185
interpretation, 140–41
intuition. *See also* moral intuition: The Child Who Is Drowning

in a Pond thought experiment, 12–13; consequentialist, 32–33, 140–41; deontological, 34, 140–41; "ordinary," xx–xxi, 27; rules and, 131–33
Is a Short Mediocre Life Preferable to No Life at All? thought experiment, 2, 71–72
It Is Harder to Do Good Intentionally Than It Is to Do Evil thought experiment, 3, 107–8
I Would Have Preferred Never To Have Been Born thought experiment, 73–75

justification: about, 140; of hypothesis, xvii–xix; of moral theories, moral intuitions in, 133

Kant, Immanuel, xix, xxii, 14, 29, 59–60, 102, 183, 203n11
Kant's razor, 161–62
The Killer Trolley thought experiment: explained, 1, 5; scenarios, 24–27
Killing the Pedestrian scenario, 7–8
Knobe, Joshua, 107–8
Kohlberg, Lawrence, 121, 201n13

law of talion, 62
learned morality, 142
"liberty," "nature" and, 78
"Life Raft" experiments, 2
"limit" cases, 76–77
linguistics, 143
liquidation, 86–88

"marginal" cases, 76–77

maximalism: about, 47–49, 177;
versus minimalism debate, 50
metaethics, defined, 185–86
method: about, 134–35; epistemological problems, 136–37; methodological problems, 135–36
method of reflective equilibrium,
164
methodological problems, 135–36
Milgram, Stanley, 4, 118, 119, 120,
121–22, 135
Mill, John Stuart, 54
minimalism: about, 45–47, 177;
versus maximalism debate, 50
modularity, debate concerning,
148–49
modules, 52, 144–48
Monsters and Saints thought
experiment, 112–28
moral arguments: elementary rules
of, 163–72; reasons for being,
57–59; simplicity of, viii–ix
moral instincts: about, 142; goodbye to, 149–50; innate morality,
142–44; learned morality, 142;
modularity, 148–49; modules,
144–48; virtues and, 175–76
moral intuition: about, viii, 131,
138–40, 178–79; in construction,
justification, and critique of
moral theories, 133; defined, 186;
elementary rules of, ix; fragility
of, 39–41; interpretation, 140–41;
justification, 140; poverty of,
37–39
morality: domain of, 47, 176–78;
ethics and, 184; innate, 142–44;
learned, 142; reasons for, 57–59;
ways of conceiving, xix–xx;

without "foundations," 173–
75
morally flawed actions, 60–62
morally neutral actions, 60
moral modules, defined, 186–87
moral questions, in The Child Who
Is Drowning in a Pond thought
experiment, 13
moral reasoning: elementary rules
of, 154–62; rule of, 132; value of
rules of, 133
moral rules, 45–46
moral theories: about, 176–78;
critique of, 133; descriptions of,
193n16
Must We Eliminate Animals In
Order To Liberate Them?
thought experiment: about,
76–78; criteria, 81–82; criterion of
pleasure and pain, 85–86; extinction, 85; individuals and species,
79; injuries and harm, 82–84;
liquidation, 86–88; "nature" and
"liberty," 78; normative conclusions, 84–85; repugnant conclusion, 86; social belonging and
bodily form, 79–81

naturalists, 164
naturalization, of minimalism versus maximalism debate, 50
"nature," "liberty" and, 78
negative responsibility, in The Child
Who Is Drowning in a Pond
thought experiment, 13
nonmoral rules, 45–46
normative ethics, defined, 187
norms, facts and, 184
Nozick, Robert, 66

Nucci, Larry, 45–46
Nussbaum, Martha, 192n5

"One Cannot Derive an Ought
    from an Is." *See* R1: One Cannot
    Derive an Ought from an Is
"ordinary intuitions," xx–xxi, 27
"ought implies being able to." *See*
    R2: Ought Implies Can

pain, criterion of pleasure and, 85–86
Parfit, Derek, 85
personal domain, 47, 176–78
personal perfection, xix–xx
philosophy, psychology and,
    xvi–xvii
Piaget, Jean, 201n13
Plato, xvi, 194n20
pleasure, criterion of pain and,
    85–86
Poincaré, Henri, 157
Popper, Karl, 157, 158
positive discrimination, 77
pride module, 52
principle of reciprocity, 62
principle of revenge, 62
psychology, philosophy and,
    xvi–xvii

R1: One Cannot Derive an Ought
    from an Is: about, 12, 156–59;
    conflicts between R2: Ought
    Implies Can and, 166–68; ques-
    tions about, 163–65
R2: Ought Implies Can: about, 12,
    159–60; conflicts between R1:
    One Cannot Derive an Ought
    from an Is and, 166–68; ques-
    tions about, 165–66

R3: Like Cases Must Be Treated
    Alike: about, 160; defending,
    170–71; questions about, 168
R4: It Is Pointless to Oblige People
    to Do What They Will Necessar-
    ily Do of Their Own Accord; It
    Is Pointless to Prohibit People
    from Doing What They Will Not
    Willingly Do in Any Case: about,
    161–62; questions about, 171–72
Rawls, John, 133, 164, 187–88, 191n2,
    194n20
reality, thought experiments and,
    xv–xvi
reasoning. *See* moral reasoning
reflective equilibrium: defined,
    187–88; method of, 164
religious theories, 176–78
The Republic (Plato), xvi
repugnant conclusion, 85, 86
respect module, 52
A Responsible Pilot scenario, 17–23
Righteous, the, 126, 127–28
rules: The Child Who Is Drowning
    in a Pond thought experiment, 13;
    intuition and, 131–33; nonmoral,
    45–46; rule of moral reasoning,
    132. *See also* moral rules
Russell, Bertrand, 164

scenarios: The Child Who Is
    Drowning in a Pond thought
    experiment, 11–12; Confront-
    ing a Furious Crowd thought
    experiment, 17–23; Emergencies
    thought experiment, 7–8; The
    Experience Machine thought
    experiment, 67–70; Failure to
    Render Assistance to a Person in

scenarios (*continued*)
Danger, 7; Frankenstein, Minister of Health thought experiment, 94–99; A Furious Crowd, 17; Incest in All Innocence thought experiment, 42–44; The Killer Trolley thought experiment, 24–27; Killing the Pedestrian, 7–8; A Responsible Pilot, 17–23; A Transplant Gone Mad thought experiment, 15–16; A Violinist Has Been Plugged Into Your Back thought experiment, 91–92; We Are Free, Even If Everything Is Written In Advance thought experiment, 110; Who Am I Without My Organs? thought experiment, 100
Schindler, Oskar, 127
Schweder, R.A., 50
Searle, John, 157–58
Singer, Peter, viii–ix, 85, 132, 205n2
"situationism," 123
"situationist" psychological theories, 123, 124, 125, 126
slippery slope: argument for, 168–70, 170–71; defined, 188
social belonging, bodily form and, 79–81
social theories, 176–78
"sorites," 216n17
species, individuals and, 79
"speciesists," 77
submission to authority, 4

talion, law of, 62
Tappolet, Christine, 193n16
Theseus, 100–101
Thomson, Judith Jarvis, 25, 26–27, 27–28, 34, 41, 93

thought experiments: democratizing, xx–xxi; explained, xiv–xv; reality and, xv–xvi; use of, xi–xiv. *See also specific thought experiments*
Tooby, John, 145
A Transplant Gone Mad thought experiment: explained, 1; scenarios, 15–16
trolleyology, 5
Turiel, Elliot, 45–46, 48

universalization, 59–60
utilitarianism, 164, 188–89
The Utility Monster thought experiment, 2, 5, 89–90

victimless crimes, 189, 200n8
victimless moral crimes, 44, 48, 49
A Violinist Has Been Plugged Into Your Back thought experiment: about, 2–3, 160; radical defense of abortion, 92–93; scenarios, 91–92
virtue ethics, defined, 3–4, 189
virtues, moral instinct and, 175–76

Wason, Peter, 145
We Are Free, Even If Everything Is Written In Advance thought experiment: about, 103, 109; scenarios, 110
"Westernization," 49
Who Am I Without My Organs? thought experiment: explained, 3; scenarios, 100
Williams, Bernard, 73–74, 169

Zimbardo, Philip, 4